Launching & Building a Brand

by Amy Will

A Wiley Brand

Launching & Building a Brand For Dummies®

Published by: **John Wiley & Sons, Inc.,** 111 River Street, Hoboken, NJ 07030-5774, www.wiley.com

Copyright © 2022 by John Wiley & Sons, Inc., Hoboken, New Jersey

Published simultaneously in Canada

For general information on our other products and services, please contact our Customer Care Department within the U.S. at 877-762-2974, outside the U.S. at 317-572-3993, or fax 317-572-4002. For technical support, please visit https://hub.wiley.com/community/support/dummies.

Wiley publishes in a variety of print and electronic formats and by print-on-demand. Some material included with standard print versions of this book may not be included in e-books or in print-on-demand. If this book refers to media such as a CD or DVD that is not included in the version you purchased, you may download this material at http://booksupport.wiley.com. For more information about Wiley products, visit www.wiley.com.

Library of Congress Control Number: 2021950437

ISBN: 978-1-119-74803-8 (pbk); ISBN 978-1-119-74804-5 (ebk); ISBN 978-1-119-74805-2 (ebk)

SKY10051016_071323

Contents at a Glance

Table of Contents

Introduction

These days, nearly everything is a brand — from large corporations to people, from products and services to government agencies, special-interest groups, and celebrities. Some organizations and people have more than one brand — a business brand, a product brand, and a personal brand, for example. Bloggers, podcasters, and YouTubers have brands. And whether you're aware or not, you have a brand too: your professional or personal reputation, which is all a brand really is.

People build and launch brands for all sorts of reasons: to sell products or services, build trust, advance their careers, promote a cause, gain exposure to new opportunities, and more. Launching & building a brand gives focus and clarity to everything you do, from defining the essence and purpose of what you're promoting to deciding what you'll do to promote it. As a result, everything you do to reinforce a positive brand image in the minds of others has greater impact.

I don't know why you're interested in launching & building a brand. My husband and I built and launched the Color Me Book brand to bring a cool product (a personalized coloring book) to market and profit from it. I launched my Girl Gang brand to promote women empowerment and connect with like-minded women. Whatever *your* reason is for launching & building a brand, you want to do it as effectively and efficiently as possible.

Welcome to *Launching & Building a Brand For Dummies.*

About This Book

Launching & building a brand isn't easy. Some people seem naturally gifted at it. They're outgoing and engaging. Their charisma is contagious, and whatever they choose to promote attracts an eager following.

The rest of us struggle. We don't even know where to start. Launching & building a brand is so overwhelming that we freeze in our tracks.

Fortunately, with the right tools and guidance, anyone can build and launch their own brand. In this book, I provide the guidance you need, and I highlight numerous tools that simplify the process. To make branding even more accessible, I break my guidance into five parts:

>> **Part 1: Getting Started with Branding** introduces key topics covered in the book and guides you through the process of creating, defining, and financing your brand; clarifying your branding goals; and getting to know your audience — the people you'll be trying to impress.

>> **Part 2: Attending to Brand Fundamentals** picks up where Part 1 left off. In Part 2, you tackle the basics of getting your brand off the ground: creating a logo and style guide, building a branded website and email account, building strategic partnerships, and taking the first steps to launch your brand.

>> **Part 3: Building a Strong Brand Presence** explains what to do to increase brand recognition and awareness, including creating in-person experiences, blogging, podcasting, posting on social media, doing email marketing, buying advertising, and building community.

>> **Part 4: Feeding and Caring for Your Brand** covers everything you need to know to protect your brand and extend its reach. Here, you find out how to scale your brand, build on existing customer loyalty, and defend your brand against threats from the competition.

>> **Part 5: The Part of Tens** covers ten ways to make a marketing campaign go viral; ten ways to differentiate your brand from the competition; and ten ways to drive traffic to your website, blog, or other online properties.

You can't get lost in this book, because everywhere you turn, you'll find valuable information and advice.

Foolish Assumptions

In this data-driven age, all assumptions are foolish. After all, who needs to make assumptions when Google knows *everything*? But to keep this book focused on the right audience and ensure that it delivers the information and insight you need to grasp a topic as complex as branding, I felt compelled to make the following foolish assumptions about you:

>> You have a great idea for a brand but little to no idea about how to get started, or you have a brand that's struggling to get traction.

>> You don't have a college degree in marketing, and you're not a self-educated marketing maven.

>> You want to brand the right way from the start and not waste time and money on a trial-by-error process.

>> You're willing to invest time and effort developing marketing skills.

Other than those four foolish assumptions, I can honestly say that I can't assume much more about you. For all I know, you could be a teenager or a septuagenarian, an intern or an executive, a work-at-home mom or dad, a doctor, a lawyer, rich, poor, or somewhere in between. You could be living in a beach house on the coast, a bungalow in a small town, or a studio apartment in a big city. Regardless of your demographic, I celebrate your interest in branding, your eagerness, and your can-do attitude. You'll be rewarded handsomely as your brand goes viral!

Icons Used in This Book

Throughout this book, icons in the margins highlight certain types of valuable information that call out for your attention. Here are the icons you'll encounter and a brief description of each.

REMEMBER

I want you to remember everything you read in this book, but if you can't quite do that, remember the important points flagged with this icon.

TIP

I've been branding for myself and various employers for more than a decade, and I've picked up dozens of marketing shortcuts and tips along the way. In this book, I share those tips with you and flag them with this icon so you'll be sure not to miss them.

WARNING

You'll find nothing dangerous about branding, but the process does have some pitfalls you'd be wise to avoid, and I use this icon to point them out.

Beyond the Book

In addition to the 300-plus pages of do-it-yourself branding advice delivered in this book, you have access to even more help and information online at Dummies. com, and that information isn't limited to branding. You can dig up all sorts of interesting stuff on a wide variety of topics.

While you're there, check out my *Launching & Building a Brand For Dummies* Cheat Sheet. No, I didn't forget to put it in the book. Making it available online is just another clever marketing ploy by the *For Dummies* brand to sell more books — a teaser, a giveaway, which is a technique I discuss in the book.

Where to Go from Here

Where you go from here is up to you. I wrote this book to be used as a reference, so feel free to skip around, following where your curiosity leads. Every part, chapter, section, and subsection is a self-standing component, so you don't have to tackle topics in some predetermined order.

If you're new to branding, you may want to head to Chapter 1, which introduces branding and key topics covered in more detail in later chapters. If you've already launched your brand and are looking to improve brand recognition and awareness, head to Chapter 6. If you're looking for branding tips and tricks, check out the chapters in Part 5.

If you're in a hurry because you're up against a deadline, or if you need urgent help dealing with a branding issue, turn to the table of contents (at the beginning of this book) or the index (at the end). Either will point you in the right direction.

Keep in mind that branding isn't a linear process. You can start just about anywhere. What's important is the collective impact of everything you do to promote your brand.

1

Getting Started with Branding

Get a quick primer on branding, including the purpose of branding, the different types of brands, what brand architecture is all about, deciding when creating a brand makes sense, and a bird's-eye-view of the 10-step branding process.

Build a brand from the ground up, starting with deciding what you're going to brand and identifying a market niche and moving on to the process of creating a business around your brand and securing the money to finance it.

Position and define your brand, which involves differentiating your brand from everything else already out there, deciding what your brand's essence will be, and coming up with a clever, catchy name for your brand that also clearly describes it.

Identify your branding goals, build a plan to meet those goals, and measure the success of your branding activities, so you can make data-driven changes to your strategy and tactics.

Define your customer avatars (after, of course, figuring out what the heck a customer avatar is). It all starts with getting to know the people in your target market and then describing them as a group in 50 words or less.

IN THIS CHAPTER

» **Grasping the purpose of branding**

» **Differentiating among brand types and why it matters**

» **Getting up to speed on brand architecture**

» **Recognizing when branding comes in handy**

» **Getting a bird's-eye view of the ten-step branding process**

Chapter **1**

Wrapping Your Brain around Branding

Because you're reading this book, I can safely assume that you want to build and launch a brand. You already have a general idea of what that entails. You create something that people value: a business, product, service, worthy cause. Then you position it as being something unique so that people will do what you want them to do: buy your product, subscribe to your service, join your cause, listen to your podcast, vote for you, whatever your goal may be.

That's what branding is all about, but to do it, you need to take a deeper dive, which is why you're reading this book. In subsequent chapters, I take you on that deeper dive. In this chapter, I encourage you to wade in slowly, building overall understanding of branding so that when you encounter the more detailed topics, you'll know how they fit into the overall picture.

Consider this chapter to be Branding Orientation Day. Here, I introduce you to the topic, explain some key concepts, and lead you through the ten-step process for building and launching a brand.

Understanding What a Brand Is and Does

A *brand* is a mental construct that identifies an entity (a business, product, service, organization, or person) as something special. As a mental construct, a brand is intangible; you can't see, hear, touch, smell, or taste it. But it can have a powerful impact on how people perceive and feel about something, such as an organization, person, or product.

Although a brand itself is intangible, several tangible items contribute to creating a brand, including the following:

>> Brand name

>> Mission and values (for corporate or individual brands)

>> Personality

>> Distinctive features (quality, design, value)

>> Visual design elements (logo, color, typography, tagline, images, packaging)

>> Content (website, blog posts, social media, images, video, white papers)

>> Customer experience (location atmosphere, convenience, customer service)

All these elements and others contribute to the perception consumers have of the brand. Just think about one popular brand: Coca-Cola. Its brand name, red-and-white Spencerian script, and unique bottle shape are recognizable everywhere in the world and have been for more than a century. But although the company is built around soft drinks, its marketing focuses on selling happiness and camaraderie and on eliciting a strong emotional response from customers.

Creating a strong emotional bond with customers is the primary purpose of a brand. But a brand also serves other purposes, including the following:

>> Differentiating an organization, product, or person from any competitors

>> Building trust

>> Building loyalty

>> Establishing credibility

>> Motivating customers to take action (buy a product or service, join a cause, vote for a candidate, watch a video, and so on)

>> Building equity or value that can ultimately be sold

BRANDS VERSUS COMMODITIES

One way to think about what a brand is and does is to compare it with a commodity:

- **Commodities** are indistinguishable goods and services that serve the same purpose regardless of who makes them, such as gasoline, batteries, dishwashing detergent, coffee beans, Internet bandwidth, and vacuum cleaners. Unless you have a good reason to buy one commodity instead of another, you buy the cheapest one.

- **Brands** are offerings that are different in some way that matters to customers or clients, such as Shell gasoline, Energizer batteries, Dawn dishwashing detergent, Starbucks coffee, Verizon Internet service, and Shark vacuum cleaners. You're willing to pay more for your favorite brands because they're different and better in your mind than the competition.

If you're not a brand, you're a commodity, and if you're a commodity, the only way you can compete in your market is to offer the lowest price.

WARNING

Don't confuse the purposes of branding with brand purpose. *Brand purpose* is the brand's *raison d'être*. The brand purpose of Starbucks, for example, is to help facilitate human connections. And although Walmart is committed to charging low prices, its purpose is to help people provide better lives for their families. To define your brand's purpose, answer the question "Why is my brand here?" When you define your brand's purpose, you don't need to be concerned too much about the competition; you just need to be sure that everything you do aligns with that purpose.

Recognizing Different Brand Types

One of the first choices you make when you decide to build and launch a brand is what to brand — your business, a specific product or service, or yourself. In this section, I describe the brand types you can build and explain how branding differs for each one.

Business or corporate brand

Small businesses to large corporations often brand themselves to

>> Differentiate themselves from competitors

>> Increase recognition among customers and clients, investors, suppliers, potential partners or associates, and other stakeholders

>> Build a strong positive reputation

>> Attract high-quality job applicants

>> Facilitate the introduction of new products

>> Generate press coverage

>> Charge a premium for offering something different and better

>> Increase the market value of the business

The focus of corporate branding is mostly on mission, values, relationships, and the business's culture. Regardless of the size of the business, the goal is to position itself as a respected and valued member of the community — the industry or market in which it operates and the world overall.

REMEMBER

Corporate brands are slow to build and slow to change. You're building the brand the entire time you're building the business. Every decision you make from the time you name the business contributes to the brand, including the suppliers you choose, the people you hire, the culture that develops within the company, how you interact with customers, and your choice of businesses to associate with.

Product brand

A *product* is anything that's manufactured for sale to consumers. A *product brand* is the distinct value of a specific product in the minds of consumers; the product is different from and better in some way than something else the consumer could spend money on. The purpose of branding a product is to

>> Differentiate it from competing products

>> Make it easily recognizable

>> Increase loyalty among consumers

>> Compel consumers to pay more for the product

The focus of product branding is *differentiation* — making the product stand out in the marketplace. You build a product brand through product development, packaging, and messaging — everything that contributes to the consumer's perception of the product.

REMEMBER

Although corporate brands are slow to build and slow to change, new product brands can be developed quickly and often undergo rebranding.

Service brand

A *service* involves doing something for someone, so how can you possibly brand a service? Usually, you brand the service provider — the business or person providing the service. The purposes of creating a service are very similar to those for creating a business or personal brand:

>> Differentiating the service and service provider from competing services

>> Building credibility (demonstrating that the service provider is qualified)

>> Building trust (showing that the service provider is reputable and reliable)

>> Charging a premium for superior service

With a service brand, your efforts focus mostly on the following credibility- and trust-building activities:

>> Earning certifications, awards, and other credentials and then getting them in front of customers, such as posting them on your website and mentioning them in brochures

>> Presenting content that demonstrates your knowledge and expertise, such as articles, blog posts, social media posts, photos, videos, podcasts, and white papers

>> Engaging with customers and prospects to answer questions and solve problems to further demonstrate your knowledge and expertise

>> Soliciting and posting testimonials or positive reviews from satisfied customers

>> Getting positive reviews from journalists, business organizations, and other trusted sources

REMEMBER

Like corporate brands, service brands are slow to build and slow to change. Your brand continues to evolve as your service evolves. As you introduce new services or develop ways to provide the same services faster, more conveniently, or more affordably, your brand evolves.

Personal brand

A *personal brand* is one that develops around a person. You already have a personal brand: your reputation. People may know you as a sharp-dressing, punctual over-achiever; a careless, fun-loving creative; a devoted parent and respected member of the community; or something else entirely. In a career or business, people develop personal brands to

>> Increase demand for a product or service they provide

>> Further their career

>> Expand their opportunities

>> Build credibility and trust

>> Establish themselves as thought leaders

With a personal brand, your efforts focus mostly on the following activities:

>> Discovering who you really are and finding your most attractive (and in-demand) traits, knowledge, and skills

>> Expressing, in a genuine way, who you are, what you do, and what makes you so special

Fake it till you make it doesn't work; people will eventually see past the façade.

WARNING

>> Being your best you — you are your business and your product, so you need to embrace learning and self-improvement

>> Building a strong portfolio, which may involve earning credentials, developing or gathering samples of your work, or soliciting customer testimonials or reviews — anything that demonstrates success in your field

>> Attending or speaking at industry events and other opportunities to get your name and face in front of people

>> Presenting content that demonstrates your knowledge and expertise — articles, blog posts, social media posts, photos, videos, podcasts, white papers, and so on

>> Engaging with customers and prospects to answer questions and solve problems to further demonstrate your knowledge and expertise

You're constantly developing your personal brand whenever you do anything that affects other people in any way. Whether you're working as an employee or free-lancer, launching your own website, posting content on your social media accounts, or driving through town, all your engagement with others contributes to your brand.

Other brand types

The brand types I've covered to this point are all business and commercial. Other brand types include the following:

>> **Public brand:** One owned by the government, such as the Internal Revenue Service, National Oceanic and Atmospheric Administration, and Central Intelligence Agency

>> **Nongovernmental organization brand:** One owned by a not-for-profit organization that isn't affiliated with any government group, such as the Cooperative for Assistance and Relief Anywhere, Ceres, and the American Heart Association (AHA)

>> **Event brand:** One created to attract participants, attendees, and sponsors, such as Burning Man, NASCAR, the Olympics, and the Cannes Film Festival

Grasping Brand Architecture Basics

If you're planning to create several related brands, you need to choose the brand architecture that establishes how they're related. You have two options:

>> **Branded house (monolithic)** consists of a master brand (usually, a company) with multiple subbrands (typically, divisions, product families, products, or services), all of which ride the coattails of the master brand. Virgin has several subbrands, including Virgin Records, Virgin Atlantic, Virgin Mobile, Virgin Comics, Virgin Wines, and Virgin Care.

>> **House of brands (freestanding brands)** consists of several stand-alone companies, product families, products, or services, each with its own brand identity, none of which refers to the corporate brand. Proctor & Gamble has a wide variety of consumer brands, including Bounty, Charmin, Gillette, Puffs, and Tide.

Most organizations and people use branded house architecture because it offers the following benefits:

>> **Easier and more affordable:** You build and manage a single brand.

>> **Stronger:** Everything you offer reinforces a single brand. Another way to look at it is that you don't have a bunch of separate brands that dilute the master corporate brand.

>> **Increased brand equity:** A single brand generally has more equity built into it and is easier to sell. With multiple brands, a prospective buyer of the business may want some brands and not others, and will expect to pay less for the business as a result.

Here are a few situations in which the house-of-brands architecture may be the better choice:

>> You have deep pockets and a large corporation with diverse companies, divisions, or families of products or services.

>> You want to introduce a new product to the market that would dilute or clash with your existing brand's identity. Suppose that an automobile manufacturer that built its brand around luxury vehicles decides to offer a line of economy vehicles. Selling economy vehicles would weaken the company's reputation for designing and building luxury vehicles, so creating a stand-alone brand probably would be best.

>> You build or are planning to build a company by acquiring multiple stand-alone brands.

REMEMBER

A key factor in successful branding is consistency, so if anything you're introducing to the marketplace is inconsistent with your existing brand, consider creating a separate, stand-alone brand around it.

Knowing When to Brand

Do you really need to build a brand to accomplish your business, organization, or career goals? Well, not really, but building a brand will generally enable you to accomplish your goals faster and raise your level of achievement. In this section, I explain situations in which building a brand is always beneficial.

Whenever you do anything that affects others, you're building a brand, regardless of whether you're aware you're doing it. A brand is simply the perception others have. The question isn't really "Do I need a brand?" or "Should I build a brand?" The question is "Do I want more control of the brand being created?" When you make a conscious effort to build a brand, you're making a decision to take a more deliberate role in influencing how people perceive your business, organization, products, services, or yourself.

Opening a new business

Whenever you open a new business, you're creating a brand, so before you even name your business, give some serious thought to how you're going to create a brand around it. Especially pay attention to the following tasks:

» Identify your niche — what your business plans to do different and better than existing businesses in the same space (see Chapter 2)

» Define your brand identity — your business's vision, mission, and values, and what makes it special (see Chapter 3)

» Clarify your branding goals, and establish ways to measure your progress toward achieving those goals (see Chapter 4)

When you create a business, you create a brand, so think about your business as a brand from the get-go. Branding shouldn't be an afterthought. If you already have a business, though, it's never too late to benefit from branding.

Promoting an existing business

People commonly launch successful businesses without branding even crossing their minds, especially freelancers and other sole proprietors or one-owner operations. Most of these same people eventually reach a plateau with their business, or they start to see that they're losing business. For whatever reason, they realize that their business needs a boost and that they need to take a more active role in promoting it. They need a brand.

Creating a brand for an existing business is nearly the same as creating one for a new business. You're essentially rebranding your business. You may keep the business name (so as not to confuse existing customers) or change the name to something that aligns more closely with your vision for the brand. But you perform the same first steps that you would for a new business: identify your niche, define your brand identity, and clarify your branding goals.

The initial steps in the branding process are about clarifying the vision you have for your brand. Subsequent steps focus on executing your vision. See "Stepping Through the Branding Process" later in this chapter for a step-by-step overview of branding.

Introducing a new product or service

If you have an existing business and are introducing a new offering, you probably don't want to rebrand your business to accommodate it. But you do need to think about how your new offering fits in:

>> Decide whether to introduce the new product or service under your existing brand or a brand of its own. If the new product or service strengthens your existing brand, introducing it under your existing brand name is probably best. If it's likely to weaken your existing brand, creating a separate brand is probably best. See the earlier section "Grasping Brand Architecture Basics."

>> Identify your market niche for introducing the new product. How is the new product or service different from and better than what's already available? If you decided to introduce it under your existing brand, how will it support and extend your brand?

>> If you're introducing the product or service as its own brand, be sure to position and define that brand. See Chapter 3 for details.

If a new product or service dilutes or clashes with your existing brand, create a new brand. Don't try to expand your offerings with something that doesn't fit.

Furthering your career

You don't have to start a business to benefit from branding. Just about anyone in the workforce who's looking to advance their career can benefit from creating and managing their own personal brand. As I mentioned previously, your reputation is part of your personal brand. You just need to be more active and intentional about the content you're putting in front of potential employers and clients. Here are a few ways you can start to strengthen your personal brand:

>> Create your own website or blog, and post regularly to it to demonstrate your knowledge, expertise, commitment, and generosity. See Chapter 7 for guidance on creating a website or blog.

Unless you're consciously building a career as a critic or political pundit, don't post negative content or attack any person, group, or organization. Remain positive. As your parents probably advised, "If you can't say something nice about a person, don't say anything at all."

>> Post a unique and engaging bio on your website or blog and all your social media profiles. See Chapter 8 for information about writing copy that promotes your brand.

>> Include your website or blog address in all your social media profiles.

>> Create a LinkedIn account. LinkedIn is the best social networking platform for professionals.

>> Join and participate in popular online discussion forums (including those on LinkedIn) that are relevant to your industry or areas of expertise.

>> Post regularly on your favorite social media platforms.

Before posting anything on any social media platform, assume that a potential employer will read it. Ask yourself whether your post would impress that person or turn them off.

>> Solicit testimonials from people you've worked with or for to post on your website or blog and social media accounts.

Becoming an influencer or a celebrity

If you're famous or influential (or want to be), building a strong personal brand is a key to your success. Your branding goal is to become popular — to have tens of thousands or even millions of followers on social media and to be in high demand due to your influence or celebrity status.

The key to building a personal brand to become famous is finding topics that resonate with large populations and that align with your own personality and goals, so that you can develop content that's both genuine and engaging.

With a personal brand, charisma goes a long way. Think about the charismatic people you know. They're confident, optimistic, approachable, engaging, and energetic; they tell great stories or jokes; they have strong convictions; they're not afraid to take risks; and they live life to its fullest. Start with those qualities, and you'll be well on your way to stardom.

Fundraising for a not-for-profit organization

People give an organization money only when they believe it's going to a worthy cause and trust the organization to use the money wisely toward that cause, so having a strong brand is essential.

When you're building a brand for a not-for-profit organization, focus on three areas:

» **Storytelling:** First and foremost, people need a compelling reason to donate to the organization. They need to believe that the organization will make the world a better place in a way that matters to them.

» **Credibility:** The organization must demonstrate that it uses money wisely to fulfill its mission. If money or projects are mismanaged, people will be reluctant to donate.

» **Transparency:** The organization must keep donors informed about where the money is going and about successful and unsuccessful projects. Transparency builds trust, and people won't donate to an organization they don't trust.

Raising capital for your business

Whether you're trying to attract private investors or planning to take your company public, branding is an important first step. You need to build a brand to convince investors that they can expect a respectable return on their investment.

When you're starting a new business, you'll be recruiting private investors, who want to see the following:

» Clearly defined products or services that have a reasonable expectation of selling well and generating a profit

» A strong management team with a track record of success or at least the knowledge and expertise to start and run a successful business

» A solid business plan, showing how the business will pursue success

» A clear and compelling brand story

» A culture of innovation to drive future growth

Only after you've created a highly successful and popular brand should you take your business public. Branding at this stage focuses on highlighting the company's track record for success, its future ambitions (such as earnings and profits projections), its innovations, and its ability to execute planned initiatives.

Expanding into new markets

If you already have a brand and are planning to expand into new markets — in different regions of the country or in different countries — consider how your current brand will play in those locations and whether any adjustments need to be made. Certain colors might elicit different emotions depending on the culture, for example. You may need to hire a marketing firm in the location you're expanding into to provide guidance on design elements and content.

Stepping Through the Branding Process

Although the approach to building and launching a brand differs depending on the brand type and purpose, the overall approach is pretty much the same and can be boiled down to ten steps. In this section, I lead you through the process. Subsequent chapters cover specific steps in greater detail.

Step 1: Creating something to brand

Before you can build a brand, you need to have something to brand or at least a concept for it: a business or other type of organization, a product or service, or yourself. This step involves the following activities (see Chapter 2 for details):

>> Deciding what to brand

>> Identifying a market niche

>> Formalizing your brand as a business (such as forming a limited liability company or corporation)

>> Coming up with the money to build your brand

Step 2: Positioning and defining your brand

This step involves clarifying in your own mind what your brand is, what it does, why it's different, and why it's better. It's all about defining your brand identity in a way that differentiates your brand from competing brands or other products or services that may attract the attention of your target market. See Chapter 3 for details.

Step 3: Establishing your branding goals

In this step, you set goals for your brand, including the following:

>> Increasing brand awareness

>> Creating an emotional connection with customers and prospects

>> Differentiating your business, product, service, or self from the competition

>> Building credibility and trust

>> Increasing sales and profitability

This step also involves building a plan to meet your branding goals and deciding on ways to measure your progress toward achieving those goals. See Chapter 4 for details.

Step 4: Defining your brand's customer avatar

A *customer avatar* is a fictional character that represents your target customers. Its purpose is to give you a sense of your audience that inspires you to create design elements and content that are likely to persuade customers to support and even promote your brand.

This step involves research and analysis to get to know the people who make up your target market, describing your avatar in your own words, and refining it to keep up with the times and any changes in your target market.

REMEMBER

You can create more than one customer avatar to represent people from different market segments you're trying to penetrate. But you want to avoid trying to be all things to all people and making an avatar so broad that your design and content have no measurable impact on anyone. See Chapter 5 for guidance on creating a customer avatar.

Step 5: Creating a brand style guide

One key factor in branding success is consistency. Every time someone encounters your brand, you have the opportunity to reinforce your brand identity in their mind. Think of your brand as being a catchy song that gets stuck in the listener's head. A *brand style guide* is a rulebook that ensures consistency by governing everything that contributes to the look and feel of your brand, including the following:

>> Corporate guidelines, including mission statement, values, and targeted demographics

>> Colors

>> Typography (typeface, sizes, and spacing)

>> Logos

>> Imagery (photos, illustrations, and infographics)

>> Tone of voice (fun, professional, caring, and so on)

See Chapter 6 for guidance on creating a brand style guide.

Step 6: Building a branded website, app, and email account

Because so many people spend so much of their time on the Internet these days, creating a strong online presence has become an important part of branding. To begin to build an online presence, do the following things:

>> Claim a unique domain that reflects your brand, such as GirlGangtheLabel.com.

>> Build a website, blog, online store, or a hybrid of those three things in that domain. This site acts as your main hub. Then you can drive traffic to your main hub from other Internet sites, such as social media platforms and discussion forums.

>> Use the domain in your email address (such as amy@girlgangthelabel.com) to reinforce your brand in every outgoing email message.

>> (Optional) Create a branded app (or hire an app developer to do the work for you) that further reinforces your brand while making it easy for customers or clients to place orders and stay connected.

See Chapter 7 for details.

Step 7: Forming strategic partnerships

One of the most powerful ways to promote your brand is to form mutually beneficial partnerships with other brands, sort of like hitching your wagon to a star. If your brand is built around retail, getting your products into popular retail chains is one approach. I was able to persuade Nordstrom to carry my Girl Gang the Label fashion line, which was mutually beneficial. The partnership generated sales and revenue for both parties, increased my brand's profile, and helped Nordstrom position itself as a hip place to shop.

TIP

Always be on the lookout for potential partnerships. Even if you're flying solo or have a small business outside the retail space, you can find partnership opportunities to extend your brand's reach and boost brand awareness. See Chapter 9 for details.

Step 8: Launching your brand

After building your brand, when you have all the pieces in place, you're ready to launch it. This step involves scheduling the launch, preparing incentives to generate interest, getting press coverage, and making it easy for users to share your content with everyone they know. See Chapter 10 for guidance on executing a successful launch campaign.

REMEMBER

At this stage in the branding process, your goal is to get your campaign to go viral. To achieve that goal, you need to do a big push in both traditional and social media channels — wherever the people in your target market go for information.

Step 9: Promoting your brand

Promoting your brand involves everything you do during and after your launch to extend your brand's reach and strengthen brand awareness. It typically involves the following activities:

>> Content marketing — sharing content that subtly promotes your brand without explicitly doing so (see Chapter 8)

>> In-person experiences, such as events, pop-up stores, retail locations, and conferences (see Chapter 11)

>> Podcasting — sharing audio presentations and interviews (see Chapter 12)

>> Social media marketing (see Chapter 13)

>> Email marketing (see Chapter 14)

>> Advertising (see Chapter 15)

Step 10: Caring for and protecting your brand

Branding is a lifelong journey — the life of the brand, that is. As long as the brand is in existence, you need to care for it and protect it, which involves the following activities:

>> Auditing and scaling your brand to increase its reach while expanding brand awareness

>> Building on customer loyalty and longevity to transform customers into brand advocates

>> Protecting your brand from competitors and anyone who may try to steal your intellectual property

REMEMBER

Attention spans are short these days. If you're not putting something fresh in front of your target customers at least a couple of times a week, they're going to forget about you.

Chapter **2**

Creating and Financing Your Brand

B randing assumes that you have something to brand — a business, a product, a service, or even yourself. You need something you can stick a label or hang a sign on. If you already have that something clear in your mind, you can safely skip this chapter. If your vision is still a little fuzzy around the edges, or if you could use some guidance on coming up with an idea or getting your idea off the ground, you've come to the right place.

In this chapter, I introduce you to the various entities you can brand, and I highlight some differences in the branding process for each type. I show you how to find or choose a niche that improves your chances of success. I explain how to register your business/brand and choose the right legal structure for it. Last but not least, I reveal a few ways to get other people to help finance what may be a risky venture.

Deciding What You're Going to Brand

You can create a brand for just about anything — products and services, businesses and corporations, performers and groups (think Cirque du Soleil), celebrities and influencers, government entities (including nations) and nongovernment organizations (NGOs), not-for-profit organizations, even places (I ♥ NY, for example). The four most commonly branded things are businesses, products, services, and individuals (personal branding).

Sometimes, the lines dividing these different brand types get a little blurry. When you *are* the business, for example, do you create a business brand or a personal brand? In this section, I introduce you to the four most common brand types so you can figure out what you're branding and how that decision will affect your approach to branding.

REMEMBER

Knowing what you're branding is important because it gives you focus and guides you in deciding what to do to build your brand. The overall approach and specific activities differ, depending on whether you're branding a business, a product, a service, or yourself.

Business or corporate brand

A *business* or *corporate brand* establishes and communicates an organization's identity to all stakeholders, internal and external, including customers, investors, executives, managers, and staff. Corporate branding involves ensuring alignment of everything that goes into defining the organization's identity, including the following:

>> **Mission statement:** The organization's overall purpose.

>> **Vision statement:** How the organization plans to develop over time.

>> **Values:** The beliefs, philosophies, and principles that guide the organization's decisions and behaviors.

>> **Core competencies:** The sets of resources and skills that enable an organization to deliver something special to the marketplace.

>> **Value proposition:** What the company delivers to the market that drives consumer demand for it.

>> **Workplace culture:** The way people within the organization generally think, behave, and interact. In a hierarchy, employees generally do what they're told by their superiors, whereas in a more collaborative culture, everyone shares in decision-making and workplace management.

>> **Business strategy:** The way an organization chooses to achieve its goals and remain competitive.

>> **Business activities:** Daily operations, including marketing, sales, financing, customer service, and supply-chain management.

>> **Affiliations:** Partnerships, associations, and relationships with other businesses and with consumers. An organization's identity is defined by the company it keeps.

>> **Brand story:** The narrative that relates the facts about a brand in a way that connects emotionally with people. (See Chapter 8 for details on how to compose a brand story.)

>> **Brand style:** Guidelines (see Chapter 6) that establish the brand's look and feel.

Note that corporate branding isn't covered in detail in this book, although some aspects of product, service, and personal branding (which are covered in this book) may apply to corporate branding as well.

REMEMBER

Corporate branding is long-term with a broad scope. Unlike product branding, which uses a narrow pitch and often adjusts its message to target different sectors and customer demographics, corporate branding strives to create a universal appeal over the long haul with strict consistency.

Product brand

A *product brand* is a set of unique qualities — including design, packaging, and advertising — that makes a consumer good easily recognizable and special in the minds of consumers. Product branding entails the following activities:

>> Designing a recognizable and appealing logo (see Chapter 6)

>> Coming up with a clever, catchy brand name (see Chapter 3)

>> Establishing branding guidelines to ensure that all marketing has a consistent look and feel, and adjusting the guidelines to keep up with the times (see Chapter 6)

>> Researching the market to better understand customers and competing products (see Chapter 3)

>> Tailoring the message to appeal to different consumer demographics (see Chapter 8)

>> Differentiating your product from competing products (see "Identifying or Creating a Niche Market" later in this chapter)

>> Marketing/advertising via email, website, blog, social media accounts, podcasts, video, and so on (see Chapters 7, 12, and 13)

Service brand

A *service brand* is a set of unique qualities, including the service type and quality. How a service provider is marketed, sold, and delivered makes it trusted and valued in the minds of consumers. With product branding, you're selling goods, whereas service branding is more about selling a relationship or an experience. Service branding involves being professional, likeable, and trustworthy at every touchpoint:

>> Marketing materials, including business cards and brochures (see Chapter 10)

>> Online marketing via email, website, blog, social media, podcasts, and video (see Chapters 7, 12, and 13)

>> Sales meetings with customers (see Chapter 3)

>> Service calls and other forms of service delivery (see Chapter 3)

REMEMBER

The bottom line is that customers will choose the service provider they know, like, and trust most, so service branding needs to focus on informing prospective customers while instilling trust and likeability.

Personal brand

A *personal brand* is a person's unique combination of skills, expertise, personality, and values that defines their identity and reputation in the minds of clients, partners, and associates and is used to advance their career. A strong personal brand positions someone as an expert in a specific field or industry or as an authority on a topic of interest. Personal branding is often used to launch a person's career as a coach, trainer, speaker, consultant, author, actor, influencer, and so on. In a way, a personal brand is a business, product, and service brand all rolled into one with a personal touch.

Effective personal branding requires the following:

>> **Knowledge, skills, or expertise:** Be good at what you do.

>> **Value:** Commit to delivering value in everything from the content you use to market yourself to the products and services you deliver or recommend.

>> **Creativity and originality:** To differentiate yourself from the competition, offer something unique.

>> **Authenticity:** Be real, not phony.

>> **Exposure:** Blog, podcast, post YouTube videos, join relevant social media communities, and make yourself available for interviews.

>> **Consistency:** Find your niche (as explained in the next section), stick with it, and make sure that all your personal branding efforts are aligned.

To create your own personal brand, follow these steps:

1. **Conduct a self-assessment to get to know who you are and what you can offer of value to others.**

2. **Decide who and what you want to be associated with (other brands, businesses, people, products, and services).**

3. **Identify and get to know your target market.**

   Who's your audience? Who's likely to follow you and why?

4. **Follow established leaders in the field you're focused on.**

   Find out what they offer of value and how they differentiate themselves. How can you differentiate yourself from them?

5. **Network with others in your industry.**

   Get involved in the communities where established leaders and your future followers hang out, keeping a low profile at first to get a feel for the culture and norms.

   WARNING

   Be careful not to step on anyone's toes as you begin to network, at least until you get a feel for the community and people get to know and accept you.

6. **Start to put yourself out there via blog posts, podcasts, social media, video, and so on.**

Identifying or Creating a Niche Market

One of the biggies in branding is *differentiation* — the process of identifying or creating and then promoting the unique characteristics of your business, product, service, or yourself. You need to figure out what's different, special, and better about what you bring to the market.

An effective approach to differentiation is going small. Instead of trying to be everything to everybody, aim to be something special to a small segment of your market. Identify or create a *niche* — a narrow opening or unique opportunity in the broader market you're pursuing. Narrowing your focus increases your impact while (counterintuitively) expanding, not limiting, your opportunities. It enables your brand to stand out in the global marketplace, which is crowded with competitors vying for consumers' attention.

To find a niche, start by answering the following questions:

>> Does your brand offer a unique solution to a problem, and if so, how is it unique?

>> What does your brand offer that competing brands don't?

>> What are your brand's use cases (different ways that my products/services can be used)? List your products/services, and identify all possible use cases for each.

>> How is your brand different from and better than the competition?

>> Does your brand fill an unmet need in the marketplace or serve an underserved group of consumers? If so, how?

>> (For a personal brand) What makes you so special? Think in terms of appearance, personality, knowledge, expertise, and skill set — every ingredient that goes into making you *you*.

>> Who's going to buy what you're selling?

>> Why do people need or value what your brand offers?

Examine your answers to these questions, and look for patterns or areas of overlap, which is usually where you'll discover your niche. For my Girl Gang brand, I knew that women empowerment was a big and growing movement and that women like to make fashion statements. In those two areas of overlap, I recognized an unmet need: Women needed a way to express and demonstrate their support for female empowerment, and they could do that through a fashion statement and by supporting women-owned businesses. I had discovered my niche.

In the following sections, I cover specific approaches to identifying or creating a niche.

Solving a difficult problem

People often ask sarcastically, "Are you looking for trouble?" as if that's a bad thing. People who look for trouble are the visionaries and inventors of the world, and they're often the richest and most successful as well. They spotted a problem, devised a solution for it, and created a lucrative niche.

Just think how many books, courses, and seminars have been sold to help couples solve their relationship issues. Consider all the commercial technologies that have been developed to solve problems in just one small area: data security. Entire industries have been created to solve problems ranging from not having enough time to shop for groceries or being unable to flag down a taxi to dealing with energy shortages and climate change.

REMEMBER

In every problem is an opportunity.

Fulfilling an unmet need (or creating one)

People often need stuff they can't get or can't get affordably or conveniently. Sometimes, they don't even know they need it or want it until you show them how much better their lives could be if they had it. Nobody really needed a camera built into a mobile phone, for example, but as soon as a mobile phone with a camera became available, *everyone* had to have one.

When you discover an unmet need or create one, you create a niche market that can be very lucrative. I once worked at Tower Paddle Boards, a direct-to-consumer paddleboard company. All the paddleboard brands in our industry sold to surf shops and outdoor retailers, so their products were pricey. But company founder Stephan Aarstol spotted an unmet need: affordable high-quality paddleboards. By selling direct to consumers, Tower Paddle Boards eliminated the retail markup and slashed prices without sacrificing quality. That's how you create a niche.

Specializing to create a new market niche

You've probably heard the expression "A jack of all trades is a master of none." You don't see a lot of demand for a jack (or a Jill) of all trades or even a business that offers everything to everyone. Some of the big players offer all things, however, and are successful. At Walmart, for example, you can find a broad selection of products, have your vision tested, get your car repaired and your hair cut, and even have your taxes done. But even many of the big players have a niche; Walmart competes on convenience and price.

When you're building and launching a new brand, you're not a big player, so don't try to be or offer everything to everyone. Eventually, you may want to reach a broader market, but start small by focusing on the needs and desires of a small segment of your market. This advice applies whether you're creating a business, product, service, or personal brand.

TIP

To create a market niche, collaborate with people who are passionate about your industry. Most great ideas are born from creative thought and discussion among people with shared interests.

Offering something unique

Niche markets are often the products of inspiration. An idea pops into your head about something unique or a twist on something that's been around for years. A case in point is the skin-care industry. Recently, this well-entrenched industry has been rocked by products with natural ingredients. Phthalates and parabens are out; fruits, veggies, and botanicals are in. The shift in demand for natural skin-care products created an opening in a very crowded market, allowing small business to make a big mark.

You can't force an idea to pop into your head, but you can create fertile ground from which unique ideas are more likely to sprout. Here are a couple methods to try:

>> **Immerse yourself in the industry or the market you're passionate about.** The more information and insight you have, the more material your subconscious mind has to work with to generate ideas.

>> **Tune in to the news, and be sensitive to growing trends.** Ideas for natural skin-care products, for example, came from concerns about potentially harmful chemicals in foods and other products.

>> **Broaden your interests; expand your mind.** Ideas for unique businesses, products, and services are often the product of diversity or convergence — viewing something from a different perspective or looking at two distinct industries or markets side by side.

Formalizing Your Brand As a Business . . . If You Haven't Already

When you're building and launching a brand, you're typically building and launching a business — a complex topic that I don't want to subject you to. But you do need to know the basics so that you start your brand/business on the right foot, avoid legal and tax issues, and ensure that your brand and other intellectual property is protected.

In this section, I explain the basics of incorporating and registering your business, and I touch on the topic of protecting your brand and other intellectual property (a topic you can find more about in Chapter 19).

Incorporating your business

Incorporating your business is the process of establishing it as an entity separate from you as a person. As a corporation, your business gains certain benefits, including legal protections and potential tax benefits. From a branding perspective, incorporating your business may help build trust and credibility among prospective customers and clients.

When incorporating a business, you decide how to structure it — as a partnership, limited liability company (LLC), C corporation, or S corporation. If you *are* your business (you're self-employed), your business is considered to be a sole proprietorship, and you stand to miss out on the benefits provided to corporations.

REMEMBER

Choosing the right corporation type now can prevent headaches and hassles later, but you can change your business structure at any time. For my first business, a wholesale hair-tie company, I started as a sole proprietor. But when I started working with larger retailers such as Zazzle and Sephora, I decided to switch to an LLC to reduce my exposure to financial risk in case someone decided to take legal action against me for some reason.

In the following sections, I weigh the pros and cons of each type of business entity.

Sole proprietorship

A sole proprietorship is the fastest, easiest, and cheapest business structure to set up, requiring no time, effort, or money. You just start doing business, and your business is considered to be a sole proprietorship. With a sole proprietorship, you have complete control of all business decisions, and you report your income (and are taxed) as an individual taxpayer. Those are the benefits. These are the potential drawbacks:

>> **Unlimited personal liability:** This one's the biggie. Nothing separates you from your business, so you're personally responsible whenever something bad happens. If your business fails or someone wins a lawsuit against your business, you can lose everything, including your home and personal possessions.

>> **Difficulty raising money to grow your business:** You can't sell stock in the business, and banks will be reluctant to loan you money.

>> **Increased burden of running the business:** With total control comes total responsibility, which can leave you feeling the heat when problems arise.

As a sole proprietor, you're not required to name the business after yourself. You can register your business under a *doing business as* (DBA) name. As a DBA, you gain no legal protection, but you appear to the world to be more of a business entity. See "Registering your business" later in this chapter for details.

TIP

However your business is structured, I encourage you to apply for an employer identification number (EIN). If you have employees, you must have an EIN to report and deposit employee payroll taxes. You don't need to be an employer or corporation to obtain and use an EIN, however. You can use an EIN instead of your Social Security number when invoicing clients and customers and paying taxes, which can help protect you from identity theft. Some businesses may also feel more comfortable doing business with you if you have an EIN because it establishes you as a business owner instead of an employee. To apply for an EIN, visit https://www.irs.gov/businesses/small-businesses-self-employed/apply-for-an-employer-identification-number-ein-online.

Partnership

If you co-own a business, consider forming a partnership. With a partnership, profits and losses pass through to the personal tax returns of the partners (so the partnership itself isn't taxed). When forming a partnership, you have two options:

>> **Limited partnership (LP)** has one general partner with unlimited liability, who has more control in the business and must pay self-employment tax, and one or more partners with limited liability and control, who aren't required to pay self-employment tax, as specified in the partnership agreement.

>> **Limited liability partnership (LLP)** is similar to an LP but provides limited liability to all partners.

Limited liability company

An LLC offers two key benefits:

>> Protection against personal liability that would otherwise expose your personal assets to risk.

>> Pass-through of profits and losses to your personal income tax return so that the LLC itself isn't subject to corporate taxes. Members of an LLC, however, like sole proprietors, are considered to be self-employed and are subject to self-employment taxes (Social Security and Medicare).

If you have significant personal assets and are doing any risky business (anything that could expose you to costly lawsuits or bankruptcy), I encourage you to do business as an LLC or as an S or C corporation, which are covered next.

C corporation

A *C corporation* (*C corp* for short) is separate from the owners and operators of the business and is subject to corporate taxes. Corporate taxation is a form of double taxation; your corporation pays taxes on its profit, and then you pay taxes on capital gains paid to you as a shareholder of the corporation. A C corp provides the strongest protections against the loss of an owner's personal assets in the event of bankruptcy or lawsuits.

One of the big benefits of a C corp is that it can raise funds by selling shares to investors. The big drawbacks are the costs and complexity of forming and managing a C corp. Although this option can be the best choice for large organizations, smaller organizations will probably want to steer clear of it.

S corporation

An *S corporation* (*S corp* for short) is a simplified version of a C corp with lower costs to set up and manage. As such, it's more attractive to smaller organizations. With an S corp, profits pass through the corporation to the owners, so it's not susceptible to double taxation.

Another key benefit is that as an owner, you can receive money from the corporation as employee pay or as dividends paid to investors. The money you take out in pay is subject to income tax and self-employment tax, whereas the money you receive in distributions is taxed at capital-gains rates (typically lower than income tax rates) and isn't subject to self-employment tax.

One important disadvantage of an S corp, compared with a C corp, is that an S corp can sell only up to 100 shares, which limits its ability to raise capital for growth by selling shares to investors.

Registering your business

Registering a business simply means establishing it as a bona fide entity with state and local licensing and taxing authorities. If you're creating a personal brand as a sole proprietorship, registering may not be necessary (depending on the jurisdiction and nature of your business), but if you're operating as a corporation, your business must be registered.

Check with your state, county, and municipal government organizations or a local branch of the U.S. Small Business Association (SBA) to find out what you need to do in terms of registration and license for the type of business you're starting.

Registering a business name

When you form a corporation or LLC, you choose a business name other than your name as part of the process. If you're operating your business as a sole proprietorship, you have the option of using your name as the business name or choosing a DBA name.

A DBA doesn't confer any legal protections, but it enables you to operate under an assumed name, which may be advantageous for branding purposes. Another benefit is that when you have both a DBA and EIN, most banks will allow you to open a separate business bank account and are more likely to consider lending you money for your business.

REMEMBER

Depending on the state or locale in which you do business, you may need to register your DBA with the secretary of state or another state agency. Alternatively, you may need to register with the county or municipality where you do business.

Registering with taxing authorities

If you operate as a sole proprietorship, you'll use your Social Security number to pay federal, state, and local taxes. If you form a corporation or create a DBA, you register your business under a separate name and can then apply for an EIN to use when you pay your taxes or withhold and pay taxes for employees.

Getting a license (or not)

Depending on the location and nature of your business, you may need to be licensed to conduct business in a certain jurisdiction. Rules vary among states, counties, and municipalities. In most states, freelancers such as writers, editors, and graphic artists don't need a license to do business, but if you plan on opening a restaurant or bricks-and-mortar retail store, or if you're a building contractor or insurance agent, you'll need a license. Again, check with your local SBA or secretary of state to determine licensing requirements.

Getting a trademark, patent, or copyright

If you're creating something unique, you need to do more than register your business; you also need to register your ideas to protect your intellectual-property rights. Depending on what your "something unique" is, obtain a copyright (for books and other publications), patent (for inventions), or trademark (for a business or brand name, logo, or design). You may need all three.

You can trademark, patent, or copyright your intellectual property yourself through the U.S. Patent and Trademark Office (https://www.uspto.gov/trademarks) or hire an attorney to do the job for you. You can find plenty of law firms online that offer intellectual-property legal services. Just search the web for "how to" followed by "trademark," "patent," or "copyright" to pull up a list.

REMEMBER

I cover this topic in greater detail in Chapter 19, but I mention it here because depending on your business and brand, it may be a crucial part of the getting-started process. You don't want to come up with a multimillion-dollar idea only to have it stolen.

Financing Your Business/Brand

Depending on the business/brand you're building and launching, you may be able to work with on a shoestring budget of your own money, or you may need to find additional sources of cash. If you're creating a personal brand to promote yourself as the world's leading expert on raising chickens, you can probably do that (or at least start) with a website, blog, and podcast, which don't require much money. By contrast, if you're aiming to create your own clothing line or build an international dog-grooming franchise, you'll need to scrounge up the money by recruiting partners, borrowing money (from individuals or banks), or selling shares in your company to investors.

In this section, I introduce you to various sources of financing. But before you even think about exploring available financing options, create a budget so that you'll know just how much money you'll need.

Budgeting for your business/brand

To budget for your business/brand, create a list of everything you need to make it a success, research prices, and then add everything up. Table 2-1 contains a list of items to get you started. Depending on the business/brand you're creating, you may need to add to the list or cross off some items. When you have a comprehensive list, research the cost for each item/service (on the web or by calling around), and write the estimated cost in the right column.

TABLE 2-1

Business/brand budget

Item	Cost
Legal fees (for incorporation, registration, licenses, and intellectual-property protections)	
Accounting fees (if you plan to hire an accountant)	
Brand design (logo and graphics)	
Website/blog (design, build, and host)	
Marketing/advertising (online ads)	
Materials/equipment/supplies	
Manufacturing/product sourcing (if you'll be selling an original product)	
Staff (if you're planning to hire people)	
Rent (for a bricks-and-mortar business or retail store)	

CREATING A SELF-FUNDED BRAND

A *self-funded brand* isn't one that funds itself, but one that you fund. The benefit of creating a self-funded brand is that you have total control of all business/brand decisions, and you get to keep 100 percent of the profits. Woo-hoo!

Unfortunately, the potential benefits are outnumbered by the drawbacks:

- You're responsible for all business/brand decisions.

- You suffer 100 percent of any losses.

- You have limited access to financing to fuel growth and pursue opportunities.

TIP

If your plan is to sell a unique product you're going to manufacture, that plan can get expensive fast. And unless you're 100 percent certain that the product is going to sell like hotcakes, manufacturing thousands of units can pose a huge financial risk. To reduce the risk, consider launching a preorder campaign. Make a small batch, and wait till the orders come in to make larger quantities. The down sides to this strategy are that customers may have to wait longer to receive their orders, and you may have to pay more in manufacturing costs per item. This strategy is just a test run, however. You can go all in when you see how popular your product is.

Creating a business plan

When you're seeking any type of financing for your business/brand, a business plan is essential. Nobody (except maybe your parents or your rich Aunt Matilda) will hand you money just because you ask for it. Banks, investors, and organizations want to know that their money will be put to good use. Banks want some assurance that your loan will be paid back. Investors want a reasonable expectation that they'll receive a return on their investment.

If you don't already have a business/brand in place to demonstrate a proven track record of success, you need a convincing business plan. Creating a business plan is beyond the scope of this book, but make sure that your plan contains the following key elements:

>> **Summary:** The summary should include what your business/brand is and does, and why it's better than the competition; your bio and experience (and that of any partners or associates); the products/services you offer; and why you think your business/brand will be successful.

>> **Strategy, goals, objectives, and activities:** Your strategy is your big plan or idea of how you're going to achieve success. Goals are what you need to accomplish to execute your strategy. Objectives are measurable milestones you must meet to reach your goals. And activities are what you'll do to meet your objectives.

>> **Market/competitive analysis:** This analysis describes the industry or market and any existing competition, and shows how your brand is different from and better than what's already available.

>> **Financial projections:** This element is your budget to start and run the business (costs), how much money you're expecting to pull in (revenue), projected profit (revenue minus costs), and how you plan to pay back any loans or reward investors. Prepare for setbacks, unexpected costs, and missed goals to protect yourself from underdelivering. It's best to set benchmarks that have a margin for error to make sure everyone involved can understand the full scope of the plan.

For detailed guidance on creating a business plan, check out *Creating a Business Plan For Dummies*, by Veechi Curtis (John Wiley & Sons, Inc.).

Getting grants

Depending on your business/brand, you may be able to get a grant to finance it. A *grant* is free money; you never have to pay it back! Organizations offer grants for all sorts of reasons, such as to stimulate the economy, improve communities, and empower certain demographics (such as women in business).

The first step in getting a grant is finding one you qualify for. Here's a short list to get you started:

>> **Government grants:** Federal and state agencies make a point of stating that they're not sources of free money for most business startups, but they offer limited grants to fund scientific or medical research and community, educational, and environmental programs. Here are a few resources for finding out more about government grants:

- SBA Grants page (https://www.sba.gov/funding-programs/grants)

- U.S. Economic Development Administration's Funding Opportunities page (https://eda.gov/funding-opportunities)

- The State Business Incentive Database from the Council for Community and Economic Research (www.stateincentives.org)

- The SBA's Small Business Development Centers database, which you can search at https://www.sba.gov/local-assistance

- Your state's .gov website

>> **Demographic-specific grants:** If you're a woman, veteran, or minority business owner, you may be eligible for grants from corporations, special-interest groups, or the SBA. Search the web for "business grants for" followed by your demographic, such as "business grants for women."

>> **Corporation grants:** Many corporations offer small-business grants or sponsor contests to encourage innovation in their industry or help entrepreneurs in certain groups start a business. Check with the big players in your industry to see whether they offer any grant programs or contests, or search the web for "corporate small-business grants."

WARNING

Be careful of any person or organization that offers help to get grant money. Some may be legitimate; others are scams.

For more about getting grants, check out *Grant Writing For Dummies*, 6th Edition, by Beverly A. Browning (John Wiley & Sons, Inc.).

Financing with debt and equity

Traditionally, businesses obtain the money they need to start and grow with either debt or equity. In other words, they borrow money from banks or sell a stake in their business/brand to investors. When you're creating a business/brand, you have the same options.

Financing with debt: Borrowing money

If you don't have enough money to build and launch your business/brand, or if you prefer not to risk your own money, you may be able to borrow money from people or banks. The people may be family members, friends, or venture capitalists. You meet with them to pitch your idea, and if they think it has potential for success (and trust that you'll pay back the loan), they'll agree to loan you the money. They may charge interest, or they may not.

If you don't like that option, you can try pitching your idea to a bank, which *will* charge you interest. Before approaching a loan officer at the bank, prepare for a meeting by gathering the following items:

>> Your business plan

>> The specific amount of money you need to borrow

>> Legal documents pertaining to your business, including your articles of incorporation or DBA; any licenses you need to operate; your EIN; and any applicable patents, trademarks, or copyrights you own or have applied for

>> Your credit score

>> Your net worth (the value of everything you own minus what you owe), along with a list of assets and debts

>> Proof of any money you have in savings, such as recent bank statements

>> Proof of any income from sources such as your day job and investments (pay stubs or recent tax returns)

REMEMBER

Lenders want assurance that you'll be able to make the monthly payments on the loan and eventually pay it back in full. You can provide that assurance by pitching an awesome business plan or by showing that if your idea fizzles, you have the collateral to pay back the loan. *Collateral* is anything of value that the bank can take from you if you default on the loan, such as your house in the Hamptons, your Tesla, or your private jet.

Financing with equity: Selling a stake in your business/brand

An alternative to borrowing money is selling a stake in your business/brand to investors. You can offer your sister-in-law 30 percent ownership of your koi-pond business in exchange for $50,000, for example. If you do something like that, of course, I strongly encourage you to hire an attorney to draw up an agreement.

You can also sell shares in your business, which is way beyond the scope of this book. To sell shares, your business needs to be structured as a C corp or S corp. You can sell various types of stock in a business, including common stock, preferred stock, and convertible preferred stock, to name a few. If your head is spinning, that's my point: Consult an attorney or a stockbroker to explain your options and suggest what's best for your particular situation and preferences.

Exploring alternative financing options

TIP

Private individuals and banks aren't the only source of business loans. Here are a few alternative financing options you may want to consider:

>> **Merchant cash advance:** If you're selling stuff online and need some quick cash to cover an unforeseen expense, such as the cost of additional product when you experience a bump in sales, consider a merchant cash advance — a

financing option offered by companies such as Kabbage (https://www.kabbage.com) through Shopify. Here's how Kabbage works: You apply for a loan, and if it's approved, Kabbage deposits the money in your bank account. Then it takes a percentage of your Shopify sales until the loan is paid off.

>> **Online business line of credit (LOC):** Banks offer LOCs, but if your business needs some additional cash flow in a hurry, consider an online business LOC, which is easier and faster to get. With an LOC, you're approved for a certain maximum loan amount and draw money out as you need it, paying interest only on the money you borrow. An example of a company that offers online business LOCs is OnDeck (https://www.ondeck.com), which offers an instant funding option that provides access to up to $10,000.

>> **Business credit cards:** One common but often-overlooked option for short-term financing is credit cards, particularly business credit cards, which work just like personal credit cards but for businesses. Search the web for "business credit card," and you'll find a host of options.

>> **Microloans:** *Microloans* are small loans with relatively low interest rates offered by traditional lenders, individuals, or groups of people. These loans are good options to consider if you don't have much collateral or credit history. They're typically prioritized for entrepreneurs in undeveloped countries and communities and for minority business owners. You can find microlenders through organizations such as Headway Capital (https://www.headwaycapital.com/microloans) and Accion (https://www.accion.org).

>> **Crowdfunding:** With crowdfunding, you get a lot of people to donate, lend, or invest small amounts of money in your business. One of the most popular crowdfunding sites for businesses is Kickstarter (https://www.kickstarter.com). With Kickstarter, you post your project, your funding goal, and your deadline, and members can choose to chip in to make it happen. Financial backers get nothing in return, except maybe a T-shirt, a sample of your product, or a copy of a book you wrote. Mostly, they get the satisfaction of having helped bring something of value, fun, or interest into the world.

IN THIS CHAPTER

» Exploring brand positioning strategies

» Differentiating your brand to highlight its unique attributes

» Composing a brand positioning statement

» Clarifying your brand's identity for yourself and others

» Coming up with a catchy, descriptive brand name

Chapter **3**

Positioning and Defining Your Brand

When you get to the point of thinking about building and launching a brand, you usually have a brand in mind, but the concept may still be a little (or very) fuzzy. You may have a clear vision of the business, product, or service you're bringing into the world, but you've given little thought to how your brand will compete with everything else that's vying for people's attention . . . and money.

What is your brand about? What's its essence? How is it different from and better than what people can already get? What do you want your branding efforts to inspire people to do (buy your product, hire you, join your cause, or spend their vacations in your state)?

To answer these questions, you must position, define, and name your brand. Clarify your brand concept in your own mind so that you can clarify it in the minds of others. In this chapter, I explain how to do just that.

Positioning Your Brand

Jockey for position is an old phrase from horse racing that means getting into a better place near the beginning of a race. When you're building and launching a brand, you need to move your brand to a position that gives it the greatest chance for success. This process usually involves identifying or developing brand attributes that enable you to outcompete what's already available.

Suppose that you're planning to open a restaurant in your neighborhood, which already has plenty of diverse restaurants — fine dining, fast food, Chinese, Mexican, Italian, Thai, Greek, Japanese, cafés, bars and grills, buffets, you name it. How can you possibly compete? You look for ways to make your restaurant different and better, such as the following:

>> Higher-quality food

>> Generous servings

>> Superior service

>> Relaxed atmosphere

>> Convenient location

>> Lower prices

>> Free entertainment

Then you can begin to market these attributes to build brand recognition and awareness. (*Brand recognition* involves the ability to identify a brand by its logo, colors, slogan, tagline, jingle, or other brand attribute. *Brand awareness* is deeper knowledge of the brand, such as its mission and the products or services offered.)

In this section, I lead you through the process of positioning your brand.

Choosing a brand positioning strategy

You start the brand positioning process by choosing one or more brand positioning strategies. A *brand positioning strategy* is an approach to differentiating something from what's already available. A brand positioning strategy could be to offer the lowest prices or the highest-quality product in its class.

When choosing a brand positioning strategy, think about your brand's *unique selling proposition* (USP) — what makes your brand different, better, and more attractive to customers.

In this section, I highlight several brand positioning strategies, but this list isn't exhaustive by any means.

REMEMBER

Some brand positioning strategies apply regardless of the business/organization and product/service; others depend to some degree on the entity you're branding. Location may be important for bricks-and-mortar businesses, for example, but not for businesses that operate primarily online.

Product/service features and benefits

Brand positioning often focuses on the product or service itself, specifically on the following attributes:

>> **Features:** Characteristics of the product or service that make it different from and better than what's already available

>> **Benefits:** How what's different and better about the product/service is advantageous to the customer

Consider a hybrid gas–electric vehicle. The feature is a vehicle that uses gas to create electricity that powers the vehicle. The key benefits are that it enables the driver to travel farther on a tank of gas and save money on fuel, it's cleaner for the environment, and it requires less engine maintenance.

Product class

A *product class* is a category of products. Videogames is a product class with several subclasses, including action games, adventure games, role-playing games, and strategy games. You can compete within a product class or subclass or outside it, but you're competing by product class only when you compete outside the class or subclass — positioning a strategy video game as a better alternative to a strategy board game such as chess, for example, or positioning video games as a better alternative to other forms of entertainment, such as movies.

Application or use

When a product or a nearly identical version of it has multiple applications or uses, brands often develop around the different uses. Consider Gatorade and Pedialyte. Both beverages are used for rehydration and replenishing electrolytes. But Gatorade is higher in sugar and is marketed as a sports drink for teens and adults, whereas Pedialyte is lower in sugar and higher in potassium and sodium and is marketed to prevent dehydration in children suffering from fever, diarrhea, and vomiting.

Customer service

Some businesses pride themselves on delivering superior customer service. Examples that come to mind include Nordstrom, Visa, and Trader Joe's. Providing quality customer service is a priority for any business or organization, of course, but you must decide on the degree to which you want to market superior customer service as one of your brand's essential qualities.

REMEMBER

Regardless of whether you want to highlight customer service, you must deliver at least industry-standard customer service. Failure to do so will result in customers associating your brand with *poor* customer service.

Convenience

In some industries, such as fast-food restaurants, convenience stores, meal-delivery services, and banks, convenience is essential. Convenience may involve choosing an accessible location, making it easier or faster to do something, eliminating a time-consuming or onerous task, rearranging items in a store, or streamlining the purchase process (online or in stores).

Quality

If you're making a conscious decision to offer premium products or services, quality is essential to your brand and something to prioritize in your marketing.

TIP

This brand positioning strategy enables you to charge more than your competitors and attract quality-conscious customers. An even more powerful strategy is to combine quality with low cost. If you can deliver higher-quality products for less money, customers won't have much reason to buy from your competitors.

Cost and value

Many brands choose to compete simply by offering the lowest prices, and some are successful at it — Walmart, for example. This strategy generally undermines the purpose of branding, however. It's the right approach if you're selling a commodity (something that's pretty much the same regardless of who's making it or selling it), but it's usually the wrong approach for a brand (something distinct that people are willing to pay more for).

Competing on value is usually a more effective strategy as long as you consider the cost to you. With the value strategy, you're offering people more for their money. But adding value doesn't necessarily cost *you* more. You may be able to introduce a superior product or service that doesn't cost you more to produce but that you can charge more money for.

WARNING

Competing on cost alone is usually a loser's game that drives down revenue across an industry, but it can work with the right strategy.

Credibility and trust

For career, service, and some personal brands, credibility and trust are top priorities and are high on the list of brand positioning strategies. You build credibility by demonstrating your knowledge and expertise via website and social media content, speaking engagements, podcasts, and videos. You build trust by being reliable and trustworthy and by demonstrating a track record of serving customers successfully, earning high ratings, positive reviews, and glowing testimonials.

Checking out the competition

When positioning a brand, you're doing so relative to competitors — anyone and anything that draws attention and money from your brand. Competitors can be direct or indirect:

>> A *direct competitor* offers pretty much the same thing you do.

>> An *indirect competitor* presents alternatives to what you offer.

For an airline, another airline is a direct competitor, whereas high-speed rail would be an indirect competitor — one that offers an alternative to flying.

When you're creating a brand, you need to know what you're up against, so check out the competition. Here are a few ways to identify your competitors and find out how they're positioning their brands:

>> Search the web for what your brand offers to find brands that offer the same thing or something similar.

>> After finding potential competitors via a web search, explore their websites to see how they're positioning themselves. Check out their mission and value statements, their visuals, their blog posts, and any testimonials they've posted.

>> Use Similarweb (https://www.similarweb.com) to identify sites similar to those of brands you've already identified as competitors (or sites that are similar to your own). Similarweb provides analytics for popular websites; if you're researching smaller brands, you may find little to no info about them there.

>> Check out your competitors' social media profiles, posts, and comments from their followers or fans.

>> Shop in your competitors' stores; buy and use their products and services. Experiencing your competitors as a customer can provide fresh insight into what they do better than you, and vice versa.

Identifying what makes your brand different and better

Brand positioning is all about *differentiation* — demonstrating that what you offer is special. Think in terms of your industry, the specific market segment you're targeting, the features and benefits of what your brand offers, and the emotion you want people to feel when they encounter your brand. Complete the form shown in Figure 3-1 to identify what makes your brand special (different and better). As you complete the form, refer to the following descriptions of each field in the form:

>> **Your brand's name:** You name your brand later in this chapter. For now, just enter a tentative or placeholder name — something that describes your brand.

>> **The classification of what you're offering:** Enter the industry, market, or product/service class, such as grocery delivery service, family dental practice, or online sports betting.

>> **Your brand's distinction:** Enter a word or phrase that distinguishes your brand in its class, such as *first, best, fastest, most highly rated,* or *coolest.*

>> **Your brand's unique features and benefits:** Briefly describe what makes your brand distinctive in terms of features and benefits. See the earlier section "Product/service features and benefits" for details.

>> **Your target customers' profile:** Briefly describe the people you want to be most enthusiastic about your brand, such as parents committed to their children's health, strong women dedicated to the environment, seniors who want to stay fit, or people who are afraid of being attacked or robbed in their own homes.

>> **The emotion you want your customers to feel when they encounter your brand:** Specify how you want customers to feel about your brand, such as safe, secure, confident, successful, comfortable, or pampered.

The completed form reveals what makes your brand different and better in the eyes of those who matter most: your target customers.

What Makes Your Brand Special?	
Your brand's name:	
The classification of what you're offering:	
Your brand's distinction:	
Your brand's unique features and benefits:	
Your target customers' profile:	
The emotion you want your customers to feel when they encounter your brand:	

FIGURE 3-1: Determine what makes your brand special.

Identifying your place on a brand positioning map

One of the most effective tools for brand positioning is a *brand positioning map* (or *perceptual map*), which illustrates the relative position of two or more brands with respect to two attributes that are key to the success of those brands, such as price and quality, healthy and tasty, reliability and luxury, or customer experience and location.

Figure 3-2 shows a brand positioning map for various automobile manufacturers, showing their relative positions in terms of how consumers may perceive their price and reliability.

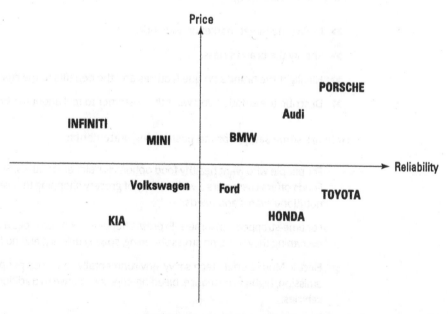

FIGURE 3-2: A brand positioning map.

To create a brand positioning map, take the following steps:

1. **Choose two brand attributes that matter most to your brand in the competitive environment in which it exists (or will exist).**

2. **Draw a two-axis grid with an axis for each attribute, and label the extremes on each axis.**

   You might label one end of the axis Expensive and the other end Inexpensive, for example.

3. **Plot points for your brand and competing brands on the grid to show their positions with relation to the two attributes.**

Repeat this exercise for several key attributes.

TIP

Consider plotting two points for your brand to show where it's positioned now and where you'd like it to be positioned 6 or 12 months down the road. The space between the points will provide a general measure of how much progress you need to make and in which directions.

Writing your brand positioning statement

After analyzing your brand and competing brands and their relative positions, you should have a pretty clear idea of how you want to position your brand as something special. Now you're ready to write your brand positioning statement to delineate precisely what makes your brand special. A brand positioning statement must do the following:

» Define the target market or audience.

» Specify the brand's class.

» Highlight the brand's unique features and the benefits to the customer.

» Describe the emotion you want the customer to feel about the brand.

Here are some sample brand positioning statements:

For people who want healthy food options for diet alternatives, Super Healthy Foods offers customers a wide variety of grocery shopping that can accommodate nutritional wants and needs.

For time-strapped consumers, Express Shopping Today provides a one-stop shop for everything they need, no-stress shopping, speedy delivery, and no-hassle returns.

Electric Motors offers tech-savvy, environmentally conscious people a zero-emission, high-performance, bleeding-edge alternative to traditional gasoline vehicles.

Use the following fill-in-the-blanks template to create your own brand positioning statement:

> *[Your brand's tentative name]* is the *[first, best, only]* *[brand class]* to offer *[unique features and benefits]* to *[customer profile]* making them feel *[emotion about the brand]*.

REMEMBER

Your brand positioning statement doesn't have to be so formulaic. Just try to keep it brief while detailing what makes your brand special to your target customers.

Defining Your Brand Identity

Brand identity is the personality and physical manifestation of a brand that makes it recognizable in people's minds. Think of it as your own identity — everything that defines you, such as your physical appearance; how you move, dress, and speak; your values, interests, knowledge, and skills; your personality; your purpose in life; and so on.

REMEMBER

You'll also encounter the term *brand image*. *Brand identity* refers to how you want people to perceive your brand. *Brand image* is more about how people actually perceive it. Defining your brand identity is the process of determining how you want people to perceive your brand.

Note that many people equate brand identity with the brand's visual design elements, such as its logo, colors, and font. Not everyone experiences a brand visually, however. Some people experience it through the brand's audio assets (such as a jingle), through its messaging, or through direct engagement. Visuals are just one way of expressing a brand's identity.

Establishing your brand's mission and values

When you think about your own identity, you're usually seeking the answer to the question "Who am I?" You're trying to discover your essence — what makes you *you,*— and that's tough. You need to evaluate your belief system, your core values, and your life's purpose.

The same is true for a brand. Engage in some deep soul-searching to figure out what your brand is all about. Explore its mission, vision, and values . . . or define what you want them to be.

Describing your brand's mission

Every business and brand should have a mission statement describing its purpose — why it exists and its big goal or purpose. I strongly encourage you to write a mission statement for your brand. Here are a few examples:

Google: To organize the world's information and make it universally accessible and useful.

Starbucks: To inspire and nurture the human spirit — one person, one cup, and one neighborhood at a time.

Sony: To be a company that inspires and fulfills your curiosity. Using our unlimited passion for technology, content, services to deliver ground-breaking new excitement and entertainment in ways that only Sony can.

Water.org: To bring safe water and sanitation to the world.

What's your brand's mission?

To _____ _____

_____

_____

MISSION OR VISION?

Some brands use either a mission or vision statement and consider the two to be interchangeable. Other brands distinguish between mission and vision statements; for them, a mission statement describes the brand's current goals and its approach to achieving those goals in the near term, whereas a vision statement expresses the brand's future aspirations. The purpose of a mission statement is to keep everyone in the organization on the same page regarding the brand's purpose, whereas the purpose of a vision statement is to inspire.

LinkedIn is a brand that has both a mission and vision statement:

- **Mission:** To connect the world's professionals to make them more productive and successful

- **Vision:** To create economic opportunity for every member of the global workforce

Whether you write a mission or vision statement or both doesn't matter much, but you should write at least one to clarify your brand's purpose — its reason for being.

Defining your brand's values

Values are principles or standards that govern thinking and behaviors. A brand's values govern the organization's decisions; policies; daily operations; and engagement with customers, vendors, and partners. Whereas mission and vision describe *what* the brand is and *why* it exists, values influence *how* the brand operates.

Create a list of what your brand values most; then rearrange the items on your list from most to least important. Your list may include the following:

>> Customer satisfaction

>> Innovation

>> Continuous improvement

>> Profitability

>> Transparency

>> Flexibility

>> Personalization

>> Teamwork

>> Integrity

>> Diversity, equity, and inclusion

>> Relationships

Another approach is to write value statements, which are more like principles or policies, such as the following:

>> Do the right thing.

>> Have fun.

>> Deliver the highest-quality products and customer service possible.

>> Treat customers as they would like to be treated.

>> Protect and preserve the environment.

Exploring your brand's personality

If your brand were a person, what kind of person would it be? Sexy and sophisticated? Young, hip, and sassy? Rugged and outdoorsy? Successful and charming? Bold and creative? *Brand personality* is the set of human traits attributed to a brand.

You want your brand to have a readily identifiable personality that appeals to your target market. Here are a few brands that have strong personalities:

Brand	Personality
Amazon	Reliable, trustworthy, responsive
Apple	Cool, creative, sleek
Coca-Cola	Enthusiastic, fun-loving, social, approachable
Harley-Davidson	Rugged, rebellious

One way to identify your brand's personality is to look at brand archetypes (common personality types), such as the following:

>> Artist/inventor

>> Caregiver

>> Explorer

>> Friend

>> Smart

>> Hero(ine)

>> Innocent

>> Magician

>> Minimalistic person

>> Confident

>> Leader

Writing your brand identity statement

When you have an intimate understanding of "who" your brand is — its mission, vision, values, and personality — you're ready to formalize it in the form of a brand identity statement. In this section, I lead you through the process.

REMEMBER

Clarifying your brand's identity in your own mind and the minds of your team members is important, because brand identity drives the look and feel of the brand and ensures that everything you do to project its identity is consistent. If you don't have a clear idea of what your brand's identity is, your brand assets and messaging will be inconsistent, reducing their impact and causing confusion in your target market.

Covering the essentials

When writing your brand identity statement, make sure that it includes the following essential elements:

>> **Your brand's name or tentative name:** Discussed in the later section "Naming Your Brand"

>> **Your brand's point of differentiation:** What your brand offers that's better than the alternatives

>> **Your target market:** The people you most want to be enthusiastic about your brand

>> **Your brand's mission or vision:** Its purpose

>> **Your brand's values:** The one or two at the top of your list

>> **Your brand's personality:** Traits that you express in words or in the tone of your brand identity statement

Structuring your brand identity statement

Your brand's identity is its essence — its lifeblood. This identity is communicated through the brand's name, logo, tagline, content marketing, advertising, signage, and public engagement.

Your brand identity statement guides everything you do to develop the brand identity you want to project. This statement must cover all the essentials listed in the previous section clearly and succinctly. Here's a template for structuring your brand identity statement, but don't feel locked into it:

> [Brand name] offers [point of differentiation] to [target market]. We are committed to [mission] through [values] with our [brand personality].

Here's an example:

> Athletipro offers a quick and easy online shopping experience and speedy delivery of equipment and supplies to amateur and professional athletes and everyone in between. We're committed to empowering each customer to achieve optimal health, fitness, and performance through research and innovation with our unequaled passion and drive.

Testing your brand identity statement

Before you invest time and effort developing a brand consistent with your brand identity statement, put it to the test. Seek feedback from others within your organization and from people outside your organization, preferably from existing or prospective customers in your target market. But you can consult friends and family members if the other options aren't available.

As you gather feedback, use it to answer the following questions:

>> Does your brand identity statement resonate with people and appeal to what matters most to them? If not, find out what would appeal to them.

>> Is the promise (mission) conveyed in your brand identity statement realistic, and can your brand deliver it consistently? If you're talking to existing customers, ask them whether they think your brand is living up to its promise.

>> What's the brand's perceived personality, and how does it compare with how you want your brand to be perceived?

>> What do you think you need to do to bring people's perception of your brand more in line with the brand identity you envision?

Naming Your Brand

Now more than ever, you need to catch the attention of prospective customers quickly and hold it for more than a few seconds. People are constantly being inundated with advertisements and offers, so your brand name needs to stand out. Choosing a brand name is one of the most important branding decisions you'll ever make.

Maybe you have a brand name in mind; maybe you don't. Either way, work through the brand-naming process described in this section. If you don't have a name in mind, this process will stimulate your creativity. If you already have a name in mind, this process will put it to the test and perhaps even lead you to a much better name.

The process of naming your brand can influence your decisions about brand positioning and identity; it can elevate your concept of the brand and its mission and values. Outdoor Voices, an athleisure brand, was inspired by adults encouraging children to use their "inside voices." Outdoor Voices encourages the opposite. Its mission is "to get the world moving" with active wear for both indoor and outdoor recreation. The brand targets teens and adults who want to step outside their comfort zones.

Following brand naming parameters

Before you start thinking about naming your brand, be aware of the following characteristics of a good brand name:

>> Positions your brand advantageously

>> Clearly communicates your brand's identity

>> Reflects your brand's promise or offerings

>> Is easy to say and spell

>> Is unique — available to trademark and available as a domain name (for use as a website address and part of your email address)

>> Is memorable and concise

>> Accommodates future expansion

>> Is consistent with your chosen brand architecture — a branded house or a house of brands (see Chapter 1)

Here are a few examples of descriptive brand names to use as inspiration:

>> AutoZone vehicle parts and supplies

>> Energizer batteries

>> Drano drain opener

>> Mr. Clean household cleaner

>> Ziploc storage bags

>> Windex glass cleaner

>> Dairy Queen ice cream

REMEMBER

A descriptive brand name can certainly help, but it's not essential. Plenty of successful brands have nondescriptive names, such as Google, Target, and Louis Vuitton.

Brainstorming brand names

Brainstorming is a creative activity in which you suspend critical thinking and give your right brain free rein. It's generally a group activity involving several team members gathered in a conference room with a whiteboard and markers, calling out and jotting down ideas that pop into their heads.

I encourage you to take the same approach, alone or with others, to come up with a long list of possible brand names. Suspend your critical mind, and jot down any brand names that pop into your head or the heads of other participants. There should be no criticizing, ignoring, scoffing at, or crossing off any ideas.

TIP

Encourage everyone to participate, consider alternative perspectives (such as the target customer's), and explain their thinking. Sometimes, digging into the thought process behind a suggested brand name can spark additional ideas.

Choosing the best brand name

When you have a long list of brand-name candidates, narrow it down to three to five names. At this point, you switch from right-brain (creative) mode to left-brain (critical) mode.

You can start by crossing obviously lousy names off the list, but as you cut more names, competition for the top spot stiffens. Evaluate the remaining names based on the criteria presented in the earlier section "Following brand naming parameters."

When only a few brand name candidates remain, you can debate the merits of each in the hopes of narrowing the list further. If that approach doesn't work, you may want to engage in another brainstorming session.

WARNING

Try to avoid choosing a brand name by popular vote. That approach often results in choosing a brand name that's simply not as bad as the others. Instead, continue debating which brand name candidate is best, or conduct another brainstorming session to generate fresh ideas to consider.

WARNING

Once you've landed on a name you'd like to use for your brand, you need to make sure it is not trademarked and that you can legally use it. For more information on trademarking, go to Chapter 19.

Chapter 4

Clarifying Your Branding Goals

One of the biggest mistakes people make when they start branding is that they start branding. I know that sounds odd, but my point is that most people start by creating a website or blog or podcast before they have any idea of what they're trying to accomplish. As a result, they work too hard at it, everything they do has little or no impact, they have nothing in place to figure out why, and they begin to wonder what they're doing wrong. What they did wrong is that they started branding when they should have started planning.

As Steven Covey, author of the best-seller *The 7 Habits of Highly Effective People*, advises, "Start with the end in mind." After all, how can you hope to get where you're going if you don't even know where that is?

In this chapter, I encourage you and guide you through the process of starting with the end in mind by establishing branding goals and figuring out the best methods to achieve those goals. Then I proceed to explain how to put a system in place to measure success and identify what's working and what's not so you can make well-informed adjustments moving forward.

Identifying Your Branding Goals/Objectives

Ultimately, many people have the same branding goals: a better, richer life: more money; more free time; enjoyable, rewarding work; and delighted customers/clients. We can all dream, right? Unfortunately, "a better, richer life" doesn't cut it as a branding goal because it's not SMART:

>> **Specific:** The goal of "a better, richer life" is vague. Specifically, what do you want to accomplish? Increased sales? Lucrative speaking engagements? More and better clients for your consulting business? Book deals with major publishers?

>> **Measurable:** Setting a measurable, quantifiable goal provides a way to evaluate success. A better goal than "increased sales," for example, would be "a 10 percent boost in sales over last year."

>> **Attainable:** Aim high, but make sure you're setting up goals along the way. Smaller goals that help you achieve your end objective are important to keep momentum going in building a brand. If you have high goals, simply make a roadmap to help get there.

>> **Relevant:** Be sure that your goal will strengthen your brand. You must have a good answer to the question "If I achieve this goal, how will it improve my brand?" Be mindful that as your brand evolves, so do your goals and your relevance.

>> **Time-based:** Specify a deadline for achieving your goal. Otherwise, procrastination is too easy.

In the following sections, I introduce five branding goals/objectives to consider and present different ways to achieve each one. These goals/objectives are just a small sample to get you pointed in the right direction and spark your creativity.

REMEMBER

Goals and objectives are basically the same, and I use the terms interchangeably, but I draw the following distinction in the context of planning to meet goals: A *goal* is the one big thing you want to accomplish, whereas an *objective* is a smaller goal that you need to accomplish to meet your big goal. Suppose that your goal is to increase sales by 20 percent over last year. Your objectives could be to increase direct traffic to my website by 10 percent, grow your email contact list by 5 percent, and increase positive word of mouth on social media by 20 percent.

Increasing brand recognition and awareness

A top goal of all branding is to increase brand recognition and awareness. *Brand recognition* is the ability of consumers to identify a brand by its attributes, such as its logo or distinctive colors. You may see the familiar green-and-white mermaid logo, for example, and instantly recognize it as the Starbucks logo. *Brand awareness* is the extent to which consumers understand what a specific brand represents or stands for. You see the Starbucks logo and know that it represents quality coffee and a relaxing and enjoyable experience.

Brand recognition and awareness are fundamental to a brand's success. After all, if people don't know about your brand, it's not much of a brand. Brand recognition and awareness can open doors to customers, opportunities, and partnerships. These factors are especially important if you're hoping to partner with large corporations because they'll want social proof of your brand's intrinsic value, such as number of friends and followers.

TIP

If you're looking to form strategic partnerships or get your products into the big-box retailers, building brand recognition and awareness is the way to do it.

When building brand recognition and awareness is the goal, you may find the following branding activities to be particularly useful:

>> **Giveaways:** A *giveaway* is just what it sounds like: providing free merchandise or services to consumers. Giveaways may involve swag, such as branded pens, key chains, koozies, and retail bags; sample products or services; free trial subscriptions; or contests. You can do giveaways alone or in conjunction with partners (see Chapter 9). You can do them at physical locations (see Chapter 11), online via your website or blog (see Chapter 12), or via social media (see Chapter 13).

>> **Press releases:** Harnessing the power of the press (print, television, radio, and online news) is a great way to create buzz with very little effort. All you need to do is plan something newsworthy, such as an exciting event or a product launch, and distribute a press release about it. (See Chapter 10 for more about teaming up with the media.)

>> **Influencer campaign:** An *influencer campaign* is a marketing tactic that involves recruiting or hiring people who are well known and trusted in target markets to give their endorsements. See Chapter 13 for guidance on how to launch an influencer campaign of your own.

Whenever I add a new product to my Girl Gang brand, I initiate a small, organic influencer campaign. Over time, I've developed strong relationships with a small group of influencers, who contribute significantly to the success of every new product release.

TIP

You may be able to expand your brand's reach with one macro influencer or multiple micro influencers. A *macro influencer* is someone with celebrity status (a household name) — someone with tens of thousands to millions of followers on social media. A *micro influencer*, on the other hand, has followers in the range of 10,000 to 50,000. Micro influencers charge significantly less for their services and may even promote a brand they really like for free.

>> **Brand partnerships:** A *brand partnership* is an agreement between at least two businesses that want to help each other increase their brand exposure. Teaming up with a brand that has an audience you're hoping to reach can be very helpful. Strategically partnering with another brand can bring in a new audience, create sales opportunities, and offer brand exposure for both companies. (See Chapter 9 for details about building strategic partnerships.)

Impossible Foods, a vegan food company famous for its plant-based burger patty, teamed up with Burger King to create the Impossible Whopper. This brand partnership is a great match because each company is reaching a new market. Burger King is adding a menu item for vegetarian customers who previously wouldn't buy its beef burgers, and Impossible Foods is reaching customers at a popular fast-food chain who may not have tried its product.

>> **Traditional advertising:** Depending on the product or service you offer, traditional advertising in the right outlet can help create brand awareness. If you're launching a coaching business, taking out an advertisement in a magazine or journal that's popular in your industry can give you exposure to precisely the market you're trying to reach.

TIP

Before buying any ad space, check out the publication's circulation, which provides insight into the maximum number of people who will see the advertisement, as well as the demographic, which is the target audience. Use these to make sure the reach and target demographic align with your goals. For the purpose of increasing brand awareness, this metric (measure of value) is key.

THE POWER OF THE PRESS

To promote my husband's Color Me Book brand (personalized coloring books), we created a press release and posted it to one media outlet: BuzzFeed Books. After the press release was picked up and trending on the main BuzzFeed website, we started attracting more interest for interviews and features.

To make it easy for others to discuss the launch of our company online (on their websites, blogs, and social media accounts), I posted our press release and media kit on our website in a section titled About Us. This material included the basic info, logos, and high-resolution photos needed to produce articles and other content about the Color Me Book brand quickly and easily.

I also included an email address dedicated to press inquiries that journalists and bloggers could use to contact us for interviews. As soon as news of his product hit the press, it went viral, and orders started pouring in.

Creating an emotional connection

In many ways, building a strong brand is about building strong relationships. People form relationships with one another based not so much on what they think about each other but on how they feel toward one another. The same is true of relationships that people create with their favorite brands. It's not so much what they know about your brand but how they feel about it that keeps them coming back and endorsing it.

One of your top branding goals should be to create an emotional connection with existing and prospective customers and clients. Stop thinking so much about what your brand is and what it offers, and start thinking more about how prospective customers and clients feel about it. How does your brand affect their lives? Get personal. Taking a more personalized approach enables you to nurture an emotional connection between your customers and your brand.

Here are a few suggestions for getting your customers, clients, and prospects connected more emotionally to your brand:

» **Get connected to the people in your market.** When you're connected to others, you're in tune with their needs and desires, what they like and dislike, and who they are. You "get" them, and when you do, you intuitively know what to do and say to get them to love your brand. Maybe they appreciate a good laugh. Maybe they're afraid of what's going on in the world. Maybe they have a common cause.

When you know what makes your customers tick, you can market more effectively to them. If you're serving a community that's committed to environmental issues, you could post blog entries about environmental issues and perhaps offer products made from recycled materials.

» **Share real stories.** People like to see brands in a real-life context, so look for opportunities to tell customer stories. Better yet, encourage customers to share their experiences with your brand. You can take advantage of this type of user-generated content (see Chapter 13) in your social media, website, and newsletter.

» **Add a personal touch.** Nothing makes a person feel more emotionally connected to a brand than being acknowledged and appreciated personally. Adding a personal touch can be as simple as addressing customers by name, calling them on the phone when they have a complaint, or liking and sharing their social media posts about your brand.

REMEMBER

Strive to personalize your brand's voice, as explained in Chapter 8, especially when you're scaling up and having to delegate or outsource some or all of your marketing. Creating a brand style guide, as explained in Chapter 6, can help ensure consistency in your brand's voice when you're having to distribute your workload.

Differentiating your business, product, service, or self

Brand differentiation involves setting your brand apart from the competition, and it's one of the most important branding goals. You want to plant the perception in the minds and hearts of existing and prospective customers and clients that your brand is different from and better than the alternatives. Otherwise, people have no reason to do business with you instead of one of your competitors.

To differentiate your brand, find or create a unique selling proposition and a value proposition. A *unique selling proposition* (USP) is a statement about what makes your brand different from and better than competing brands. A *value proposition* is a clear statement of the tangible benefits of your products and services.

Here are a few ways to differentiate your brand with USPs and added value:

>> **Narrow your target demographic.** New brands may not be able to win a war against bigger, well-entrenched brands, but they can win some battles to gain a foothold and start building momentum. Narrowing your target demographic enables you to differentiate your brand in a smaller market.

>> **Create a different price point for a popular product.** Notice that I said *different*, not *lower*. Your price may be lower to appeal to the budget-conscious or higher to appeal to the quality-conscious.

WARNING

Don't start a price war with well-established brands. Why not? Well, for one thing, you'll lose, and in the process, everyone in your industry will lose because you're all trying to undercut one another.

>> **Focus on customer service.** Promising and delivering superior customer service is a great way to differentiate your brand when your brand is nearly identical to competing brands.

Differentiation is all about creating a market niche, as explained in Chapter 2.

Building credibility and trust

People buy only the brands they believe and trust, so one of your branding goals should be to build credibility and trust and not do anything that undermines these attributes. Here are a few ways you can build credibility and trust in your brand:

>> **Demonstrate your knowledge and expertise.** Use *content marketing* (valuable, relevant content that doesn't explicitly promote your brand) to show that you know your stuff. You can distribute content in the form of web pages,

blog posts, email messages, newsletters, press releases, podcasts, videos, and more.

>> **Keep your promises.** Salespeople have a motto: "Underpromise and overdeliver." Don't make your customers expect more than you can reasonably deliver. Do what you say you're going to do. If you launch a preorder, be sure that the date you promise to ship the product is realistic; then meet or beat that date. If an unforeseen delay arises, keep your preorder customers informed so that they know what to expect.

>> **Use customer and client testimonials.** Include testimonials and positive quotations about your brand on your website or blog and in your marketing materials. Testimonials are especially effective for business-to-business brands because they show that you have a track record of delivering quality products or services.

Business-to-consumer businesses can also benefit from testimonials. After launching our brand Color Me Book, we reached out to satisfied customers to request testimonials, which we then posted on our site.

>> **Embrace transparency.** Be open and honest. If you say or do something wrong, own up to it, apologize, and try to undo any damage. Denial and shifting the blame may work in politics, but they'll destroy a business.

Driving sales

Often, the goal of branding activities is to drive sales. Some activities drive sales directly, and others do so indirectly. Here are a few direct approaches for motivating customers and clients to buy what you're selling:

>> **Advertise your brand.** Traditional and online advertising are great for building brand recognition and awareness while driving sales. See Chapter 15 for details about using advertising to promote your brand.

>> **Offer freebies and promotional deals.** The best way to persuade prospects to buy your product is to get them to experience your brand's value. To do that, you need to get your foot in the door. Offering a sample product, a free consultation, or a 100 percent money-back guarantee are all ways to reduce customers' exposure to risk, so they're more likely to give you a chance.

>> **Create a loyalty program.** A loyalty program rewards customers for repeat business, and every encounter you have with a customer or client is an opportunity to prove your brand's value.

Creating Your One-Year Branding Plan

With branding goals in place, you're ready to build a plan for achieving those goals. Start by outlining your plan. Create a document that includes the following sections:

>> **Goal:** What you hope to accomplish by the end of the year, such as 25 new clients or $100,000 in sales revenue. Make sure that your goal is SMART, as explained in "Identifying Your Branding Goals/Objectives" earlier in this chapter.

>> **Objectives:** Mini goals that you must achieve to meet your overall goal, such as increasing brand recognition and awareness among millennials.

>> **Strategy:** A *strategy* is nothing more than a big plan. Suppose that your goal is to increase your brand's market share by 10 percent over last year. You could use different strategies to achieve that goal, such as positioning your brand as being the highest-quality or marketing your brand as the most socially conscious.

>> **Tactics:** *Tactics* are specific activities for executing the strategy, such as launching a website, creating five branded social media properties, or buying $5,000 in online advertising.

>> **Timeline:** Break down your one-year plan into more manageable milestones. What do you need to accomplish in three months, six months, nine months, and 12 months to reach your goal? Or what do you need to accomplish each month to reach your goal?

>> **Budget:** How much money do you plan to invest in your brand over the coming year? If you're just getting started, this amount will be a fixed dollar amount; later, it could be a percentage of sales revenue.

Monitoring and Evaluating the Success of Your Branding Efforts

Whether you set personal, professional, or business goals, having a way to measure your success in meeting those goals is essential. Otherwise, you're flying blind; you have no idea whether what you're doing to achieve your goals is working and no insight into what you could be doing differently or better.

To measure success, you need two things: metrics and analytics. *Metrics* are quantitative measures used to track performance, such as sales revenue, customer retention, and online sales conversions. *Analytics* involves examining the metrics in various ways to gain insight into what you can do to improve performance.

In the following sections, I explain how to use metrics and analytics to monitor and evaluate the success of your branding efforts.

The purpose of metrics and analytics is to enable you to make data-driven decisions instead of relying on hunches or guesses.

Choosing metrics and key performance indicators

The first step in measuring and monitoring performance is figuring out what you're going to measure. Here are some important branding metrics:

>> **Brand recognition:** The extent to which people in your market recognize your brand when they see your product or logo

>> **Brand awareness:** The extent to which people in your market understand what your brand represents or stands for

>> **Brand consideration:** The percentage of customers who would be open to the possibility of buying your brand

>> **Perceived quality:** The extent to which people in your market associate your brand with high quality

>> **Sales:** Metrics that reflect a brand's success, including the following:

- Number of sales

- Sales conversion rate

- Customer lifetime value

- Average order value

>> **Net promoter score (NPS):** NPS is a measure of brand loyalty on a scale of 1 to 10. NPS may be measured in return sales, referrals, or answers to survey questions (such as "On a scale of 1–10, how likely are you to recommend our brand to a friend or family member?").

Note that metrics have no specific value attached to them; they're just measures, like inches and pounds. To make them meaningful for tracking the success of your branding activities, you need to turn them into *key performance indicators* (KPIs) — specific goals, such as a 10 percent increase in brand consideration or an NPS of 8 or higher.

Collecting and analyzing data: The tools of the trade

To use metrics and analytics most effectively, become familiar with the tools of the trade for collecting and analyzing data. Here's a list of tools to consider:

» **Google Analytics** (https://analytics.google.com) is great for collecting and analyzing data on websites and blogs. All you do is insert a line of code into your website's header, and Google Analytics starts collecting data, including number of users, new users, and average engagement time on the site.

» **SurveyMonkey** (https://www.surveymonkey.com) makes creating surveys and collecting and analyzing survey data a snap. Surveys are valuable in analyzing key metrics, such as brand recognition and awareness.

» **Sprout Social** (https://sproutsocial.com) is one of many social media management platforms. It enables you to streamline and scale engagement efforts via various social media platforms; plan, create, schedule, and publish content to your brand's social media accounts; and analyze customer engagement data.

» **Asana** (https://asana.com) is a full-featured project management platform that includes marketing tools for planning and tracking marketing campaigns, new product launches, and more.

» **Salesforce** (https://www.salesforce.com) is a full-featured customer relationship management platform that includes multiple marketing-specific tools, including an email marketing platform, a Journey Builder (for tracking your developing relationships with customers), Interaction Studio (to visualize, track, and manage real-time customer experiences), and Datorama (for managing marketing data, KPIs, and decisions). It also includes tools for managing social media accounts, personalizing mobile interactions, and advertising to customers individually.

» **Geckoboard** (https://www.geckoboard.com) is an analytics dashboard that enables you to visualize and share data, metrics, and KPIs. (*Data visualization* involves presenting data in charts, graphs, maps, and other graphic forms to make the data more meaningful.)

Chapter **5**

Defining and Refining Your Customer Avatars

The ultimate goal of branding is to establish an emotional bond between your brand and consumers. To accomplish that feat, you need to know your prospective customers — their likes and dislikes, where they go for information, where they shop, what they do for a living, what they like to do in their free time, their values and political affiliations, and more. The better you know your prospective customers, the more effectively you'll be able to reach them via the media channels they use and bond with them via marketing and advertising.

One way to get to know your target customers is to work through the process of creating *customer avatars* — fictional characters that represents your ideal customer. In this chapter, I lead you through that process.

REMEMBER

Customer avatars are useful in marketing/branding, product development, and rebranding. They can inspire new products and help guide product design and development.

Discovering Who Your Target Customers Are

The first step in creating a customer avatar involves identifying who your target customers are and gathering information about them. Think of this process as a reconnaissance mission; you scout the market looking for a niche and then find out all you can about the consumers in that niche. As you gather information, you begin to recognize patterns across the consumer group that you can use to create a customer avatar.

Ultimately, you want to create at least three distinct customer avatars to accommodate a broad enough market. Focusing on only one customer type in a given niche results in missed opportunities. If you try to promote your brand to everyone, however, your messaging will lack impact; it'll be all over the place and be unlikely to resonate with any group.

REMEMBER

If you don't know the people you're marketing to, you'll have more difficulty creating content and campaigns that attract customers.

As you gather data as described in the following sections, complete a form like the one shown in Figure 5-1 to create a record of your customers' interests and values, where they go for information, and so on.

Name:
Age:
Gender:

GOALS AND VALUES

Goals:

Values:

INFORMATION SOURCES

Books:
Movies:
TV Shows:
News Outlets:
Social Media Accounts:

CAREER AND EDUCATION

Job:
Income:
Education:

LIKES AND DISLIKES

Likes:

Dislikes:

FIGURE 5-1:
Gather
information
about your target
consumers.

Identifying your target customers

In the early stages of building and launching a brand, you may need to rely on guesswork or your gut to identify your target customer, at least tentatively, so that you can begin to focus your research efforts on a specific group. Jot down details about who you think your target customer is or will be. Here are a few areas to address:

>> Career or business

>> Demographics (age, gender, income level, education, marital/family status, geographical location)

>> Psychographics (interests, hobbies, lifestyle, opinions, aspirations)

>> Challenges, problems, or pain points

>> Where the person goes for information (news outlets, social media platforms, websites, books, magazines, and so on)

>> Where the person shops (bricks-and-mortar retail stores, websites, specific stores)

>> Reasons why the customer may not buy your brand

REMEMBER

The purpose of this general information is to narrow the focus of your research so that you'll know whom to gather data from and where to find the right people to research and survey. In other words, this general information helps you gather the specific information you need to create a detailed customer avatar.

Gathering and analyzing data about your target customers

Whether you've already launched your brand and have customer data to analyze internally or have no internal data source, you can gather data about your target customer.

If you have customers, you can use the following techniques to collect customer information and feedback:

>> Sales and marketing associates and customer service personnel probably have valuable data based on their interactions with customers.

>> Interview or survey existing customers to find out what they think.

>> Examine your website and social media analytics to gain insight into people who visit your online properties. (See Chapter 7 for information about web analytics and Chapter 13 for details on social media analytics.)

>> Examine your email analytics to find out what works and what doesn't in terms of communications with existing customers. (See Chapter 14 for information about email analytics.)

If you haven't launched your brand, you have no internal data to draw on, but you can research external data to find out more about your target customer. Here are a few approaches to consider:

>> Survey your friends and followers on social media.

>> Examine your competitors' blog and social media properties to find out who's engaging with their brands.

>> Participate in industry blogs and forums to get a general idea of who's active in those communities.

>> Identify social media influencers (see Chapter 13) in the market you're pursuing, and check out their followers and fans. You can also follow influencers and engage with them to get a better feel for prospective customers.

Conducting a focus group

A *focus group* is an assembly of people who gather to answer questions, offer input, and engage in discussion about a product, service, brand, political campaign, television series, and so on. Conducting a focus group to gather feedback about your brand is a great way to obtain information about your target customers.

To set up and conduct a focus group, take the following steps:

1. **Come up with a list of questions to ask members of the focus group, such as the following general questions:**

   - What are your favorite TV shows, movies, or podcasts?
   - How do you spend your weekends?
   - Which social media platform are you most active on?
   - What's your highest level of education?
   - What is your dream vacation?
   - What are your favorite magazines?

- Where do you do most of your shopping?

- Currently, what's the biggest challenge you face or your biggest source of worry?

If focus group members are existing customers, ask more targeted questions about your brand, such as the following:

- How did you find out about us?

- When, how, and where do you use our products or services?

- What makes our products stand out from competition?

- What other brands do you think of when you think about our product?

- Would you recommend our brand to a friend?

2. **Create an incentive for participants.**

You can choose to pay people to participate (money or a gift card); offer a free product or discount; or offer some swag, such as a branded tote bag, umbrella, T-shirt, or coffee mug.

TIP

If you're gathering feedback about a specific product or product changes under consideration, gifting your product and getting honest feedback is a great way to find out whether your brand is heading in the right direction.

3. **Choose a location that's convenient for participants, comfortable, and free of interruptions and distractions.**

If you have a physical location, great. Another option is to conduct a focus group online, allowing people to participate remotely via conferencing platforms.

4. **Implement a way to record your focus group session so that later, you can closely analyze what participants said, how they said it, and how they interacted with one another and with the moderator.**

5. **Recruit participants.**

You can recruit via email, phone, text, or social media, or use a recruitment firm such as FieldworkHub (https://fieldworkhub.com) or Focus Insite (https://focusinsite.com), to connect with participants who meet your criteria.

6. **Schedule your focus group, and send out invitations specifying the date, time, and location.**

7. **Conduct your focus group.**

Here's a sample outline:

- *Introduction:* Introduce yourself, thank the participants for coming, describe the purpose of the focus group, and explain how the session will be conducted.

- *Icebreaker:* Have the participants introduce themselves and say something interesting about themselves, such as what superpower they'd most like to have.

- *Questions/discussion*: Pose your questions to the group, and lead the discussion. Be sure that everyone participates and nobody monopolizes the discussion.

- *Wrap-up:* Thank everyone for participating in the focus group, and distribute any promised incentives.

Conducting a survey

Surveys enable you to obtain feedback without having to gather people and lead a discussion. All you do is call, email, or present the survey questions online or on location, instructing participants to answer the questions.

You can recruit participants by using the same methods you would use for a focus group and ask the same questions, as explained in the preceding section. Several online platforms facilitate the process of creating and distributing surveys and tabulating the results, including the following:

- » SurveyMonkey (https://www.surveymonkey.com)

- » SoGoSurvey (https://www.sogosurvey.com)

- » SurveyAnyplace (https://surveyanyplace.com)

Evaluating your customers' interests

Evaluating your customers interests enables you to create products and content they enjoy and value. If you have an athleisure (athletic–leisure) brand, and you know that your brand is popular among yoga enthusiasts, you can incorporate yoga imagery, articles, and tutorials in your content marketing. (See Chapter 8 for more about content marketing.) When doing a photoshoot for your products, you might consider doing it on location in a yoga studio.

TIP

Knowing your customers' interests also enables you to target paid advertising campaigns more effectively. Instead of advertising to everyone, you advertise only to those who are most likely to respond positively to your ads. In addition, you can create ads that are more likely to appeal to your target customers. (See Chapter 15 for more about paid advertising.)

To gather information about a customer's interests, ask questions in a broad range of categories in your focus group or survey. Categories may include food and drink, entertainment, travel, fashion, home decor, health and fitness, hobbies, and values/causes. Ask specific questions to elicit more details from each participant. For the food and drink category, you might ask the following questions:

>> Do you consider yourself to be a foodie?

>> Do you prefer local restaurants or large franchises?

>> When you're choosing a restaurant, what's more important: good taste or good health?

>> Do you have any diet restrictions?

>> What's your favorite meal?

>> What's your favorite nonalcoholic beverage?

TIP

As you evaluate customer interests, think about how those interests align with your brand's identity and may influence the brand identity you're trying to create. In 2013, in response to demand for healthier foods, McDonald's began working with the Alliance for a Healthier Generation to provide customers greater access to fruits, vegetables, low-fat dairy products, and water, especially in Happy Meals, which are marketed to children. Instead of merely changing its marketing, McDonald's changed its brand.

REMEMBER

Tying customer interests to your content marketing and paid advertising demonstrates to your customer base that you're paying attention to them and are committed to serving their needs and preferences. It can also communicate subtly that your customers are a part of something bigger — a community that's built around your brand. If you don't try to appeal to specific customer interests, your efforts may not resonate as much with your target market.

YOU CAN'T PLEASE EVERYONE

You can't please everyone, and if you try, you'll fail to attract the customers who are most likely to buy what you're selling (and pay a premium for it). Your messaging will lack impact and may even cause confusion. Focus on your customer avatars' needs, interests, and challenges so that you can speak to your target audience about what matters to *them*.

(continued)

(continued)

When my husband and I launched Color Me Book, a custom coloring book, we hoped to offer competitive pricing, quick turnaround times, and a quality product. Doing all the above is nearly impossible with a custom product. We decided to focus on serving two customer types and figure out how to satisfy their needs:

- **Customer Avatar 1, a business-to-business (B2B) customer:** We created our first avatar to focus on serving a customer who's ordering our product in bulk for events and marketing initiatives. We wanted to go after high-end clients and were able to attract the Shops of Pebble Beach Resorts and The Beverly Hills Hotel, among others. For this customer type, the most important factor is quality. These customers are willing to pay a higher price to get quality goods. Turnaround time wasn't an issue, because most of our B2B customers planned well in advance, and we could deliver on a three-week production schedule, with an option to pay a rush-production fee.

- **Customer Avatar 2, a consumer purchasing the product as a gift:** The second customer we decided to target was someone purchasing a Color Me Book as a gift. Further, we targeted specific occasions when people might give such a gift: holidays, first-year wedding anniversaries (which is paper), and Mother's Day. Like the first avatar, Customer Avatar 2 focuses primarily on quality. When presenting a gift to a loved one, people are generally willing to pay more for a higher-quality present. Again, turnaround time was not an issue for these customers; holidays and special occasions are typically well publicized at least a month in advance and within the limits of our production times.

By targeting these specific groups and not trying to please customers who want the cheapest and quickest product, we were able to make our business more profitable and scale with a smaller team.

Finding out where customers go and what they do

Where your customers go and what they do, online and off, matters more than what they say, so put some effort into researching consumer behaviors. One way to research behaviors is to ask consumers questions, such as the following:

- » Where are you located?
- » What do you do in your free time?
- » What are your primary sources of news and information?
- » What's your favorite form of exercise?

>> Where do you socialize online?

>> Where do you socialize offline?

You can also gain insight into customer behaviors by buying and analyzing location and transactional data from data vendors, such as Exact Data (https://www.exactdata.com) and Complementics (https://www.complementics.com). To extract insight from the data, however, you need to have data analytics software and know how to use it.

REMEMBER

Actions speak louder than words. Near the beginning of the COVID-19 pandemic, the media led people to believe that consumers were divided into two camps: the safety-conscious and the scofflaws (those who repeatedly and knowingly violated the rules). Location data collected from smartphones, however, painted a far different picture. Early in the pandemic, most people headed to the grocery store, came home, and voluntarily or otherwise sheltered in place. In short, you may get totally different answers to your research questions if you study the data instead of asking people.

Describing Your Customer Avatars in Your Own Words

After gathering customer data, you're ready to describe your customer avatars in your own words. Write them as you would write a short biography of someone you know and love, including as much detail as possible from the data you gathered. Here's an example:

Jenae Greene is 30 years old and lives in Los Angeles, California. She graduated from San Diego State University, where she majored in marketing. She's an entrepreneur and a project director for a company that develops products to enhance meditation. Her goal is to serve others while having the financial stability to travel in her free time. When she's not working, she enjoys practicing yoga, spending time outdoors, and hanging out near the ocean.

Jenae's favorite TV shows and movies are comedies. She also loves listening to thriller podcasts.

She enjoys reading when she has the time and finding ways to optimize her time so that she can make more room for what she enjoys. Jenae is a big fan of standup comedy, having lightly explored it as a career herself.

Her favorite restaurant is Jones Italian Food and Veggie Grill.

She listens to Alabama Shakes.

Whenever she has time off work, she heads to the beach or buys a plane ticket to somewhere in the world she's never been.

She posts regularly on Instagram, where she has 2,500 followers.
She loves to shop at Nordstrom.

Fill in as much detail as you can about your customer avatar; then use this avatar whenever you're putting together branding campaigns, developing new products or services, and creating content.

Redefining Your Customer Avatars As They Evolve

In a way, your initial customer avatars are preliminary snapshots of your target customers. As you begin to sell to and to engage with customers, your customer avatars should evolve, becoming increasingly fleshed out with detail. The more data you gather from real consumers, the more you can fine-tune your avatars. In addition, times change, and people change with the times. The customer avatars you create today may no longer be relevant 12 to 18 months in the future. Keep revisiting your customer avatars as your business and the world in general evolve to ensure that you're speaking to the needs and preferences of your current customers.

The online job board Girlboss (https://www.girlboss.com), for example, has evolved considerably over the years, both in terms of the brand and its customer avatar. Originally, Girlboss sold tickets to events that helped aspiring female entrepreneurs obtain the tools and resources to succeed. Its marketing targeted millennial women, and the brand was known for creating a hue of pink later coined "millennial pink." Although the brand still appeals to female entrepreneurs, it has expanded to women who excel in their side hustles and pivot their careers. Now the brand is for women of various ages at various stages of their careers. As the brand's customer avatar changed, so did its voice and content, expanding beyond its initial demographic, enabling Girlboss to connect with new customer groups that were previously overlooked and underserved.

REMEMBER

If you're going through a rebrand or getting ready to launch a new product, conduct additional focus groups and surveys, and make any adjustments necessary to remain relevant in the current market. Keep in mind that the speed of change is constantly accelerating.

Putting Your Customer Avatars to Work

Now that you have fully fleshed out customer avatars, you're ready to put them to work for your brand. Imagine that your avatars are real customers whom you consult whenever you do anything related to your brand, such as the following:

>> Developing a new product or service or improving an existing one

>> Rebranding (changing the brand's image in some way)

>> Developing content such as blog posts, social media posts, articles, podcasts, images, and videos

>> Developing a paid advertising campaign

>> Prioritizing your marketing focus (such as deciding whether to put more effort and money marketing on Instagram or Facebook)

>> Identifying potential partnership opportunities with other brands

REMEMBER

Your customer avatars enable you to connect with customers more effectively. The customer avatar for Jenae Greene in "Describing Your Customer Avatars in Your Own Words" earlier in this chapter tells me that funny ads would probably appeal to my target customers, as would beach scenes and music by Alabama Shakes. And because my customer avatar loves to shop at Nordstrom, getting my brand into Nordstrom's stores is a priority.

Putting Your Customer Avatars to Work

Now that you have fully fleshed out customer avatars, you're ready to put them to work for your brand. Imagine that your avatars are real customers whom you consult whenever you do anything related to your brand, such as the following:

- Developing a new product or service or improving an existing one

- Rebranding (changing the brand's image in some way)

- Developing content such as blog posts, social media posts, emails, podcasts, images, and videos

- Developing a paid advertising campaign

- Prioritizing your marketing efforts, such as deciding whether to put more effort and money marketing on Instagram or Facebook

- Identifying potential partnership opportunities with other brands

Your customer avatars enable you to connect with customers more effectively. The customer avatar for Jenae Greene in "Describing Your Customer Avatar x in Your Own Words" earlier in this chapter tells me that a fancy ads would probably appeal to my target customers, as would headsets, hats and music by Alabama Shakes. And because my customer avatar loves to shop at Nordstrom, getting my brand into Nordstrom's store is a priority.

2

Attending to Brand Fundamentals

Create a brand logo, style guide, media kit, and branded templates, all of which you'll use to give your brand a unique and consistent look and feel. A brand style guide establishes guidelines for colors, fonts, graphics, voice, tone, and more.

Build a branded website, app, and email account, so that all your online branding points back to whatever address you choose for your website, blog, online store, or a combination of the three.

Compose valuable, relevant content to build brand recognition and awareness. This process includes content marketing — delivering free content that attracts customers and clients, demonstrates your brand's value, and proves that your brand can be trusted.

Engage and partner with other strong brands to create powerful, mutually beneficial marketing synergies. Find out how to pitch your brand to prospective partners, draw up a contract, and steer clear of common partnership pitfalls.

Plan and execute a successful brand launch and improve its chances of going viral. This process includes scheduling all your branding activities, getting the press involved, and masterfully managing your launch campaign.

Chapter **6**

Creating a Brand Style Guide, Media Kit, and Templates

uccessful branding centers on projecting a consistent look and feel across all marketing and advertising content and materials — from business cards and letterhead to websites and social media accounts. Consistency reinforces your brand identity at every touchpoint, whether you're interacting with customers or reaching out to the media.

To ensure consistency, start with a clear and comprehensive brand style guide, media kit, and templates. These three items keep you from wandering off course. They also save you time, energy, and focus communicating your design specs to vendors, bringing journalists up to speed on your brand, and creating branded marketing assets such as business cards and websites.

In this chapter, I lead you through the process of developing your own brand style guide, media kit, and templates to lay the foundation for your future marketing and advertising initiatives.

Creating a Brand Style Guide

A *brand style guide* is a rulebook that governs everything that contributes to the look and feel of your brand, including the following:

>> Corporate guidelines, including mission statement, values, and targeted demographics

>> Colors

>> Typography (typeface, sizes, and spacing)

>> Logos

>> Imagery (photos, illustrations, and infographics)

>> Tone of voice (fun, professional, caring, and so on)

Often referred to as a *brand bible*, your style guide contains all the specifications needed to ensure consistency and to strengthen the impact and influence of your brand in the marketplace.

REMEMBER

As you create your brand style guide, focus on your mission and how to bring it to life. (See Chapter 3 for more about defining your brand.) The values your brand stands for and your brand's aesthetics are just as important as the products and services you sell and the marketing content you produce.

Appreciating a style guide's value

The primary purpose of a brand style guide is to ensure consistency, but it delivers other benefits as well: It strengthens your brand identity, helps you maintain quality control as your organization grows, and supports your overall branding strategy.

In this section, I describe these benefits in more detail.

Strengthening your brand identity

When scrolling through my Instagram feed, I frequently recognize the brand behind a photo even before I check to see who posted it. Something about the look and feel of the photo are unique to that brand, expressing the brand's personality. That's a sign of a strong brand identity, and it's no accident.

People who create strong brands (or the designers they hire) work hard to arrive at the right combination of colors, graphics, fonts, and editorial style to convey the personality of the brand they want to project. Dry Bar, a blow-dry hair salon chain that focuses on blowouts, uses yellow to enhance its brand identity. Outside the logo and brand assets, you'll find that specific shade of yellow everywhere the brand is. From retail experience to social media posts and products, the company makes sure that its brand is intertwined with Dry Bar yellow.

Color is a fun way to give a brand personality because it can be used so many ways in marketing, from the color of the store décor and the uniforms employees wear to business cards, packaging, the brand's website, and more. You can even stage events around a brand's unique color.

Facilitating quality control

When you conceive the look and feel of your brand, you have no trouble remaining consistent with your vision. You know which colors you want to use, how you want the logo to look, and the tone of any content you post or share. But as you grow and start to delegate or outsource some of your branding responsibilities to vendors or employees, maintaining consistency becomes a challenge.

A brand style guide helps you meet that challenge by ensuring that everyone involved in producing marketing materials is on the same page. They're all working from the same rule book.

Guiding your selection of partners and opportunities

When you come to know yourself well — who you are, what you stand for, and what you want — you waste a lot less time on unproductive relationships, dead-end jobs, and the pursuit of fruitless opportunities. Likewise, when you have a well-defined brand, you can make decisions and choices much faster and more easily. You can instantly tell which partners and opportunities are a good fit and which aren't. When you come to a fork in the road, your brand points you in the right direction.

At my brand, Girl Gang, we established in our brand style guide that we want to work exclusively with female-owned companies and to interview only women on our podcast. This decision helped us narrow the focus of our podcast (*Girl Gang the Podcast: A Show by Women for Women*) and decide on the types of partnership opportunities we wanted to pursue — with female entrepreneurs who share our values and the communities we want to reach. When we partner with female-led companies, our partnerships are more successful because our shared customer base values female-owned brands.

Your brand guide can give you a clear rationale for pursuing certain partnerships and steering clear of others. If you own a reusable-water-bottle company, for example, and sustainability is your key value, when you decide to team up with influencers, you can quickly narrow the field of candidates to those who frequently post about environmental issues. If you're looking to partner with other businesses, you can rule out those that have a poor track record for sustainability.

Setting corporate guidelines

Corporate guidelines consist of everything that goes into defining your brand and the way you do business (see Chapter 3 for details):

>> Mission

>> Values

>> Brand differentiators

>> Brand guardrails — which organization types you do and don't do business with, what your brand does and doesn't do, and areas where you won't compromise

>> Target customer

REMEMBER

Corporate guidelines are the heart and soul of your brand. They work behind the scenes to influence every aspect of your brand — from the selection of your brand's color scheme to the voice and tone of every piece of content you publish.

Creating a color palette

Imagine your high-school colors. Chances are good that you didn't have to think too hard, because those colors are etched in your memory. In the same way, you want your brand's colors to be etched in the minds of your customers, making your brand easily recognizable.

Brushing up on color associations

Colors communicate and evoke specific thoughts and emotions, so be aware of the following color associations when creating your color palette:

Color	Association
Yellow	Sunshine, warmth, positivity, happiness, caution
Red	Action, adventure, aggression, danger, energy, love, passion, vigor
Blue	Trustworthiness, success, confidence, calmness, serenity
Green	Growth, freshness, serenity, healing, wealth, nature
Purple	Royalty, nobility, fantasy, sophistication
Orange	Warmth, energy, enthusiasm, lightheartedness
Pink	Romance, softness, innocence, gratitude, gentleness
Brown	Earthiness, richness, simplicity, subtlety, utility
Black	Power, mystery, secrecy, authority, class, distinction, formality, seriousness, tradition, death

Understanding hues, tones, tints, and shades

As you choose colors, brush up on the following concepts and terms related to variations of color:

>> **Hue:** *Hue* is a color variation. Azure, cyan, cerulean, and turquoise are all hues of blue.

>> **Tone:** *Tone* is lighter or darker version of the same color created by adding white or black to the color.

>> **Tint:** *Tint* is a lighter version of a color created by adding white.

>> **Shade:** *Shade* is a darker version of a color created by adding black.

Picking your colors

Several online tools can help you choose colors that work well together. Canva's Color Palette Generator (https://www.canva.com/colors/color-palette-generator) features several ways to create a four-color palette:

>> Upload an image and have the Color Palette Generator extract four colors from it that work well together.

>> Explore a library of color combinations.

>> Create a custom color palette. For this option, you choose one color to start and then choose one of the following options to generate the other colors that make up the palette (see Figure 6-1):

- *Complementary:* Complementary colors are opposite each other on the color wheel, such as green and red, blue and orange, and yellow and purple.

- *Monochromatic:* A monochromatic color palette consists of different shades of a single color, such as dark blue, blue, and light blue.

- *Analogous:* Analogous colors are next to each other on the color wheel, such as yellow and orange, purple and blue, and green and yellow.

- *Triadic:* A triadic color scheme uses three colors that are equally spaced on the color wheel, such as yellow, red, and blue.

- *Tetradic:* A tetradic color scheme uses four colors that form a rectangle on the color wheel.

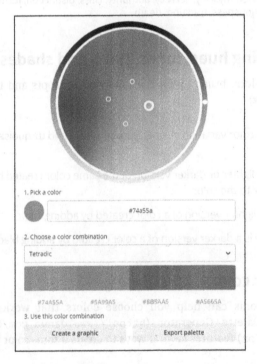

FIGURE 6-1:
Building a custom color palette on Canva.

REMEMBER

Note that the Color Palette Generator includes both the name of each color and its *hex code* — the six-character code that identifies the color, such as #ff0000 for pure red. When creating a color palette for your brand style guide, be sure to include the hex codes for the colors you choose. Specifying hex codes ensures that your colors will be consistent on every brand asset you create.

Picking dominant and accent colors

When creating your brand's color palette, specify which colors are dominant and which ones are to be used as accent colors:

>> *Dominant colors* are the one or two main colors in your logo and design.

>> *Accent colors* are all the colors in your color palette except the dominant colors. Accent colors may be complementary or analogous to your dominant colors, or they may be different tones, tints, or shades of your dominant colors.

Establishing typographical guidelines

If your brand design calls for any text, such as your business or brand name, you need to specify exactly how that text is to be presented. Provide specifications for every aspect of the font and formatting, including the following:

>> **Typeface:** The *typeface* is the font, such as Times New Roman, Arial, or Calibri. Choose only a few typefaces, and specify how they're to be used. You may want to use a different font on web pages from the one you use for items in your media kit, for example, because what looks good on paper may not look as good when viewed on a computer monitor or mobile device.

>> **Size:** *Size* refers to how large the print is, and it's typically expressed in points. (For reference, an inch is 72 points.) Specify the sizes or range of sizes and how different sizes can be used. You may want to use smaller print on a business card than in an infographic, for example.

>> **Weight:** *Weight* refers to how thick or thin (light or bold) the print is. Normal is 400, but weight ranges from 100 to 900. In your brand style guide, specify the allowed and preferred weights and how different weights are to be used. You might specify a weight of 800 for headings and 300 for normal text, for example.

>> **Color:** Color is obvious, but be sure to choose one or more colors that are already in your approved color palette and specify how text colors are to be used. You might use different colors depending on whether the background is light or dark.

>> **Alignment:** *Alignment* specifies whether and in what situations text can (or should) be aligned left, right, or centered and how it should be wrapped around any images.

>> **Spacing:** *Kerning* determines the distance between characters — whether you want them to be elbow-to-elbow, comfortably separated, or socially distanced. Certain letter pairs (such as *Tr*) often appear to be too close together or too far apart, so the spacing between them may need to be tweaked; if so, list that requirement in your brand style guide.

Most word-processing, graphics, and page-layout programs include a broad selection of fonts, but if you're looking for something unique, check sites such as FontSpace (https://www.fontspace.com) and Dafont (https://www.dafont.com) for custom fonts. FontSpace can also put you in touch with font designers if you have something special in mind.

TIP

Note that in most cases, free fonts aren't actually free for commercial use; you need to purchase a commercial license to use them legally on your website and on any branded items.

Designing a logo

Getting a logo designed for your brand is easy. You can do the work yourself or outsource the job at a minimal cost. The hard part is conceptualizing the design. To get your creative juices flowing, start by checking out other brands in your industry and any related industries. Then start doodling ideas with the intention of designing a logo that meets the following criteria:

>> **Consistent:** Your logo must be consistent with your brand's color and fonts and its tone. Do you want it to convey a sense of fun or the fact that your brand is engaged in serious business?

>> **Distinctive:** Your logo needs to be unique and make your brand stand out from the crowd.

>> **Memorable:** A glance at your logo should stamp it on the brain of the person who looked at it. Think about it. Memorable logos leave a lasting impression. Cases in point include the Shell, McDonald's, Coca-Cola, and Starbucks logos. They're what you're shooting for.

>> **Representative:** Develop a design that conveys what your brand is all about. IBM's logo is all business. Nike's swish logo conveys a sense of speed and is consistent with the name. (In Greek mythology, Nike is the winged goddess of victory.) BP's logo is shaped like the sun, with shades of yellow and green to signify different forms of energy. Admittedly, not all logos have a deeper hidden significance; many are merely formed from one or more the letters of the company's name.

- **>> Simple:** Most logos are simple, consisting of a basic shape, maybe a few letters, and one or two colors. Keep your logo simple. Any intricacies will weaken the logo's impact.

- **>> Versatile:** Your logo should look good wherever you use it — on a sign outside your business, your business cards, a web page, products, packaging, wherever.

- **>> Visible:** A good logo pops out at you and is easy to discern even against an otherwise-distracting background.

TIP

If you're part of a team, brainstorm ideas with team members. If you're flying solo, reach out to friends, family members, and associates for their input. If you already have a brand and some customers, consider hosting a Design Our Logo contest, thereby harnessing the collective creativity of your customers while driving further engagement with your brand.

Rolling your own logo

If you have a good eye for graphic design, plenty of free online tools can help you design your own logo, including Wix.com (https://www.wix.com), which is for website design and has options to make your own logo, Canva's logo maker (https://www.canva.com/create/logos; see Figure 6-2), and Vistaprint's logo maker (https://www.vistaprint.com/logoMakerService). Just search the web for "logo maker tool," and you'll find plenty to choose among.

FIGURE 6-2:
Canva's logo
maker.

If you're looking for a higher-level graphics tool to meet all your branding needs, I recommend Adobe Creative Cloud (https://www.adobe.com/creativecloud) — a suite of powerful programs that can help you with photos, graphic design, video production, illustration, user interface design, and more. If you're not familiar with computer graphics fundamentals, however, you'll have a steep learning curve to climb.

Hiring an artist

Hiring a talented artist to design a logo or take on any graphics project has never been easier or more affordable. Several online logo design services allow you to specify your preferences, including foreground and background colors, fonts, and industry, and one or more artists will present you several options. If you don't like any of the choices, you can usually send the artist back to the drawing board, or you won't be charged anything.

Another option is to avoid the intermediary and contract directly with a freelance artist through a freelance marketplace such as Upwork (https://www.upwork.com) or Fiverr (https://www.fiverr.com).

Either approach — using a logo design service or a freelance artist — is an inexpensive alternative to contracting with a creative agency to design your logo and brand assets. But if you have a fat budget and want a more personal touch, hiring a creative firm is certainly an option.

Specifying guidelines for photos, illustrations, and other artwork

When you're choosing photos, illustrations, and other artwork, you may have a clear idea of what's appropriate for your brand, but anyone else who's creating or contributing visuals may not. Be specific in your brand guide about the content and the look and feel of all graphics. Here's a list of criteria to get you started:

>> **Composition:** Include the minimal amount of detail possible to communicate the thought or concept.

>> **Point of view:** Scenes shouldn't appear to be staged, and all subjects in the foreground should be in focus.

>> **Mood:** Photographs should be light and positive, conveying a sense of fun and confidence.

>> **Lighting:** Lighting should be natural. Avoid dark scenes.

>> **Portraits:** Any portrait photos should be casual and candid, with a consistent background and natural lighting.

- **Community:** Photos of two or more subjects should convey a sense of diversity and inclusion in a warm, welcoming, and casual setting.

- **Events:** All photographs of events should focus on a specific person or object to avoid appearing overly busy.

- **Overlays:** Use brand overlays sparingly, limiting them to one or two of the brand's dominant colors.

- **Illustrations:** Use the minimal amount of detail necessary, and when possible, use colors from the brand's color palette.

Photo and illustration guidelines also contain minimal quality standards. You may want to specify that any digital graphics used in printed materials be 300 dots per inch (dpi) or higher-resolution and any images used online be at least 72 dpi. You may also specify a preferred file format, such as JPG, PNG, or TIF.

Setting guidelines for voice and tone

As part of your branding guidelines, specify the voice and tone for all communications (text, audio, and video):

- **Voice:** *Voice* is your brand's personality — witty, considerate, genuine, fun, friendly, positive, and/or elegant. Your brand's voice remains consistent throughout all your brand messaging.

TIP

  Picture yourself as your brand ambassador talking with a customer. (Read more about how a brand ambassadors factors into your content marketing strategy in Chapter 12.) How would you describe your personality? Are you friendly and helpful? Are you making your customer laugh? Are you all business? What personality types are your customers most attracted to? Which do they respond best to?

- **Tone:** *Tone* is your brand's mood — serious, happy, confident, certain, and/or afraid. Your brand's mood may change depending on the message. When you're composing content to promote your brand, consider the mood you want to convey. Are you excited about a new product you're offering? Are you confident that your service can help customers address a challenge? What mood do you want to express or evoke?

The clothing rental company Fashion Pass uses voice and tone very effectively in its advertising. The company speaks directly to its target demographic — young, style-conscious women — and frequently signs off its social media posts with "babe." Using "babe" is one way that the company establishes its voice — a voice that makes customers feel more like they're chatting with a girlfriend than listening to a sales pitch.

TIP

Follow Fashion Pass's lead by adopting a few signature words or phrases that communicate your brand's voice.

Assembling and Using a Media Kit

A *media kit* is a document or collection of materials that provide all the key information about a brand, including the company's mission and vision, details about the products or services offered, and contact information.

Early in the process of launching a brand, you should assemble a media kit that you can send to journalists and any prospective partners, just as you might hand a business card to someone you meet at a party. Having a media kit readily available enables you to reply to media requests in near real time without concerns about omitting anything important.

In this section, I provide guidance on assembling a media kit and knowing when to do it.

Creating your own media kit

A media kit can range from a single page to a folder full of documents. It may even include one or more digital videos (or links to them) that introduce the recipient to your company and brand.

Make your initial media kit all-inclusive, containing everything you may want to send to any media outlet or prospective partner. Then you can whittle it down whenever necessary. In your all-inclusive version, include the following elements:

>> **Contact information:** This information should include your phone number, email address, and mailing address.

>> **Company bio:** The bio is a brief description of your company or brand.

>> **Website address:** A website can provide information that's not included in your media kit. (See Chapter 7 for guidance on creating a website, blog, or online store.)

>> **Mission:** Your brand's mission is its *raison d'être* (purpose for being). You may include your mission statement in your company bio or as a separate entry.

TIP

If your mission is a charitable cause, set it off by keeping your mission statement separate from your company bio.

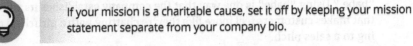

- » **Media coverage:** Include any notable media coverage that your brand recently received. Specify the media outlet, and include a quote from the article. My *Girl Gang the Podcast* was featured in *Marie Claire* as one of the "33 Best Podcasts of 2020," for example, so I mentioned that in the media kit. I also make to highlight that bit of information whenever I pitch to my brand to people I want to appear as guests on the podcast.

- » **Logos:** Include all forms of your logo — full-color, monochrome, logo by itself, the fonts alone, and logo plus fonts.

- » **Lifestyle photos:** If applicable for your brand, include some lifestyle photos or user-generated content of customers using your product in real life.

- » **Customer testimonials:** If you have a service-based business, include testimonials from customers who have used your service.

- » **Links to videos:** If you have any video introducing people to your brand, include links to those videos.

Targeting your media kit to your audience

A media kit is like a résumé: You customize it every time you send it out so that it speaks directly to your audience and has the greatest chance of achieving the desired outcome. If you're sending your media kit to recruit experts to serve as guests on your podcast, you might include statistics about how many listeners subscribe to your podcast. If you have a fashion brand and are sending your media kit to editors at style magazines, you'll want to include photos of your latest designs or clothing lines.

REMEMBER

Consider the needs of the person on the receiving end of your media kit, and provide everything that person needs. If you're sending a media kit to an online publication, you need to provide the editor all the information they need to write a decent article. You may even want to draft the article to make publishing it super-easy. Include photos and clever quotes, and volunteer for an interview.

Also, you want to build momentum with existing media coverage. If you already have some coverage of your brand, include it in your media kit. People want to know what others are saying about your brand. If you have no coverage, include customer testimonials. Getting testimonials from real users of your product or service can be very effective.

REMEMBER

People are busy, so keep your media kit short. My typical media kit is a one-page PDF with a link to my brand's website, where the recipient can go for more information.

Deciding when to send a media kit

Now that you have a media kit, you'll be eager to send it to *everyone*. One word of advice: Don't. For the initial (cold) contact, keep your pitch short and sweet without the media kit. Why? Two reasons:

>> Too much information can be a turn-off.

>> A cold email with an attachment is likely to get flagged as spam, in which case the recipient will probably never see it.

Keep your pitch short, and end with an offer to provide more information upon request, such as "I'd love to send more details and our media kit if you're interested." This approach gives the recipient the freedom to opt in and increases the likelihood that they will read the info you send in response.

If you have a hit list of journalists who already know you, sending a media kit whenever you launch a new brand is a good idea.

TIP

Extend the use of your media kit beyond the media. A media kit is helpful when you're pitching an opportunity for a strategic partnership (after your initial contact). Your kit can provide a snapshot of your brand's mission and values, along with additional information the recipient may need to decide whether to partner with your brand.

Creating Your Own Branded Templates

Consistency is crucial in creating a strong brand, and branded templates can simplify the task of maintaining consistency. A branded template contains your brand's logo and conforms to all the design specifications you've established, so all you need to do is tweak the content. I encourage you to create branded templates for all the marketing materials you create, including the following:

>> Announcements

>> Banners

>> Brochures

>> Email messages

>> Flyers

>> Infographics

- » Invitations
- » Invoices
- » Letterhead
- » Memes
- » Menus
- » Newsletters
- » Presentations
- » Press releases
- » Social media ads and posts
- » Video intros

You have several options for creating branded templates:

- » Online advertising programs, such as Google Ads and Facebook Ads, provide their own templates.
- » Email marketing tools, such as Mailchimp, feature a selection of templates.
- » You can hire a designer to create a set of templates to meet your needs.
- » You can use online design applications to design your own templates.

Here's how easy it is to create a custom template in Canva:

1. Go to https://www.canva.com/templates.

2. Scroll through the list of categories, and select the category that most closely matches the item you want to create, such as an infographic, meme, or Instagram story.

3. Select the theme you want to customize, as shown in Figure 6-3, and then select Use This Template.

   The selected template appears, with customization options displayed on the left side of the screen (see Figure 6-4).

4. Follow the onscreen prompts to use the available tools to customize the theme.

5. Click Download (in the top-right corner of the page) to download your new template.

REMEMBER

When creating templates, follow your branding guidelines. Adhere to your specified color palette, and include your logo, if appropriate, to reinforce your brand identity.

FIGURE 6-3:
Select a predesigned template.

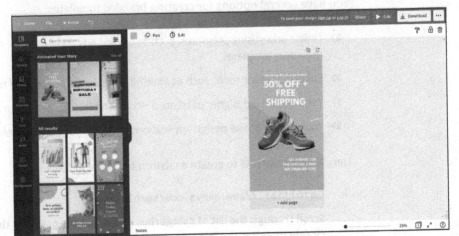

FIGURE 6-4:
Customize your template.

IN THIS CHAPTER

» Registering a domain name that promotes your brand

» Building your own website or outsourcing that job

» Using website analytics to monitor traffic on your site

» Getting an email address that matches your domain name

» Building a branded app or hiring a developer

Chapter **7**

Building a Branded Website, App, and Email Account

F or any brand to be successful in today's world, it must have a strong online presence. When you tell people about your brand, the first question they typically ask is, "Do you have a website?" And my answer is always, "Yeah, GirlGangTheLabel.com. You should check it out." Then, of course, I hand them my business card, which has my website and email addresses on it.

Even if you do most of your business at a physical location, having a website is useful for keeping customers informed and attracting new customers. If you have a physical store, an e-commerce-enabled website enables you to sell products and services to people in remote locations and to those who are unable (or unwilling) to visit your physical location. A website significantly extends your reach.

In this chapter, I explain how to begin the process of establishing an online presence by building a branded website, online store, or blog (or a combination of the three); creating a branded email address (such as amy@girlgangthelabel.com); and, if you're truly ambitious (and it makes sense to do so), launching your very own branded mobile app.

REMEMBER

Don't feel intimidated by the technology. In this chapter, I provide the guidance you need and introduce numerous tools and services that simplify these projects.

Going It Alone or Hiring a Developer

After you decide to build a website, online store, or blog, the next question is whether you're going to do the work yourself or hire a designer/developer to do it for you. The answer usually comes down to time and money:

>> **If you have time but not enough money to hire a pro, do it yourself.**
If you've never created a website before, you can find plenty of tools and resources to do the job (many of which are free), but getting through that learning curve will take more of your time than hiring someone to do it for you.

>> **If you have the money, hire a pro, regardless of whether you have the time to do it yourself.** A professional designer/developer can probably build a better site faster than you can. You still need to provide the developer guidance and most (or all) of the content, but a professional delivers the expertise and does most of the heavy lifting.

In the following sections, I take a deeper dive into the question of whether to build your own website or hire a pro.

Doing it yourself

You can build a decent-looking website, blog, or online store yourself quickly and easily. Readily available and often free or inexpensive themes, graphics, and tools are available to facilitate the process. Here's a list of what you need to build your own branded website, blog, or online store:

>> **Website host:** A *website host* is where all the files and functionality that make your website work will be stored on the Internet. See "Claiming Your Domain Name and Choosing a Hosting Service," later in this chapter, for more about hosting services.

>> **Content management system:** A *content management service* (CMS), such as WordPress, is software that enables you (or your developer) to build a website, blog, or online store and that presents your site to visitors. Think of a CMS as being a desktop publishing program, such as Microsoft Publisher, specifically for creating and publishing websites.

>> **Theme:** A *theme* (template) controls the layout and appearance of a site's contents, making it as easy to change the appearance of your site as it is to change your clothes. Thousands of custom themes are available for popular CMSes, such as WordPress.

REMEMBER

Choose a mobile-friendly theme — one that automatically adjusts your site's layout and formatting to make it look and function properly regardless of the device on which it's being viewed. More than half of users now browse the web on mobile devices, so your site needs to adapt to their needs and preferences.

>> **Plug-ins or apps:** Third-party providers develop plug-ins or apps for popular CMSes that you can use, typically for free or a small fee, to add functionality to your site, such as enabling e-commerce for online shopping, securing and backing up your site, or adding a discussion forum.

>> **Content:** Content is everything you bring to the table — text, logo, graphics, audio, video, product catalog, and anything else you want to include on your site.

Some platforms contain nearly everything you need to get started. Just add content. Here are a few of my favorite all-in-one solutions:

>> **Shopify** (https://www.shopify.com/domains) is great for building an online (e-commerce) store. A Basic account starts at $29 per month and includes a selection of free themes, an overview dashboard, financial reporting, customer profiles, product and order management, email carts, gift cards, discount codes, and more. Shopify also has more than 6,000 apps that integrate with and add features and functionality to your business.

Shopify Lite ($9 per month) is a plan for merchants who sell in person or simply want to add a Buy button to their existing site. Using Lite, you can turn any website into an online store, accept credit card payments anywhere from an iOS or Android device, and prepare and send invoices. You can't build an online store with the Lite version.

>> **Squarespace** (https://www.squarespace.com) is a combination website hosting service and CMS. It features attractive themes for building a professional-looking website, online store, blog, or portfolio (to let freelancers o showcase their creativity). It also features search engine optimization (SEO) tools that improve your site's search engine rank and analytics that show out where your

website traffic is coming from, what your visitors are looking for, and how they're navigating and interacting with your site. Plans range from Personal ($12 per month) to Business ($18 per month), Basic Commerce ($26 per month), and Advanced Commerce ($40 per month).

>> **WordPress** (https://wordpress.com) is a combination hosting service and CMS. Like Shopify and Squarespace, it provides the tools you need to build and manage a website, blog, or online store. It offers several plans ranging from Free or Personal ($4 per month) to Premium ($8 per month), Business ($25 per month), and e-commerce ($45 per month).

REMEMBER

Popular e-commerce platforms such as Shopify integrate easily with WordPress sites. With a few clicks, you can generate a special code on Spotify and paste it into a page on your WordPress site to feature a product you sell on Spotify along with a Buy button customers can click to order the product.

See "Claiming Your Domain Name and Choosing a Hosting Service" and "Walking Through the Basics of Building a Website," later in this chapter, for more about building a website, blog, or online store.

Hiring a developer

If designing and building a website is a project you prefer to outsource, you'll need to find a qualified website developer. Start by creating a list of everything you want your site to have and to do. Your list should contain the following items:

>> **Your business's or brand's background:** Include customer demographics, a description of your industry, and names of any competitors.

>> **Your site's primary and secondary goals:** You may have a primary goal of building a strong brand identity and a secondary goal of selling lots of merchandise, for example. If you're a service provider, your primary goal may be to spread the word about your business, with a secondary goal of building trust.

>> **A sitemap:** A *sitemap* is an outline of your site, listing all pages you want and how they'll be organized.

>> **A few examples of existing sites you really like:** List their addresses, along with what you like and dislike about each one.

>> **Project scope, functionality, and deliverables:** Create a list of everything you expect the site to have, such as the following:

- Static content on 10 to 12 pages
- Blogging functionality

- E-commerce functionality

- Ability for customers to choose a preferred store location

- Content development (will you supply text and graphics, or are you depending on the developer to do that?)

- Ability to collect information from forms

- SEO

- Content migration

TIP

You can save yourself and your developer time, money, and aggravation by nailing down exactly what you need before you start. Otherwise, you're susceptible to *scope creep* — the phenomenon in which a project continues to change and grow far beyond what was planned.

» **Deadline and milestones:** Specify when you'd like to launch your site, and create a realistic timeline for completing different stages of the project.

» **Budget:** Be up-front about how much you're willing to spend. As you start your search for a qualified developer, you can adjust your budget or the scope of the project according to what you find out about the going rates for developers.

When you have a fairly clear vision of your site, you'll be well prepared to start looking for and contacting prospective developers. If you don't have anyone in mind, consider the following resources:

» Search a freelancer marketplace such as 99designs (https://99designs.com) or Toptal (https://www.toptal.com).

» Check the platform you want to use to build and host your site for developers who are familiar with the platform. Squarespace Marketplace can match you with a developer based on your needs and preferences, or you can browse its developer directory. Likewise, the Shopify Experts Marketplace can connect you with a trusted freelancer or agency.

» Reach out to your personal network by asking for recommendations from your contacts on social media platforms such as LinkedIn, Instagram, and Facebook.

Examine potential developers' portfolios closely to determine whether they have the skills necessary to develop the site you want. Have they created any online stores? How effective are the sites they've developed at projecting brand identity? Check references to see what their clients have to say about their work.

REMEMBER

Don't expect the developer to do *all* the work. You'll need to provide raw content for the site (info, images, and video), write some copy, supply your product database (for an online store), and offer guidance and feedback.

Claiming Your Domain Name and Choosing a Hosting Service

Choosing a domain name and hosting service is like buying a lot on which to build a home. The domain name is your site's unique address, and the hosting service is the computer server on which your site will be built. The domain name for my Girl Gang brand, for example, is GirlGangTheLabel.com, and the site is hosted on servers maintained by Shopify. My domain name is also part of my email address (amy@girlgangthelabel.com), which strengthens my brand identity.

In this section, I explain how to choose and register a domain name, and how to find a reputable and reliable hosting service that meets your branding needs.

Choosing and registering a domain name

When your goal is to build brand recognition, you want to choose a domain that matches or reflects your brand name. You also want a name that's short, easy to remember, easy to type, and difficult to mistype. Having .com at the end is a plus but not necessarily a deal-breaker if you can't get it.

To find and register a suitable domain name, use a domain-name registrar. I use GoDaddy (https://www.godaddy.com) to register and mange my domains, but you can choose among dozens of reputable registrars, including the following:

>> Squarespace (https://www.squarespace.com/domain-name-search)

>> Shopify (https://www.shopify.com/domains)

>> WordPress.com (https://wordpress.com/domains)

>> Bluehost (https://www.bluehost.com/domains)

>> HostGator (https://www.hostgator.com/domains)

>> Google Domains (https://domains.google)

When you arrive at any of these sites, you're greeted by a search form. Type the domain name you want (including .com, .org, or whatever), and click the Search button (or its equivalent). The search results indicate whether the domain is available and provide alternatives if that domain is already taken. You may have to search several times until you find a suitable domain name.

TIP

Be flexible and creative. If the domain name you want is already taken, search for something similar. If winecircle.com is taken, consider winecircle.net or winecircle.store. Finding an available domain name may even be a good opportunity to rethink your brand name and come up with something entirely different, such as Wine Sprites at WineSprites.com.

Choosing a hosting service and plan

A web hosting service provides the Internet servers on which your website lives. Whenever someone visits your site, these servers deliver the content and coding that enable the visitor's web browser to display the contents of your site as you designed it to be viewed.

Most hosting services are similar and offer comparable plans, but they can vary a little or a lot in terms of speed, reliability, security, features, and cost. Here's a checklist you can use to be sure you're getting a hosting provider and plan that meets your needs and can handle your brand's growth:

>> **Reputable:** Search the web and your social media accounts for ratings, customer reviews, and testimonials. If anyone has anything bad to say about a hosting service, it's likely to pop up in a general search.

>> **Reliable:** Whenever your site goes down, you lose opportunities and customers. Find out what the hosting service's uptime percentage is, and remove from your list any candidate with less than 99.9 percent uptime. Uptimes may be posted in articles on the web or on the hosting provider's website.

>> **Fast:** Several factors determine how fast your site loads on a device, including how it's built, the size of the files being transferred, the speed of your hosting provider's servers, the connection speed between the server that delivers the site and the client that receives it, and the speed of the client's device. You don't want your hosting service to be the speed bump in that chain of delivery. Compare average speeds of all hosting services on your list. You can usually find a hosting provider's average speed, typically measured in milliseconds (ms), through a simple web search.

>> **Scalable:** Hosting providers must be prepared to scale to meet not only your needs, but also the needs of their growing customer base. There's no easy way to check scalability, but if a hosting provider isn't scaling effectively, customers will start to complain online about its reliability and speed.

Beware of hosting providers that limit bandwidth (the amount of data your site transfers) and restrict access to your site or slow the flow of data if your site exceeds a certain bandwidth limit. Look for hosting providers that offer unlimited bandwidth.

>> **Secure:** You can take steps to protect your own site, your data, and your customers from nefarious hackers and malware, but hosting providers can help. Choose a provider that stresses security and offers features such as free malware scanning, automated software updates, site backups, free Secure Sockets Layer (SSL) certificates, and distributed denial of service (DDoS) attack mitigation. You don't need to know what these things are; just make that sure your hosting provider stresses security in its marketing.

>> **E-commerce-enabled:** Most hosting providers feature tools for building online stores, but some are more geared to e-commerce than others. Shopify and Squarespace, for example, cater specifically to customers who sell products and services.

>> **Easy to use:** All hosting providers have a control panel or some other interface that simplifies access to what it offers. You can usually find information or tutorials in the provider's help system that demonstrate how to navigate and use popular tools and features. Check out these guides to get a taste of a provider before subscribing.

>> **Feature-rich:** Before choosing a hosting provider, make sure that it offers everything you need, such as domain name registration and management, email accounts, sufficient storage, ability to migrate your site easily (if you have an existing site with a different hosting provider), and support for the CMS you want to use (such as WordPress).

>> **Quality technical support:** When your site goes down or you're having trouble getting a tool or feature to work as it's supposed to, you need quick and easy access to technical support. When you're screening different hosting providers, investigate how much they emphasize technical support, and see what their customers (or former customers) have posted about it online.

>> **Affordable:** Most hosting providers offer different plans at different prices, so when you're comparing providers, look at comparable plans. Plans typically vary based on the number of websites you have; the amount of storage and bandwidth you need; and whether you want any special features, such as automated backups and site analytics.

All web hosting services offer promotions in the form of credits and free services, providing an affordable way to compare options. However, compare what you'll be paying *after* the promotional period expires, and be sure you can easily transfer the site you're developing to another service if this one doesn't work out.

A key consideration in choosing a plan is which server type you want or need:

>> **Shared server:** On a *shared* server, your site shares storage and computing resources with multiple other sites, so if any of those sites is hogging resources, it could negatively affect your site's performance.

>> **Virtual private server:** A *virtual private server* (VPS) dedicates a portion of a shared server's resources to your website to help reduce competition for resources. The server is shared, but it acts more like a server that's dedicated to your site.

>> **Dedicated server:** With a *dedicated* server, your websites don't share resources with other sites. This option is the best one, but it's also the most expensive.

>> **Cloud server:** Some hosting services run on giant public cloud servers, such as Amazon Web Services and Microsoft Azure, which have virtually unlimited storage and computing resources and can scale up and down automatically to meet changes in demand.

Walking Through the Basics of Building a Website

When you have a domain name and a hosting provider, you're ready to start building your website, blog, online store, or combination of the three. I can't possibly cover the process in detail for two reasons:

>> It would require an entire book.

>> It varies considerably according to the hosting service, the site you decide to build, and the tools you use. Building a website on Shopify is different from building a site on WordPress.com, for example.

What I can do is walk you through the basics so you have a general idea of what's involved before you get your hands dirty.

Choosing the right site type and elements to include on your site

Websites vary considerably according to form, function, and content. An artist or architect may build a site that serves as a digital portfolio, whereas a retailer builds an online store to sell merchandise, and a consultant builds a blog to establish themselves as a thought leader in their industry. These sites would look and function very differently from one another, even though they can all be used to build brand identity.

When you have a general idea of what you want your site to be and do, start thinking about its purpose and the components it needs to fulfill that purpose, such as the following:

>> Web pages for presenting information

>> A blog to publish posts regularly and allow visitors to comment on them

>> A product catalog and shopping cart to enable visitors to shop for, order, and pay for merchandise

>> A portfolio to showcase your creativity and expertise

>> A contact form so visitors can get in touch with you via email

>> A calendar for scheduling appointments

>> Forms (registration, application, appointment request, request for additional information, and so on)

>> A discussion forum to build a community where members can interact

TIP

Think about why customers and prospects will be visiting your site. If you created one product and are offering a preorder, you'll want a minimalistic design with only a few pages. If you sell a variety of products, you'll want a template that makes it easy to create a catalog. For a service-based business, you may be able to get by with a landing page to describe the services you offer, a testimonials page, and a contact form. Check out some websites for brands like yours to get ideas about what to include on your site.

Installing a CMS (or not)

Depending on what your hosting provider offers and how it's set up, you may not need to install a CMS on your hosting provider's server to start building your site. (With some hosting providers, the CMS is fully integrated, and you just choose an option to build a site.) If you need to install a CMS, the process can be complicated, but nearly all hosting providers offer installation wizards that make the process as simple as installing new software on a computer. On Bluehost, for example, you log in, click Advanced, click WordPress Manager by Softaculous, click Install, and complete an installation form (see Figure 7-1).

FIGURE 7-1:
Installing
WordPress on
Bluehost.

The form prompts you to enter your preferences, such as the site's URL (address), name, and description; your username, password, and email address; any plug-ins you want to install to add extra features; and the theme you want to start with (which you can easily change later, as explained in the next section, "Choosing a theme").

At the bottom of the form is an Install button; click it to commence the installation.

After installation, you can log into your site's dashboard (see Figure 7-2), to create pages and posts, modify the site's appearance, install plug-ins, monitor comments posted by visitors, and more. Use the navigation bar on the left side of the screen to choose what you want to work on.

Navigation bar

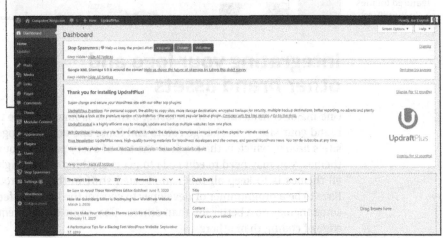

FIGURE 7-2:
The WordPress
dashboard.

Choosing a theme

A *theme* is a template that controls the layout and appearance of your site — its colors, fonts, number and sizes of columns, line spacing, margins, you name it. Some themes add features and functionality to your site as well, such as an email form, share buttons, survey forms, and drag-and-drop page builders. (To add an image, text, or other content to a page, you drag it from your computer and drop it in place.) WordPress provides access to thousands of free themes, and thousands more are available for purchase.

To change themes in WordPress, click Appearance (in the navigation bar on the left), click Themes, and choose the theme you want to use. To view more themes or install a theme, click Add New. A collection of featured themes appears, as shown in Figure 7-3. Use the navigation bar above the collection to view Popular or Latest themes, filter themes by desired features, or search for themes. (You can search for e-commerce themes, for example, or themes for consultants or musicians.)

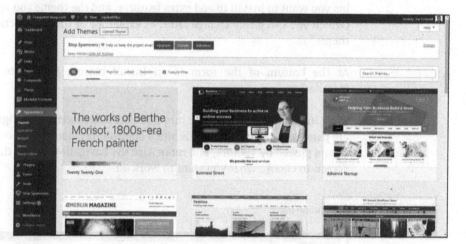

FIGURE 7-3:
A collection of featured themes in WordPress.

Integrating your logo and other brand assets

One major consideration in choosing a theme is how easy the theme makes it to brand your site — to change colors and fonts and add your logo (typically to the site's *header*, which is the block at the top of every page on your site). With some themes, you may need to edit code to get everything to look right. The purpose of all themes is to keep all this complicated stuff in the background, so you don't have to be a programmer or developer to control the look and feel of your site, but some themes do a better job than others. Also, some themes require more knowledge of coding than others.

Divi, a WordPress theme from Elegant Themes, does an excellent job of keeping the coding behind the scenes. In WordPress, when you choose to customize the appearance of the Divi theme, your site appears as shown in Figure 7-4, with a navigation bar on the left that enables you to control everything from the header and footer to the color scheme, menus, and more. As you enter your preferences, your site's appearance changes, so you can preview the effects of changes before accepting them. When everything looks just right, click the Publish button (above the navigation bar) to save your changes.

Options for customizing the theme

FIGURE 7-4:
You can easily customize the Divi theme.

REMEMBER

Be sure to add your logo to the header and change the color scheme to comply with your brand's style guidelines (see Chapter 6).

Note that at the bottom of the navigation bar in Figure 7-4 is Additional CSS. If you know Cascading Style Sheets (CSS) and want to fine-tune your site beyond what Divi's menu-driven options offer, you can click this link to enter your own custom CSS.

Posting content

When you have your site roughed out, you can start posting content — pages, blog entries, images, audio, video, and so on. A CMS makes posting content as easy as working with a word processing or desktop publishing application. You simply enter the content and then format it by using the formatting tools in the CMS. In the following sections, I show you what to expect.

Creating web pages

The CMS and theme you choose determine what tools you have for creating, formatting, and publishing web pages, but the overall process is fairly standard. In WordPress, you mouse over Pages and click Add New. A blank page appears, prompting you to add a title for the page and start typing content (see Figure 7-5).

Type a title

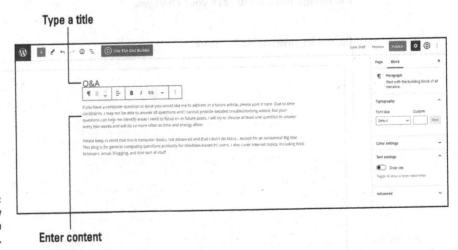

FIGURE 7-5: Creating a new web page in WordPress.

Enter content

Your theme's settings control the format of your page title, so you can't change the title's format when creating or editing a page. But when you start typing in the content area and select text, a toolbar appears just above the content area, providing options for formatting text, creating links, and adding media. Another toolbar appears on the right side of the screen, with additional options for controlling specific attributes of the page or the block of text you're working on.

When you're done creating the page, you can click the Preview button (top right) to see how it'll look when published or the Publish button to add the page to your site.

You can edit a page at any time by returning to the WordPress dashboard, selecting Pages, and clicking the page you want to edit.

Posting blog entries

In WordPress, the process for posting blog entries is nearly identical to that for publishing pages. The main difference is how you start the process. To create a new post, go to the WordPress dashboard, mouse over Posts, and click Add New. Follow the steps in the previous section, "Creating web pages," to add a title and to add and format text.

You may see some different options in the toolbar on the right side of the screen. On a blog's Page tab, for example, is a Categories option that enables you to assign the post to specific categories you create. Categories help visitors find posts on specific topics of interest and help search engines properly index the content you post.

Adding images

To add an image to a page or post, position the insertion point where you want the image to appear and then click the Add Media button (in the toolbar above where you're entering your content). The Add Media window appears, with the Media Library tab selected. Click the Upload Files tab and use the options on this tab to drag and drop image files or select them from a folder.

Click the Media Library tab (see Figure 7-6) and select the image you want to insert. Enter additional information about the image in the form on the right side of the tab, including alt text (for people who can't view the image); an image title, caption, and description; and how you want text to wrap around the image. Then click the button for selecting or inserting the image.

FIGURE 7-6:
Add an image to a page or post.

Adding videos

To add a video to a page or post, first upload the video to YouTube, Vimeo, TikTok, or a similar site dedicated to playing video (see Chapter 12). Then access the video on that site, and look for the embed-code option. An *embed code* is text pasted into a web page or blog post that brings in content from another site. (If you can't find the embed-code option, check the video sharing site's help system.)

To add the video to a page or post on your site, copy the embed code, as shown in Figure 7-7. Then return to the page or post you're creating and choose the option to edit the page or post in Hypertext Markup Language (HTML) mode, which displays all the complex formatting tags you usually want to keep hidden. Position the insertion point where you want your video to appear, and paste the embed code there. Then change back to Edit Visually mode to hide the HTML codes.

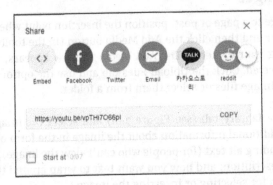

FIGURE 7-7:
Copy an embed code for a YouTube video.

Making your site easy to navigate

As soon as you have some content posted, you can create one or more menus to enable visitors to navigate your site. Your CMS or theme contains a feature for creating and editing menus (see Figure 7-8). You can use this feature to create a menu from the names of pages you created, rename menu items, rearrange items, and even create submenus.

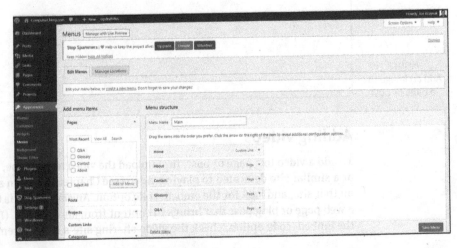

FIGURE 7-8:
You can create menus from the names of existing pages.

When creating a menu, follow these guidelines to make your site easy to navigate:

>> Limit your top-level menu to seven items visitors will click to access the most important content on your site — such as Home, Blog, Testimonials, Shop, Support, Contact, and Locations.

>> Use clear, concise names for menu items.

>> Follow the three-click rule: Visitors should be able to get to what they want on your site with the fewest clicks possible, preferably no more than three.

>> In your site's footer, include links to all the most popular pages on your site. If necessary, group the links by category, such as About, News, and Support.

Driving Traffic to Your Site

When your site is as close to perfect as you can make it, start promoting it. The situation isn't like that Kevin Costner movie *Field of Dreams*, in which the voice from beyond says, "If you build it, he will come." You can build a fantastic site, but if you don't help people (and search engines) find it, nobody's going to come.

In this section, I offer a few suggestions on how to start driving traffic to your site.

Making your site attractive to search engines

Prospective customers are most likely to find your site through one of the big search engines, such as Google, Bing, Yahoo!, and DuckDuckGo. Think of a search engine as being part phone book and part referral agency. If you want people to find you, the major search engines need to index your site and give it a high rank among similar sites for the content, products, and services you offer.

Every developer is in search of the secret sauce for improving their search engine rank, but the most effective techniques are the most basic:

>> **Embrace mobile-first web design.** I can't stress enough the importance of designing a mobile-friendly site — one that adjusts automatically to look and function properly on any device used to access it. A mobile-friendly design makes your site accessible not only to more users, but also to search engines: If your site's not mobile-friendly, search engines may not include it in their search results for mobile users.

>> **Post relevant, quality content.** On the web, the sites with the best content win. Search engines look at how long users spend on your site and how frequently they return to it. If few users visit your site and spend only a few minutes (or seconds) there, search engines take that fact as a sign that your site doesn't offer anything of value. You want to get people's attention and keep it.

>> **Keep it fresh.** Update your site regularly by posting fresh content. One of the best ways to keep your site populated with fresh content is to add a blog to it and post something interesting and relevant to your brand at least a couple times a week. If people comment on your posts, all the better; they're keeping your content fresh without your having to lift a finger. But you should engage with commenters by posting responses to show that you're listening and are interested in what they have to say.

>> **Use SEO, but don't overdo it.** Use relevant search terms throughout your text, especially in the titles and headings of web pages and blog posts. Use meta text to describe every page and post. *Meta text* is descriptive text that visitors don't see but search engines check to help identify the nature of content. Your CMS or theme provide meta-text fields to fill out whenever you create a page or post.

WARNING

Don't overdo SEO. Unnaturally packing a page or post and its metadata with keywords to trick search engines into giving content a higher search rank than it deserves (a technique called *keyword stuffing*) can backfire. Search engines penalize sites suspected of using this technique. Don't do it. (See Chapter 8 for more about SEO.)

>> **Label content with headings.** When composing web pages and blog posts, break up the text with plenty of headings that describe the content accurately. Generally, the higher the heading level (heading 1, heading 2, and so on), the greater its importance in the eyes of search engines.

>> **Use alt text for images, audio, and video.** People with impaired vision or hearing may be unable to experience certain media, such as graphics, audio, and video, so they rely on your verbal descriptions of such content: alternative text (*alt text* for short). Whenever you add media to a page or post, be sure to complete the alt-text fields. Also helpful are transcripts for any audio or video content. Search engines rely heavily on text to determine the contents of nontext media.

Building incoming links

Search engines often determine a site's status by the company it keeps — specifically, by the status of other sites that link to it. Here are a few ways to start creating incoming links:

- >> **Post awesome content.** When your site is established as a thought leader in a specific field or industry, people will start to refer to it via their own blogs and social media accounts.

- >> **Add your site to your social media profiles and pages.** Most social media sites allow members to provide the address of their website or blog. Check your profiles and any pages or other properties you own to make sure that you've included your site address.

- >> **Link your blog to your website, and vice versa.** If you have a separate blog and website or store, link the two.

- >> **Add your site address to any business listings.** If you have a business listing on Yelp, for example, be sure to include your site's address.

- >> **Link to your site any content you contribute to another site.** If you write articles or posts for other online publications, request (or demand as a condition) that the content include a link to your site.

- >> **Trade links.** If you know other people with sites that contain content relevant to yours, ask whether they'd be willing to include a link on their site in exchange for your linking your site to theirs.

See Chapter 22 for more suggestions.

Promoting your site

When your site is ready for prime time, stage a grand opening by letting everyone know about it. Here are a few ways to start promoting your site:

- >> **Link to your site in your email signature.** Every email client allows you to create a signature that's inserted automatically at the bottom of every outgoing message. Include a link to your site in your signature. (Search your email client's help system for "signature" to find out how to create a signature.)

- >> **Let everyone know about your site.** Send an email blast to all your contacts, blog about your new site, and post about your site on all your social media accounts. When people ask what you do, be sure to include your site address in your *elevator pitch* — a statement about your brand that's brief enough to deliver in full during a brief elevator ride.

- >> **Add your site address to all your marketing materials.** Your site address should be on your business card, all press releases and press packets, on every package you ship, on any company vehicles, in all your advertisements online or off, and anywhere else you can think to put it.

> » **Start an online ad campaign.** Create a paid ad on Google or Facebook (or other online advertiser) offering a discount or other promotion to people who visit your site. Start with Google Ads at https://ads.google.com.

Using Web Analytics to Improve Your Online Branding Activities

Web analytics involves the collection, reporting, and analysis of traffic in and around a site to gain insight into user behavior, the effectiveness of a site's contents, the effectiveness of ad campaigns, and other metrics. Measuring and analyzing these metrics provide the insight you need to increase the number of visitors to your site and keep them engaged. Using web analytics, you can discover the following:

> » The number of people who visit your site daily

> » Which pages on your site draw the most traffic and engage visitors longest

> » Where visitors to your site are coming from and where they go when they leave your site

> » Your site's *bounce rate* — the percentage of visitors who land on a page and then leave without doing anything else

> » The effectiveness of your ad campaigns

Most hosting services provide one or more web analytics tools. The tools may be integrated into the platform, or you may need to access them via the provider's control panel after logging in. Your CMS or theme or available plug-ins may also provide the means to easily add web analytics to your site and access data and reports.

One of the most popular web analytics tools is Google Analytics. In the following sections, I explain how to add it to your site and use it to gain insight into your site's performance and other metrics you can use to improve what you're doing online to strengthen and grow your brand.

TIP

Before you go through the trouble of adding Google Analytics to your site, check your hosting provider, CMS, theme, and available plug-ins for easier methods.

Setting up Google Analytics

With Google Analytics, you copy and paste a unique code into the header or footer of your site so that the code is added automatically to every page. Google Analytics uses this code to measure, collect, and analyze the traffic into, around, and out of your site.

The procedure for adding the code varies depending on how your hosting provider is set up or which CMS you're using. The steps for obtaining a tracking code and adding it to a WordPress site go like this:

1. **Go to `https://analytics.google.com`, set up a Google Analytics account, and enter details about the site you want to track.**

   For guidance on how to create an account and add your site, click the question-mark icon in the top-right corner of the Google Analytics screen.

2. **Log into your account, and choose Admin.**

3. **Select the property (site) you want to track.**

4. **Select < > Tracking Info and then Tracking Code.**

   Google displays a tracking code to place on your site.

5. **Copy the tracking code (see Figure 7-9).**

FIGURE 7-9:
Copy the code in the Global Site Tag box.

6. **Log in to your site as an administrator.**

7. **Paste the global site tag you copied as the first item after the opening `<head>` tag on every page and post of your site.**

   How you do this varies depending on how your site is set up. The Divi theme, for example, has an Integration tab with a special field for adding codes to the head of your site (see Figure 7-10). You can also find Google Analytics plug-ins for WordPress and other CMSes that simplify the process.

8. **Save your site to save your changes.**

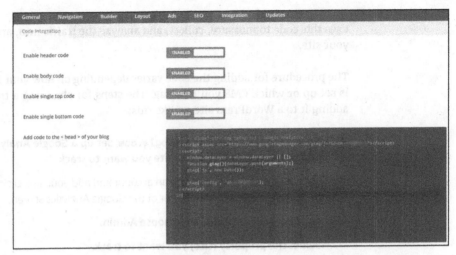

Checking out your site's Google Analytics

As soon as you add your Google Analytics tracking code to your site, Google starts to monitor your site and gather visitor and traffic data. You can access this data by logging into your Google Analytics account:

1. Go to `https://analytics.google.com`, and log in if you're not already logged in.

2. Open the menu to the right of Analytics (in the top-left corner of the page), and select the account, property (site), and view you want to see, as shown in Figure 7-11.

   You can have multiple Google Analytics accounts with multiple properties (sites) in each. You can create different views for each property to filter data.

3. Use the menu bar on the left side of the screen to view reports on a variety of metrics and to access other Google Analytics features (see Figure 7-12).

   Be prepared to spend some time on Google Analytics exploring its many reports, features, add-ons, and customizations. Consult the help system for details. To access the help system, click the question-mark icon near the top-right corner of the dashboard.

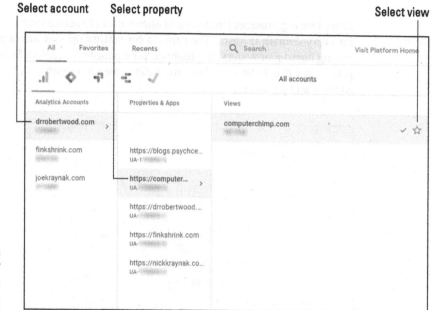

FIGURE 7-11:
Select your
analytics account,
property,
and view.

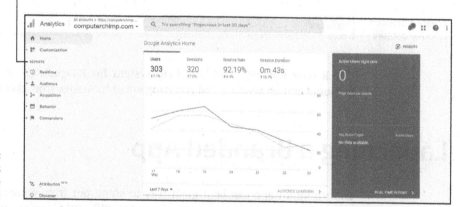

FIGURE 7-12:
Google Analytics
displays site
metrics.

Establishing a Branded Email Account

I often encounter people who have a branded site address but continue to use their Gmail address for correspondence — a big mistake, and a common one too. After you go through all the trouble of finding and registering a domain name for your brand, you should use it in your email address as well. My Girl Gang the Label site address is GirlGangTheLabel.com, for example, and my email address is amy@ girlgangethelabel.com.

Every hosting provider I'm aware of allows users to set up multiple email accounts for every domain it hosts. The process for setting up new email addresses varies among hosting providers. In Bluehost, for example, you select Email in the control panel, click Create New, and use the form shown in Figure 7-13 to specify an email address and password.

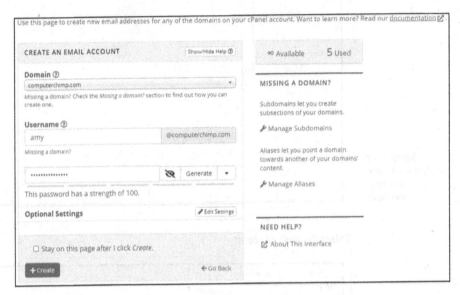

FIGURE 7-13: Create a branded email account.

Check your hosting provider's help system for instructions on creating email accounts and on sending and receiving email messages from those accounts.

Launching a Branded App

Launching an app can be a great way to stand out from competitors, deliver a unique experience to your customers, and significantly increase engagement with your brand. In addition, an app provides an easy way for you to contact your customers (via notifications) and collect more detailed behavioral analytics.

My company, Girl Gang, created a directory of female-owned businesses. Now I'm developing an app that makes it easy for users to find female-owned businesses near them — businesses in our directory. To experience the full effect, users must opt in to share their locations, which enables us to collect location data about them. We'll be monetizing the app by partnering with businesses to offer discounts and other incentives, which can be sent via real-time notifications.

Several online tools are available for developing and distributing custom apps, including the following:

- **Appery.io** (https://appery.io) is a cloud app development builder for creating cross-platform apps that run on iOS, Android, and other devices. It's billed as a low-code app development platform with visual drag-and-drop creation and editing.

- **Mobile Roadie** (https://mobileroadie.com) is a custom app development service. You present your idea, and the development team works closely with you to develop your app for use on iOS and Android devices.

- **GoodBarber** (https://www.goodbarber.com) is a low-code, drag-and-drop development tool for creating e-commerce apps. You can make your app available in Apple's App Store and Google Play or create a progressive web app (PWA) that's designed to work on any device — smartphone, tablet, or desktop. You subscribe to the surface (starting at $25 per month), which provides you access to the builder and support.

- **Appy Pie** (https://www.appypie.com) bills itself as the number-one no-code development platform. It prides itself on simplicity, providing a development platform that enables you to drag and drop your way to mobile apps, websites, automated tasks, chatbots, and live chat applications. You can even transform an existing website into an app.

TIP

If you prefer to outsource your app development, you can find plenty of skilled, affordable development professionals who are eager to take on the project. Some app development platforms can refer you to developers, or you can search for freelancers on websites such as DevTeam.Space (https://www.devteam.space) and Toptal (https://www.toptal.com).

IN THIS CHAPTER

» **Using various types of content to promote your brand**

» **Choosing to write your own copy or outsource it**

» **Staying on track with an editorial calendar**

» **Writing copy that attracts and engages your target market**

» **Driving search engine traffic to your content**

Chapter **8**

Writing Copy That Supports Your Brand Messaging

To build and launch a successful brand, you must be able to produce good *copy* — text — either by writing it yourself or collaborating with editors and copywriters. After all, nearly all marketing content requires copy — web pages, blog posts, social media, advertisements, white papers, podcasts, even videos. They all start with concepts and words and must do the following:

» **Entice:** To be effective, copy must capture the attention of the audience. If your audience isn't interested, you have zero chance of leaving a positive impression.

» **Engage/entertain:** To engage or entertain simply means to hold a person's attention. Engagement/entertainment can range from creating content that is viewed in storytelling form in an Instagram story to running a workshop that engages with your audience.

>> **Educate:** Most marketing copy educates customers in some way. It may inform customers of a new product/service or a new technology they weren't already aware of, for example.

>> **Impress:** Good copy leaves a positive impression of the brand in the minds of customers.

>> **Influence:** Ultimately, all marketing copy is designed to influence the customer's thoughts or behavior. You can also think of it as persuasion.

In the following sections, I introduce the types of content for promoting a brand, help you decide whether to write your own copy or outsource it, lead you through the process of creating an editorial calendar, offer some suggestions on how to write copy that meets the five criteria described above, and explain how to integrate search engine optimization into your copy to get it in front of more people.

Exploring Types of Copy You Can Use to Promote Your Brand

When I mention writing copy, you may wonder what I'm talking about specifically. The copy I'm referring to is *marketing copy* — any text used to promote your brand or influence a person's thinking, behavior, or decision process. It includes everything from advertisements and email messages to podcast and video scripts, white papers, and books.

In the following sections, I cover the entire spectrum of marketing copy you can use to promote your brand.

REMEMBER

Whatever you write is probably going to end up online at some point in some format, so as you write, be sure to include keywords that people are likely to search for to find that type of content. For more about including keywords in your copy to make it more search engine–friendly, see the later section "Maximizing Your Reach with Search Engine Optimization."

Advertising copy

The most obvious type of copy used to promote a brand is *advertising copy*, text used in a paid advertisement, which includes the following:

>> Headline and subheadline

>> Slogan

>> Body copy

When writing advertising copy, you don't have much space or time. Copy must be relevant, concise, and catchy to achieve maximum impact. See Chapter 15 for more about increasing brand awareness with paid advertising.

Audio/video scripts

Copy for audio and video marketing must account for the fact that most people will be *hearing* the words, not reading them. Here are a few suggestions for taking advantage of this important difference:

>> Include voice directives to cue changes in voice inflection, such as italicizing or underling words and phrases that should be stressed.

>> Tell stories to express yourself in an engaging and entertaining way that's easy to understand.

>> Use metaphors and similes to illustrate your point by comparing the unfamiliar with the familiar. Metaphors and similes are useful in any copy but particularly in scripts, because when people are processing audio content, keeping it simple is key.

>> Use mirroring, when relevant, to demonstrate that you understand the listeners' needs and concerns. You might tell a story about a common challenge you faced, one that resonates with your audience, and the solution you discovered or developed to overcome it.

>> Engage listeners in a visualization exercise in which they imagine having overcome the problem or challenge you describe.

WARNING

Don't assume that everyone will be listening to the words. Many people who are hearing-impaired rely on written transcripts. When posting audio or video content online, be sure to include the written transcript.

Blog posts

Blog posts provide a valuable means to impart information while building trust and credibility. They're also helpful for building a strong web presence because search engines love blogs. And what's not to love? Blog posts tend to feature fresh content that speaks directly to a specific audience's needs and desires.

WHERE IN THE WORLD IS SUP?

When I worked for Tower Paddle Boards, we were committed to being pioneers in the stand-up paddleboard (SUP) industry. Our business model was based on selling paddleboards directly to customers instead of to retail outlets, such as sporting-goods stores.

To establish ourselves as leaders in the industry, we hosted a blog that included a regular feature called "Where in the World Is SUP?" Every segment focused on one or more other paddleboard companies around the world to inform readers about how the sport was growing. Very subtly, it communicated our involvement in the community that formed around the industry and our generosity in sharing our platform with some of our competitors.

Because all our posts applied to the SUP industry, our blog attracted the attention of search engines, boosting our search engine ranking for relative keywords such as *SUP* and *stand-up paddleboard*.

REMEMBER

With blogs especially, quality content is the key to success. People are drawn to blogs that deliver fresh, relevant, and informative content — tips, tricks, techniques, insights, entertainment, guidance, and inspiration — that matters to them and that they can't get anywhere else. But blog posts must also be well-written and carefully edited to demonstrate the care and consideration that went into writing them. See Chapter 12 for more about blogging.

TIP

Guest blogging (contributing content to other relevant blogs) is another great marketing tool, enabling you to extend your brand's reach to audiences built by other bloggers, establish yourself as a thought leader, and network with others in your industry. To get started with guest blogging, take the following steps:

1. **Create a list of the leading blogs in your industry — the blogs that appear near the top of the search results whenever you search for a topic related specifically to your industry.**

2. **Read and follow the blogs on your list that you'd like to guest-blog for so that you're familiar with the content that's typically posted and the audience being served.**

3. **Obtain contact information for every blog on your list, including the blogger's name and email address.**

4. **Write your value proposition, which explains what you bring to the table by describing how you can benefit the blog and serve the needs and interests of its audience.**

5. **Email your value proposition to the blog's owner.**

Whenever you contribute content to another blog, post about it on your own blog and social media accounts to drive traffic to the *other* blog. This technique serves two purposes: It increases traffic to the other blog to demonstrate the value you deliver as a guest blogger, and it advertises that you're available for guest blogging gigs, which can begin to generate requests for you to share content on other sites.

Books

Most people don't think of books as marketing copy, but they can be very powerful for that purpose. Some marketing experts refer to books as business cards on steroids. If you want to be known as an expert and thought leader in the carbon-capture industry, what better way to do that than by writing a book on the topic and having a leading publisher behind it? Then you can post about the book on your blog, sell or hand out copies at major industry events, and use it as leverage to get speaking engagements and media appearances.

REMEMBER

When writing a book to establish yourself as an expert or thought leader, the key is to present valuable information, insights, and guidance in a way that's easily accessible to your audience. If you've ever wondered why the *For Dummies* brand has been so successful, that's why.

Catalog copy: Product descriptions and listings

Whether you sell products or services online or in person, you need to be able to describe them in words. The most effective product descriptions are generally those that enable the customer to envision not only the features, but also the benefits of the product or service. Your product (or service) description must answer the customer's burning question: How is this going to improve my life?

TIP

Most product/service listings are dull. They merely describe the product's features. Look for ways to jazz up your listings by helping the reader envision the potential improvements to their lives. Instead of describing a device that saves electricity as a "performance booster," say something like "Slash your electric bill by 30%" or "Imagine paying 30% less per month on electricity."

Email messages

Email is a very effective and cost-efficient way to keep your brand in the minds of existing and prospective customers. Many sales teams use automated email campaigns to lead new customers gradually through their *sales funnel* — the path customers take from initial awareness of a solution to their purchase decision. You can use a similar approach to generate awareness and interest in your brand and then lead customers to perform your desired call to action, whether it's purchasing your product or service, signing up for your monthly newsletter, joining your cause, or something else. See Chapter 14 for more about email marketing.

Press releases

Whenever you write a press release, you're creating marketing copy for other content producers, especially journalists. The relationship is mutually beneficial: You give them something to write about (or talk about on radio or video broadcasts or on podcasts), and they publicize your brand. . . for free!

As you write a press release, follow these guidelines:

>> Keep it short — a single page, 500 words maximum. The recipients can contact you if they need more info.

>> Make their job easy. Write your press release as a news story so that journalists can use it pretty much as is, expanding it if necessary to meet their word-count requirements.

>> Include a compelling headline that clearly and concisely describes the topic. Keep the headline in the range of 50 to 150 characters.

>> Include the location and date of the press release.

>> Write three to five paragraphs, leading with answers to the questions Who? What? When? Where? Why? and How? Follow up with supporting material, such as statistics and quotable quotations from people in the know.

>> Add contact information at the end, including your name and title, telephone number, email address, and website/blog address.

TIP

Approach each press release as an opportunity to express your brand's personality, whether it's button-down professional, fun and sassy, gritty, or something else. See Chapter 3 for more about brand personality.

Social media profiles and posts

When using social media to promote your brand (see Chapter 13) all text is marketing copy. Obviously, this maxim applies to the content you post and your responses to your followers' comments, but it also applies to your profiles. Everything from your brand name to your bio to your website or blog URL is an opportunity to reinforce your brand identity in readers' minds.

Web pages

Creating and managing a branded website is an excellent way to promote your brand, especially if you treat all your website copy as marketing copy. As you create web pages, follow these best practices to ensure that all copy projects the desired brand identity:

>> As you write, pretend that you're carrying on a conversation with your customer avatars — your imaginary "ideal" customers. This technique helps make your copy engaging, clear, and relevant to customers' interests and needs.

>> Follow your brand's style guide regarding voice and tone. If you're projecting a playful image, avoid wording that sounds dry or businesslike. Read about creating a brand style guide in Chapter 6.

Voice and tone express your brand's personality.

>> Include keywords that are indicative of your brand so that search engines can properly index and rank your site in their search results for those words.

>> Edit and proofread carefully, and ask someone else who's skilled with spelling and grammar to check all your web copy. As professional journalists often advise, "Never proofread your own work."

REMEMBER

Although all copy on your website is marketing copy, three pages in particular provide ideal branding opportunities: the About page, the product page, and the frequently asked questions (FAQ) page, as discussed in the following sections. (See Chapter 7 for more about building a website.)

About page

If you have a website, blog, or online store, it should have an About page, typically called "About Us." This page provides you a golden opportunity to tell visitors about your business and brand, information that goes beyond what you're selling, including the following:

>> Your brand's story/history

>> Your mission statement (see Chapter 3)

>> Your qualifications and areas of expertise (for a personal brand)

>> Your bio and bios of any team members, along with a photo of each person

>> Location and contact info

Products/services page

Your product/services page showcases what you're selling, whether it's all-natural ice cream toppings or airboat tours of the Louisiana bayou. Here, you describe your product(s) or service(s) in words, pictures, and maybe even video, incorporating words and phrases consistent with your brand's identity.

TIP

Be concise. If you think that visitors may want additional information about a feature or benefit, you can create a link to your FAQ page, discussed next.

FAQ page

Your FAQ page answers questions that people commonly ask about your brand or that you expect them to ask, such as the following:

» When can I expect to receive my order?

» How do you handle returns, refunds, and exchanges?

» Where can I go for product support?

REMEMBER

Write a clear, concise answer to each question in your brand's voice and tone. If you have the resources, consider including a live chat option or an email link that visitors can use if their questions aren't included in the FAQ. Keep a record of these questions and add them to your FAQ if they're asked frequently enough.

White papers

A *white paper* is an in-depth, authoritative report on a specific topic that typically educates readers about a challenge and explains or promotes a technology or methodology for overcoming it — the technology or methodology the business just happens to sell. Businesses often use white papers to generate leads and capture contact information. A business may offer a white paper as a free download to anyone willing to hand over their name and a valid email address. (You can use the same strategy with a brief e-book.)

REMEMBER

White papers are a form of *content marketing* — giving away valuable information in the hopes of generating business. They're thoroughly researched technical documents that include tabulated data, charts, graphs, infographics, and other data visualizations and are often used in consulting, financial, and technology by businesses or people trying to position themselves as thought leaders.

WARNING

Avoid any high-pressure selling. Using white papers to generate leads is all about soft selling; your goal is to provide valuable information that improves some aspect of the reader's life or business. Any reference to what you're selling should be very subtle.

Deciding Whether to Fly Solo or Hire a Copywriter

As with most branding tasks, the decision of whether to write copy yourself or hire a copywriter comes down to time, talent, and money:

» Do you have the *time* to write the copy yourself? If you have better, higher-level tasks to perform, such as developing new products or establishing profitable partnerships, outsource your copywriting to others.

» Do you have the *talent* to write quality copy? If you're great at writing and have a passion for it, you may want to do it yourself, especially if you tried to hire someone in the past and didn't receive copy that met your standards.

» Do you have the *money* to pay someone else to do it? If you're just getting started, you may be a one-person show. Finances often dictate what you're able to do, regardless of what you think is best.

REMEMBER

You can rarely outsource copywriting entirely. Usually, you need to provide the copywriter information and direction, which is — you guessed it — copy. Also, initially, you should carefully review all copy before it's published or posted so you know it's accurate and consistent with your branding guidelines. When you have a well-established relationship with a copywriter who has intimate knowledge of your industry, brand, and customers, you can begin to relax your oversight.

You can find freelance copywriters on sites such as Upwork (https://www.upwork.com) and Fiverr (https://www.fiverr.com). If you're looking for a full-time or part-time copywriter, consider posting a job opening on LinkedIn (https://www.linkedin.com) or Indeed (https://www.indeed.com).

Whether you hire a copywriter as a freelancer or employee, provide the writer a copy of your branding guidelines (see Chapter 6). Whenever you delegate a writing project, be clear about your audience, word-count requirement, deadline, and payment, and allow sufficient time for some back-and-forth conversation during the revision process.

Creating an Editorial Calendar

An *editorial calendar* is a schedule for creating and publishing content (see Figure 8-1). It ensures that you post or publish content regularly so that your brand is continuously and consistently reinforced in the minds of existing and prospective customers.

Editorial Schedule

PUBLISH DATE	CONTENT TYPE	TITLE	STATUS
August 2	Blog Post	Female Owned Brands in Portland	Complete
August 4	Newsletter	Weekly Newsletter, Issue #13	Finazling design
August 10	Blog Post	Podcast Recap with Teressa Foglia	Complete
August 14	IGTV	Q&A with Trish Fausset	Live (August 14)

FIGURE 8-1:
A sample editorial schedule.

At its most basic level, an editorial calendar contains the following details for each post or publication:

>> Title or headline

>> Publishing/posting date

>> Author name (who's responsible for writing it)

TIP

Consider adding details to your editorial calendar, such as the audience for the piece (if your audience is segmented), keywords to include, status, and the name of the campaign each content piece is tied to.

Crafting Brand-Boosting Copy

When you're writing copy to promote your brand, your primary goal is to shed a positive light on your brand. Depending on the piece you're writing, you may have other goals as well: encouraging readers to place an order, capturing their contact information, educating the audience on a topic of interest, persuading them to adopt a certain point of view, and so on.

To increase your chance of achieving your goals, take the following steps before writing any marketing copy:

1. **Identify the purpose (goal) of the piece.**

   What do you want the audience to think, feel, or do when they're done reading it?

2. **Define your target audience.**

   To whom are you speaking? Imagine one member of your target audience sitting in front of you. See Chapter 5 for details about defining your *customer avatars* — fictional characters who represents the people in your target market.

3. **Choose the voice and tone you want to use.**

What are your brand's voice and tone? Review your branding guidelines (see Chapter 6) to refresh in your mind the voice and tone of your brand. Also consider the topic and think about the tone it calls for (serious, gritty, sympathetic, or playful).

4. **Write down your call to action.**

What do you want readers to do after they finish reading the piece? Should they contact your office for an appointment, register for your newsletter, post a comment, or answer some survey questions?

I can't possibly cover everything that goes into writing effective marketing copy in a brief section on the topic, but I can offer the following suggestions:

>> Be clear and concise.

>> Choose the best words. Use a dictionary and thesaurus in tandem to find the words that most clearly and concisely express what you're trying to say. The more precise the words you use, the fewer words you'll need.

>> Write in active voice. Try to start each sentence with a descriptive noun followed by a specific action verb (other than *is* or *was*). Avoid starting sentences with weak constructions such as *There is/are* or *It is*.

>> Pretend you're speaking to a customer sitting right in front of you.

>> Even if you're not technically telling a story, think about each piece as a story with a beginning, middle, and end.

>> Express or evoke emotion, especially if you're concluding your piece with a specific call to action. People are most likely to think, feel, or do what you want them to if they feel compelled by a strong emotional response.

Here are a few formulas for writing marketing copy that may help you structure pieces that have a clear call to action:

>> **Attention, Interest, Desire, Action (AIDA):** Grab the reader's *attention,* build their *interest* in what you're selling, increase their *desire* (imagine how their lives will be better with your brand), and then deliver your call to *action.*

>> **Problem, Agitate, Solution (PAS):** Describe the *problem, agitate* the reader into feeling how frustrating or painful the problem is, and then deliver the *solution.*

>> **Features, Advantages, Benefits (FAB):** Describe your product/service, showcasing its unique *features;* explain the *advantages* of the product or service (over competing brands or older versions of the product); and demonstrate how the features and advantages *benefit* customers by improving their lives in some way.

TIP

If you're creating a playful brand, consider using cheeky words and phrases to reflect its personality. At Girl Gang the Label, we're primarily targeting strong, confident women who have a sense of humor, so we address members of our target market as "babe" or "girl." When we're leading shoppers through the purchase process, instead of using phrases such as "Add to cart" and "Check out," we use "You got this" and "Keep going." Creating a branded language within your community can boost engagement and sales.

Maximizing Your Reach with Search Engine Optimization

Search engine optimization (SEO) is anything and everything that's done to increase organic traffic quantity and quality from search engines to specific websites. (*Organic* means natural, as opposed to traffic from paid advertisements.) Another way to look at SEO is as a way to increase a website's search engine ranking when users search for keywords relevant to the website.

As you write copy, you want to weave keywords into your text that are relevant to your brand so that when people search for those keywords, your site will appear at or as near as possible to the top of the search results.

REMEMBER

SEO is about much more than keywords. It includes making your site mobile-friendly, getting other sites to link to yours, posting quality content that's in high demand, and doing so regularly (at least twice a week). See Chapter 7 for general coverage of SEO.

In this section, I focus more on integrating SEO into your copy.

Recognizing the difference between discovery and search

Before I dive into the topic of SEO, I want to call your attention to the distinction I draw between discovery and search. Both are part of a marketing strategy, but knowing the distinction can help you prioritize your time and focus:

>> **Discovery** occurs when someone encounters your brand by happenstance, either physically or digitally. Customers can discover your brand when passing by your retail location, hearing about it from a friend or influencer (word of mouth), or having a recommendation pop up on their screens based on their past purchases. Discovery tends to feel seamless and natural.

>> **Search** occurs when someone actively seeks out what your brand offers. Depending on the product or service, search varies in importance. If you're a hairstylist in Santa Barbara who specializes in weddings, search is a huge priority, because people in and near Santa Barbara are likely to search for "hair stylist near me" or something similar. On the other hand, if you're introducing a revolutionary new product to the market that nobody has ever heard of, search wouldn't be very helpful.

REMEMBER

If no one is searching for the product or service you're offering, spend your time on discovery. As brand awareness grows and demand increases specifically for what you're selling, you can transition to more of a search (SEO) strategy.

SEARCH VS. DISCOVERY: REAL-LIFE EXAMPLES

The difference between search and discovery is clearest when you look at real-world examples:

- **Search:** I run digital marketing for the brand Color Me Book (www.mycolormebook.com), founded by my husband, Cory Will. Customers submit their photos, and Cory's company transforms them into a personalized coloring book. We focus heavily on search because we have a specific product and clientele. When we began to see demand increase dramatically from businesses wanting to bulk-order our coloring books to promote their brands, we shifted our marketing to focus more on business-to-business (B2B) and less on business-to-consumer (B2C). We adjusted our SEO accordingly, adding keywords such as "bulk order custom coloring books" to get our brand in front of these prospective customers.

- **Discovery:** One of my close friends owns the brand Sintillia (https://www.sintillia.com), which started by making statement sunglass straps. At the time she launched, she was one of the first to market using a revamp in design for the classic accessory. She focused first on discovery (how potential customers were going to find her). By focusing on influencer marketing, photoshoots, and pop-up stores (see Chapter 11), she was able to grow sales and launch into more than 100 retail stores, including Free People. Her success in discovery increased consumer awareness of and demand for statement sunglass straps. Now that this product was a "thing," she could shift to using more SEO with keywords such as "statement sunglass straps."

Strategy time!

Building a successful online marketing strategy that incorporates SEO isn't tremendously challenging, time-consuming, or costly. All you need to do is cater to what search engines like to see. Here are a few suggestions based on my experience:

>> **Build your site on a platform that's search engine–friendly.** Look for a platform that features quick load times, mobile-first themes, secure servers, and an easy way to add *meta text* (descriptive text that visitors don't see but search engines use to index web content properly). Search engines such as Google often display the meta description in search results, which tends to increase click-through rates.

TIP

My favorite platforms are Shopify (https://www.shopify.com) for e-commerce and Squarespace (https://www.squarespace.com) for everything else.

>> **Identify and prioritize the value you plan to bring to your target market.** For my Girl Gang brand, our priorities are (1) community, (2) content, and (3) merchandise. Merchandise is our main revenue source, so why isn't it our top priority? Because we're not in business just to make a profit. But placing community and content first is also a solid approach to generating sales. By building a strong community and offering valuable content, we can drive more sales than by focusing solely on selling our merchandise. Community and content are the soul of Girl Gang. In a way, the merchandise is just window dressing. By building a thriving community of ambitious women in creative fields, our opportunities for growth and for making the world a better place are limitless.

>> **Seize every opportunity to create and share engaging and relevant branded content.** Post content to your website, blog, online store, and social media accounts; make yourself available to journalists for interviews; and offer to contribute content to popular blogs in your industry. Every chance you have to create and share relevant content is an opportunity to increase your brand's reach and awareness.

>> **Use a variety of keywords in everything you write — web copy, blog posts, social media posts, product descriptions, white papers, everything.** I recommend combining popular keywords with more unique ones that have a narrower focus. Your content may not show up in as many search results with narrowly focused keywords, but when someone searches for those keywords, your content is more likely to appear at the top of the list.

TIP

You can use a variety of keyword search tools to find out which keywords are most popular. If you have a Google Ads account, you can access its keyword search tool at https://ads.google.com/home/tools/keyword-planner (see Figure 8-2).

Keyword (by relevance)	Avg. monthly searches	Competition
Keywords you provided		
vegan food	100K – 1M	Low
dairy free ch...	10K – 100K	High
veggie burge...	10K – 100K	Low
vegan desse...	10K – 100K	Low
vegan fast fo...	1K – 10K	Low

FIGURE 8-2:
Use a keyword search tool to find common searched words and phrases.

>> **Make your images and videos search engine–friendly too.** Name your photos with descriptive keywords instead of something generic like pic0001.jpg. Use *alt text* (text that describes the image for people who can't or choose not to view images and video). Use meta tags to add a title, caption, and description. (A *meta tag* is text inserted into a website's source code that's not visible to users but is used by search engines to index and rank a site's contents.)

>> **Post content to all the popular social media platforms.** These platforms include Pinterest, Instagram, Reddit, Twitter, and Facebook. See Chapter 13 for more about promoting your brand via social media.

Search engines do a great job of analyzing content to determine how to index and rank it in the search results presented to users, but they can always use a little help. Use keywords both in the front end (the content) and the back end (meta tags) to accurately describe every piece of content you post.

WARNING

Be careful about repeating keywords in one content piece. Search engines discourage *keyword stuffing* — artificially repeating keywords in the content and meta tags to gain an unfair advantage. Search engines will penalize suspected content and either assign it a low ranking or not include it in the search results.

- **Make your images and videos search engine–friendly and.** Name your photos with descriptive keywords instead of something generic like photo1.jpg. Use alt text that describes the image for people who can't or choose not to view images and video. Use meta tags to add a title, caption, and description. (A meta index inserted into a website's source code that's not visible to users but is used by search engines to index and rank a site's contents.)

- **Post content to all the popular social media platforms.** These platforms include Pinterest, Instagram, Reddit, Twitter, and Facebook. See Chapter 2 for more about promoting your brand via social media.

Search engines do a great job of analyzing content to determine how to index and rank it in the search results presented to users, but they can also use a little help. Use the keywords both in the front-end (the content) and the back-end (meta tags) to accurately describe every piece of content you post.

Be careful about repeating keywords in one content piece. Search engines discourage *keyword stuffing* — artificially repeating keywords in the content and meta tags to gain an unfair advantage. Search engine will penalize suspected content and either assign it a low ranking or not include it in the search results.

WARNING

IN THIS CHAPTER

» **Weighing the pros and cons of partnership opportunities**

» **Choosing the right partners for your brand**

» **Persuading prospects to partner with your brand**

» **Negotiating a partnership agreement**

» **Avoiding big mistakes that can sink a partnership**

Chapter **9**

Building Strategic Partnerships

I n the business world, everyone agrees that networking is essential for further-ing a person's career. People can accomplish far more together than they can alone. Yet when the topic of developing partnerships arises, many brand own-ers express a reluctance to even consider it. In a competitive business environ-ment, partnerships can appear to be more risky than beneficial, and sometimes, concerns about the risks prove to be true. Partners don't always act in the best interests of the partnership or of one another.

But if you can create synergies with other brands and take precautions to mitigate the risks, you can accomplish far more together than the sum of what you could accomplish separately. You just need to find the right brands to partner with and agree to terms that protect each party's interests.

In this chapter, I explain how to build strategic partnerships with other brands. But first, I highlight the potential benefits and drawbacks of partnerships so that you're equipped to approach partnership opportunities with eyes wide open.

Considering Potential Benefits and Risks of Strategic Partnerships

Establishing strategic partnerships seems like a no-brainer. Except for strategic miscalculations and mistakes, nearly everything described as *strategic* can only be good, right? Well, not exactly. Like other business ventures, creating partnerships comes with both risks and rewards. Before you set out to build partnerships, weigh the pros and cons.

Potential benefits

When two brands create the right synergies, they both stand to reap the following benefits:

>> **Increased brand reach:** If each brand focuses on different market segments, it can extend its reach to the other's audience. Two brands that serve the same market segments, however, can benefit from cobranding opportunities. If the brands can identify unique factors they bring to the table, they can overlap to create new value for their customers.

>> **Increased brand awareness:** Depending on the success of the cobranding initiatives, the target audience has the opportunity to find out more about each brand.

>> **Increased sales and revenue:** Cobranding can increase sales and revenue in several ways. Some brands create a new product or product line as a part of their joint venture; others have more marketing success together than they had alone; and some brand partners extend their reach into each other's markets.

>> **Complementary knowledge and expertise:** Partners can choose to share knowledge and expertise and to work collaboratively to overcome challenges.

>> **Increased efficiency and cost reductions:** Sometimes, partnerships provide opportunities to share resources and streamline operations.

>> **Increased capital:** In some instances, one brand has money, and the other is cash-poor but has something else of value.

>> **The ability to offer customers more:** Ideally, brand partners offer different but related and even complementary products or services, enabling the brands to offer more to their customers collectively than either could as a separate entity.

>> **Shared risk, responsibilities, and rewards:** When both brands have some skin in the game, risk, responsibilities, and rewards are shared, so that the entire burden isn't placed on one brand, and both brands experience some benefit.

Possible risks

Partnering does carry some potential risks, including the following:

>> **Conflicts of interest:** When partners' goals diverge, they can begin to operate in favor of their competing interests, leading to potential difficulty in the partnership. What's in the best interest of one partner harms the other partner in some way.

>> **Lost autonomy:** Partners often must consult each other before making certain decisions or taking certain actions. When you have a partner, you can't always act independently or as quickly and responsively as you'd like.

>> **Increased complexity:** Partnerships require collaboration and coordination both of which add to operational complexity. In addition, partnerships place extra demands on management, reporting, and evaluations.

>> **Increased demand on resources:** Although partners may gain efficiencies in certain areas, they may experience a strain on resources in other areas, due to the increased demands of managing the partnership and any collaborative projects or ventures.

>> **Increased exposure to public-relations crises that are outside your control:** Your brand is judged by the company it keeps, so a partner brand that does or says something controversial can reflect poorly on your brand as well.

Finding and Selecting a Cobranding Partner

You've weighed the pros and cons of forming a cobranding partnership and have decided that it sounds like a great idea — exactly what your brand needs to move to the next level. Now what?

Well, the first step is finding the right brand to partner with. In this section, I guide you through the process.

Identifying your why

Every successful partnership has a clear purpose — a logical reason for creating it. The goals of every partnership, of course, should be to improve the partners' ability to deliver more and better goods and services to their customer base and expand that base. But I'm talking about a purpose, a *why*, that's more specific, such as the following:

>> To create a unique new product (a product development partnership)

>> To streamline the supply chain (a supply chain partnership)

>> To obtain the capital needed to fuel growth (a financial partnership)

>> To obtain the technical resources to drive innovation (a technology partnership)

>> To increase brand reach and awareness (a marketing partnership)

As you can see, many partnership types are available. Each type involves aligning the two brands in a way that elevates both brands.

Developing a list of selection criteria

A partnership is like a marriage, in that it rests on the foundation of compatibility. If two brands aren't compatible, the partnership is doomed from the start, assuming that it even develops beyond the dating stage.

To ensure compatibility, use the following criteria to evaluate prospective partners:

WARNING

>> **Comparable and complementary value:** Be sure that each brand brings something to the table that benefits the other party in a different but equal (or almost equal) way.

Don't focus solely on what your brand needs. If you don't deliver something of benefit to the other brand, the partnership will dissolve as soon as your partner realizes that it's not getting anything out of it.

>> **Shared culture and values:** Compare your mission statements, values, and cultures to ensure that they resonate with your partner's. Your "personalities" may differ, but both brands should be on the same or parallel paths and have a similar code of conduct. If one brand has a win-at-all-costs mentality, and the other values collaboration and fairness, the two brands are likely to clash.

>> **Physical proximity:** Give special consideration to brands near you. Collaborating with a local brand is always easier and often leads to better outcomes.

>> **Reliability:** Be sure that you can count on the partner you choose to deliver whatever they promise — that they not only can deliver, but also will deliver.

>> **Honesty:** Partners need to be open and honest with each other so that they both have the information they need to make data-driven decisions. If a partner withholds information or spins the narrative, it could lead you to make decisions that damage your brand.

>> **Integrity:** Partner only with brands that demonstrate *integrity* — strict adherence to their code of ethics. Brands that bend the rules may bend them to the detriment of your brand. In addition, they're at increased risk of saying or doing something that generates negative press and reflects poorly on you by association.

>> **Loyalty:** Choose a brand partner that's considerate and makes decisions not only in its own best interests, but also in yours.

Evaluating potential partners

With your list of criteria in hand, you're ready to search for and choose a strategic partner. Follow these steps:

1. **Identify brands that meet your criteria.**

   Look for areas of overlap or common ground, such as brands that share your vision, business goals, and target demographic (see Figure 9-1). These brands are more likely to provide opportunities to serve the same customers better.

   TIP

   Look within your existing network for options and referrals.

FIGURE 9-1:
Find the sweet spot where vision, goals, and target demographic overlap.

Brand Vision

Business Goals

Target Demographic

2. **Rank the brands on your list by reputation.**

At the top of your list, include only those brands that have a track record of reliability, honesty, integrity, and loyalty. Cross off any brands that have a tarnished reputation.

3. **Check for potential conflicts with current partnerships.**

If a candidate on your list is already cobranding with a close competitor of yours, don't place that candidate in the awkward position of having to deal with a potential conflict of interest.

4. **Consider proximity.**

Having a partner or brand close by can have benefits such as being able to enhance community at your location and meet frequently in person to discuss your partnership.

5. **Choose among the remaining candidates.**

You may not choose the remaining candidate at the top of your list. Make sure to identify the factors that are the most important of the benefits you've identified.

REMEMBER

FEELING PEACHY?

When you're in the market for a cobranding partner, don't overlook brands in your own industry. Case in point is Recess, a company that makes beverages and powders that help consumers feel calm and relaxed. Recess partnered with Alfred Coffee, a coffee shop in Los Angeles. Alfred used Recess Mood powder as an additive in its drinks and carried the Recess beverage in coolers at its locations. Both companies were able to focus on the brands they created to launch a unique experience born from their collaborative efforts and innovation.

As this case study proves, even brands that fall in the same industry can create win-win-win partnerships — a win for each brand and, more important, a win for the shared consumer base.

Checking out successful cobranding partnerships

Here are a few examples of successful brand partnerships:

» **GoPro and Red Bull:** These two brands represent different products; GoPro sells wearable digital camcorders, and Red Bull sells energy drinks. Both brands target energetic and daring consumers, however, and they collaborate on cobranding events such as extreme sports competitions. Go Pro supplies cameras for the athletes, and Red Bull sponsors the events.

» **Bonne Belle and Dr. Pepper:** Can you imagine Dr. Pepper–flavored lip balm? The creatives at Bonne Belle and Dr. Pepper did just that to forge a unique cobranding relationship and product: Dr. Pepper Lip Smacker. (How cool is that?) While introducing generations of lip-balm users to the unique flavor of Dr. Pepper, Bonne Belle has used Dr. Pepper's popularity to promote its own product. As one Bonne Belle ad states, "Dr. Pepper Lip Smacker. It's the super shiny lip gloss with lip-smacking flavor . . . just like the world's most original soft drink."

» **Uber and Spotify:** The road-trip playlist has become woven into America's cultural tapestry, so an audio streaming service teaming up with a rideshare company to create a cobranding relationship is no surprise. As Uber riders head to their pickup point, they're prompted to connect with Spotify to enhance their journey with an existing road-trip playlist or a creation of their own.

» **Kanye West and Adidas:** What do rapper Kanye West and German sportswear company Adidas have in common? Nothing. But that didn't stop them from collaborating on the creation of a new fashion brand: Yeezy, a high-end athletic footwear and apparel brand. Kanye's celebrity status and Adidas' reputation for quality athletic shoes proved to be a winning combination. The new brand launched in 2015, and by 2020, annual sales of Yeezy sneakers reached nearly $1.7 billion.

» **Levi Strauss & Co. and Pinterest:** Cobranding with a leading social media platform is always a good idea, and it's at the heart of the relationship between Pinterest and Levi's — the oldest and most recognized brand of jeans. The relationship gave birth to Styled by Levi's, which offers users an online styling experience along with personalized style recommendations. Based on answers to a visual questionnaire and style insights gleaned from the user's Pinterest activity, Styled by Levi's produces a Pinterest board to help customers see how they can create unique styles that include Levi's jeans.

When choosing a partner, keep your customers in mind. How will the partnership affect them? If the partnership has the potential of benefiting your customers, it has the potential of benefiting your brand. See Chapter 5 for guidance on evaluating your customer base.

Developing and Delivering a Pitch for a Strategic Partnership

Developing a strategic partnership is like developing a product; it starts as an idea to capitalize on an opportunity. Usually, that happens in a nanosecond — the speed of thought. The genius who came up with the idea for Dr. Pepper–flavored lip gloss probably didn't work long, hard hours on it. The idea came effortlessly, in a flash. It was inspired.

The time and effort come in the form of developing a delivering a pitch to the prospective partner. This work can be easy too. After all, a great idea generally sells itself. You just need to present it in the right way to the right person or people so that they can see the potential value in it for their own brand. In this section, I guide you through the process.

A strategic partnership is a business relationship between two or more brands that create value for one another. The relationship starts with one brand pitching to another. Until you ask, you don't know what brands are open to working with you. The brand you're building doesn't have to be as big as the brand you're pitching to; you just need to show its value. Your pitch is the vehicle for presenting your value proposition, and it must be clear about the goals of the partnership and what your brand brings to the table.

Determining what you want from the partnership

The first step in forming a partnership is figuring out what you want from it (your goal) and what your partner would need to bring to the table to make that happen — what your brand doesn't have and the other one does. To find out what that is, answer the following question:

> What is your brand lacking that another brand can provide to help your brand achieve the desired level of success?

Certainly, you want to improve brand reach and recognition and to increase sales and revenue, but be more specific. Here are a few examples of specific answers:

"My brand needs the credibility of a well-established brand."

"I need capital to finance my marketing efforts."

"I need distribution through a well-established retail channel."

"My brand needs product design and production capabilities."

When house-paint producer Sherwin-Williams partnered with home-furnishings retailer Pottery Barn, the relationship provided both companies increased exposure to their shared target market: people who love to furnish and decorate their own living spaces. The partners developed an exclusive line of paints to complement Pottery Barn's home furnishings, and a tool on the Pottery Barn website enables customers to coordinate paint colors with their furniture and décor.

Identifying what your brand needs enables you to focus your search for cobranding partners on brands that can deliver it.

Defining your value proposition

The term *value proposition* generally refers to the value that a company or brand promises to deliver to customers; it's why customers choose to spend money on one thing instead of something else. When you're pitching a partnership opportunity to another brand, however, you also need to present a clear value proposition. In this case, you're communicating the value that your brand brings to the table or the value that the partnership will bring to the other brand.

Be prepared to change your value proposition to speak to the needs of the brand partner you're pitching to and to the purpose of the partnership. Every partner is different, so what appeals to one may be of no consequence to another. If a brand has a much larger social media audience than yours, your modest social media following on Instagram probably won't matter to that brand.

To identify your value proposition, take the following steps:

1. **Describe your product or service, and think about what makes it valuable.**

   If you have a vegan hair-care company, the value you offer is in the form of vegan-friendly products and an eco-conscious customer base. If you're pitching a brand partnership opportunity to a large beauty and hair-care products retailer, you could highlight your brand's deep roots in the vegan community as part of your value proposition.

2. **Connect your brand's value to the major pain points of your prospective partner's customers.**

   Your value proposition might highlight the demand for vegan hair-care products along with stories from consumers who have trouble finding such products where they normally do their shopping.

3. **Highlight what your brand can bring to the table.**

   Present everything your brand offers that complements or enhances the other brand. Here are a couple of examples:

   - *A strong community:* If your brand has a large, active community of friends, followers, and fans on one or more social media platforms, that community can be a big selling point. Be sure to include specific metrics such as the number of friends, followers, and fans and engagement stats, which reflect comments and shares. Community is difficult to build, so if the brand you're pitching to has little to no social media, it'll be eager to look into any opportunity to gain a social media presence with little investment on its part.

   - *A unique design:* A unique design, a trademarked saying that can be licensed, or strong brand colors can all contribute to an effective value proposition. My Girl Gang the Label brand formed a strategic partnership with *Peanuts* (yes, the comic strip) to produce an exclusive clothing collection for Nordstrom. Our trademarked phrase and brand identity, centered on female empowerment, resonated perfectly with popular female characters from the *Peanuts* strip. In the tag, both brands are represented to show to reflect our creative collaboration.

THE BORED APE YACHT CLUB

A nonfungible token collection calling itself the Bored Ape Yacht Club (BAYC) has created a thriving community of art and culture enthusiasts, and this community alone has made BAYC a valuable asset. (A *nonfungible token* is a digital asset that can be bought, sold, and traded online like paintings and other original creations in the real world.)

Many more traditional brands are eager to partner with brands like BAYC that are trendsetters in their industry. They want to plug into that excitement and engagement to gain appreciation through association. BAYC has collaborated with apparel brands, created a shoe for community members, launched a collection of wine in Spain, and curated an auction with Sotheby's.

To pitch a cobranding partnership opportunity to a brand like BAYC, which already has a large and highly engaged community, the social media community you've built wouldn't be a strong selling point. But if you have a product that clicks with the BAYC brand and is in an industry that the other brand haven't ventured into, that selling point could be very strong.

Pitching your proposal

Pitching a partnership proposal is like networking to get a job. Emailing your proposal to the other brand's owner or chief executive officer would be about as effective as mailing your résumé. You're more likely to get your proposal accepted if you build a relationship *before* delivering your pitch. Here are some dos and don'ts for getting your proposal in front of the decision-makers:

>> **Find the right person to pitch to.** The person to pitch to depends on the size of the business/brand and the department most relevant to the partnership arrangement you have in mind. If you're reaching out to a small business or a brand owner, pitch to the person in charge. For larger companies, look for midlevel management or someone in the department you'd be working with, such as the marketing or retail manager. If you can't get in touch with someone at the top or the middle, contact another insider; an employee who's passionate about your brand may be able to influence the organization's leadership.

TIP

To obtain contact information, check the brand's or the person's website, blog, and social media profiles. I don't recommend making initial contact online unless you have no other option, but online resources can be very helpful in tracking people down.

>> **Build a relationship first.** If the two brands have a shared mission and values, building a relationship with the other brand should be easy but may take some time. Look for the brand owner or CEO online and engage with them informally via social networking.

TIP

If the other brand has employees, connect with them as well. They may not be the decision-makers, but they're insiders who have the potential to champion your partnership proposal and get it in front of the decision-makers.

>> **Don't pitch initially via email unless you have no other option.** If you're pitching your partnership idea to a popular brand, assume that you're not alone and that the person receiving your email won't welcome it. An email is the equivalent of a cold sales call. Hold off on email until the person shows some interest and you're in a position to make a more formal pitch.

REMEMBER

Even though you should hold off on pitching a partnership proposal via email, having an email template prepared in advance enables you to follow up quickly with any brands that have shown an interest in forming a partnership. See the next section for details on creating an effective email template.

>> **Connect but don't pitch on LinkedIn and other social networks.** Search for decision-makers and other insiders on LinkedIn and other social networks, engage with them, and get to know them. Avoid presenting your partnership idea until you feel comfortable with your relationships.

REMEMBER

Social networks emphasize *social*. On some social networks, such as LinkedIn, talking shop is appropriate and welcome, but don't use social networks to try to do business or sell anything outside the features designated for doing so. Selling on social networks is about as welcome as selling dietary supplements at a family gathering.

» **Meet in person if possible.** Nothing replaces in-person contact, so look for opportunities to meet in person, such as at industry events or conferences. If you're in the same location, invite your contact to lunch or coffee, and continue to work on developing the relationship. If you have a popular podcast or blog, offer your contact an opportunity for an interview or guest blog post.

» **Be genuine.** Express genuine interest in the other brand. If you're not genuinely interested, you'll have a very difficult time trying to act as though you're being authentic, and the other person will quickly sense that you're not.

» **Don't hard sell.** Ideally, your idea for a partnership should become so subtly clear to your contact that they believe they thought of it first. If that outcome is too good to be true in your case, at least present your idea in the natural course of a conversation in a matter-of-fact manner to plant the seed of the opportunity in the contact's mind.

REMEMBER

You can ease into a partnership instead of rushing your partnership proposal. Take your time to get to know each other and fully understand each other's business, brand, mission, values, and challenges. Make sure to consume as much information you can about the brands and industries you want to partner with by buying books, attending seminars and events, reaching out to ask questions, and reviewing their websites. The more you know, the better equipped you'll be to pitch your proposal effectively.

Building an email template

Having a cobranding partner pitch email template available comes in handy when you're ready to follow up with prospective brand partners who've expressed interest. You'll want to convey what you can bring to the partnership while showing proof of what you've already accomplished. Create a template that's visually pleasing and easy to digest.

One of my big selling points for Girl Gang the Label is my podcast, which highlights successful women. When pitching founders to be a guest on my podcast, I include highlights of past guests along with a template of what their feature will look like in email (see Figure 9-2).

FIGURE 9-2:
A sample
cobranding
partner-pitch
email template.

Every email pitch is different, but here are a few ideas for structuring your pitch in the hope that they'll get your own creative juices flowing:

» Present a bullet-point plan to describe how the partnership will look — what each brand brings to the table, how the brands complement each other, and how both brands will benefit. Keep the plan short and simple. Drafting a working agreement can come later.

» Deliver an elevator pitch describing your vision for the partnership — that is, a pitch concise enough to be delivered in the course of a brief elevator ride.

» Follow up your bullet-point plan or elevator pitch with any relevant examples of past partnerships that have been successful for your brand.

» Create a three-sentence pitch, including

  • Your vision for the partnership

  • What you bring to the table

  • A successful current or past partnership

» Consider including a brief statement describing the alignment of your two brands in terms of customer base, mission, or values.

Agreeing on the Terms of Your Partnership

WARNING

Although partnerships are often formed with a handshake, they're important legal agreements that can have a significant impact on your brand and business. To avoid future conflict and resolve any conflicts that can't be avoided, I strongly encourage you to hire an attorney to prepare a partnership agreement or to carefully review any agreement proposed by your future partner.

Be sure that the partnership agreement covers the following terms:

>> The partnership's goals and each party's goals if they differ in some way

>> The length of the partnership

>> Descriptions and timelines for any cobranding projects, products, activities, and events

>> What each partner promises to do or contribute toward achieving the stated goals (job duties and contributions of capital and other resources)

>> A noncompete clause to prevent either partner from entering into agreements with competing brands

>> A nondisclosure clause to protect any sensitive or proprietary information obtained in the course of doing business together

>> Data ownership and sharing agreements that cover any data collected through cobranding activities

>> Brand licensing guidelines that specify how each brand's logos, trademarks, and copyrights can be used

>> Each party's liability in the event of a lawsuit

>> A termination clause that allows either partner to end the agreement under certain conditions, such as failure to perform, failure to meet the stated goals of the partnership by a certain date, or doing anything that might harm your brand

Steering Clear of Common Partnership Pitfalls

Assuming that you and your brand partner have prepared and signed a partnership agreement and carefully considered and discussed all its terms, your agreement is the most effective way to avoid the most common partnership pitfalls.

Both parties are aware of their mutual and respective responsibilities. Now success depends on both parties delivering on what they promised.

Even with a rock-solid partnership agreement in place, however, brand partnerships can fail. Here are some of the most common causes of failure. You need to be aware of these causes so that you're prepared to avoid them:

>> **Poor communication:** One key factor in the success of any relationship is communication. Don't assume anything. Ask for clarification whenever you're unsure about something. You can't function as a unit if both parties are acting independently.

>> **Lack of transparency:** Many partnerships fail when partners aren't honest and open about everything that might affect their successful collaboration, such as a lack of essential resources, poor decisions, or behind-the-scenes business dealings. You and your partner needn't share everything, but you need to share everything that could affect your cobranding success.

>> **Lousy management:** When you create a strategic alliance, you often create a third entity that functions almost like a separate business, and like all businesses, this new one must be managed properly for it to succeed. Establish goals, measurable objectives, and detailed tactics for achieving each objective. Plan and budget carefully for every cobranding initiative, and provide the oversight required for successful execution.

>> **Diverging visions:** Partnerships often begin with a clear shared vision and goals. Over time, as the interests of one or both partners change, so do their visions for the cobranding partnership. Be sensitive to the possibility of divergence, and communicate clearly and openly with your partner throughout the partnership. Realize that at some point, your interests and goals may no longer align, in which case dissolving the partnership may be best for both brands.

>> **Inflexibility:** You and your cobranding partner must remain flexible and willing to adapt when your plans don't deliver the desired outcomes, when market conditions change, and when you disagree on the approach to take to meet your shared goals. Here, too, open, honest communication is the key to making adjustments and shifting course.

Chapter **10**

Launching Your Brand

T he process of launching your brand is where all your preparation finally comes together and the rubber meets the road. You have a clear vision of your brand's identity, what makes it special, and a clear sense of purpose; you know your audience; and you have a solid brand style guide, an Internet presence, and an email account. All systems go. You're ready to launch.

All you need now is a flight plan that leads you through the process. In this chapter, you get the information and guidance you need to develop that flight plan.

Planning Your Launch Campaign

Planning your launch campaign involves figuring out what to do, when to do it, how much money to invest in it, and how you're going to measure progress and success. In this section, I lead you through the process of planning your launch campaign. In short, that process goes like this:

1. **Decide where to launch.**

2. **Confirm your key target audiences.**

3. **Create a brand launch to-do list.**

4. **Time your launch for maximum impact.**

5. **Schedule your launch activities.**

6. **Prepare incentives for your first customers.**

7. **Choose metrics for success and establishing your benchmarks.**

8. **Budget for your launch.**

9. **Launch your brand internally, and make adjustments as needed before launching it to the rest of the world.**

TIP

Your ultimate goal is to launch your brand externally — to the outside world — but I strongly recommend that you do an internal launch first, both as a dry run and as a way to clarify your brand vision for everyone on your team. See "Launching your brand internally" later in this chapter for details.

Deciding where to launch

When I talk about where to launch, I'm referring to both online and physical venues or locations — wherever you choose to make a big splash and generate buzz. Online and physical locations may include one or more of the following:

TIP

» One or more pop-up stores (see Chapter 11).
  If you're launching in a physical location, carefully consider where you'll get the most foot traffic, especially people who are most likely to be interested in your brand.

» Retail outlets (see Chapter 11).

» Public locations, such as airports and roadsides (billboards).

» Your website, blog, or online store (see Chapter 7).

» A third-party ecommerce platform such as Etsy (https://www.etsy.com). Although you won't have your own domain, you can create a shop and open it to millions of customers in Etsy's network.

» Social media platforms, such as Facebook, Instagram, and Twitter (see Chapter 13).

» Publications — newspapers, magazines, or professional journals.

» A fundraising website, such as Kickstarter (https://www.kickstarter.com). What does fundraising have to do with branding? If you have a great idea, your fundraising effort can serve as a very effective marketing tool.

» A speakers' bureau, such as APB (https://www.apbspeakers.com) or social media influencer directory, such as Find My Influencer (https://www.findmyinfluencer.com), if you're launching a personal brand.

Confirming your key target audiences

Whenever you launch or relaunch your brand or launch any marketing campaign, for that matter, confirm your key target audiences. In Chapter 5, I guide you through the process of defining one or more customer avatars — each a composite of all the people in one of your target markets. Do those avatars still represent the people in your target markets? If they don't, now is the time to make adjustments. If they do, great; have everyone on your team study them again so you all have a clear idea of who you're reaching out to.

REMEMBER

Your key target audiences may be defined by location, demographics (age, gender, occupation, income level, marital status), psychographics (values, hobbies, lifestyle, personality, attitude, behavior), industries, buying habits, pain points, motivation, and so on.

Creating a to-do list

Launching a brand sounds so easy. After all, it merely involves announcing your brand to the world — or to the small part of the world you're reaching out to. It starts to get complicated when you ask yourself "How?" What specifically are you going to do to promote your brand during your launch?

The answer to that question depends on several factors, including the brand type (product brand, personal brand, and so on), the product or service you're selling, your target audiences, and your budget and resources. If you're launching a personal brand to market yourself as a consultant, you'll need to build a website and a social media presence, write blog posts and articles, establish media contacts, network with decision-makers, and pursue relevant speaking engagements. If you're launching a product brand, you'll need to build an online store, establish a social media presence, write and distribute a press release, send product samples to influencers, and so on.

Make a comprehensive to-do list of specific things you need to do to launch your brand. Here's a list of ideas to get your creative juices flowing (the good news is that you don't have to do all of them):

>> Create the marketing materials you need, such as advertisements, signs, posters, banners, brochures, postcards, business cards, case studies, sales sheets, testimonials, flyers, loyalty cards, branded shirts, and promotional items (branded pens, mugs, keychains, and so on).

REMEMBER

Give yourself plenty of lead time for designs, edits, approval, and printing (if necessary). See "Creating a launch calendar" later in this chapter for details.

- >> Create and distribute a press release. See "Tapping the Power of the Press to Launch Your Brand" later in this chapter.

- >> Go live with your branded website, blog, or online store.

- >> Post promotional content to your social media accounts — text-based content, discount codes, podcasts, audio, video, white papers, and so on.

- >> Execute an email marketing campaign (see Chapter 14).

- >> Launch pay-per-click advertising campaigns.

- >> Advertise in traditional media — newspapers, magazines, television, and radio.

TIP

You can create local, regional, or national ad campaigns depending on the distribution and availability of your products and services.

- >> Perform in-store product demonstrations.

- >> Conduct promotional campaigns that offer discounts, gifts, samples, or free trials.

- >> Connect and coordinate your launch with influencers. See Chapter 13 for more about teaming up with influencers.

- >> Get a booth or deliver a presentation at a popular industry event, such as a conference or trade show, that gets a lot of press, such as Comic Con or the Consumer Electronics Show. Those events may be a little ambitious for a small brand, but every industry has events large and small.

- >> Throw a launch party.

- >> Do a prelaunch campaign in the days, weeks, or months leading up to your official launch date. A pre-launch campaign is a downscaled version of the official launch designed to generate some buzz and build anticipation for a brand. It may involve creating a "Coming Soon" page, blogging about an upcoming product release, and capturing email addresses so you can execute an email marketing campaign as part of your official brand launch.

TIP

Have fun thinking up clever ideas for your brand launch. The more enthusiastic you are about your launch, the more enthusiastic your audience will be about your brand.

Timing your launch for maximum impact

What's the tenth biggest reasons why startup fail? Poor timing, according to a recent survey conducted by the Small Business Administration. Introduce your product or service too early, when customers aren't ready for it, and you won't make a splash. Introduce it too late, and your competitors may beat you to the punch. This statistic applies only to innovative product or service brands, but even so, when you're launching any brand, timing can dramatically affect your success.

When you're deciding on a launch date, consider the following factors:

» **Readiness:** For most brands, the best time to launch is as early as possible — whenever your brand is ready and you're ready.

» **Seasons:** Some things are more popular in certain seasons. If you're launching a new line of kayaks, you probably want to schedule your launch sometime during boat-show season: late fall to early spring. Likewise, launching a self-improvement product near the first of the year, when people are making their New Year's resolutions, is usually effective.

» **Industry cycles and events:** Most industries have annual cycles and specific events that drive interest in innovative products and services. In the publishing biz, BookExpo in late May or early June generates a great deal of buzz.

» **Your own product cycles:** When one product is reaching its peak, and you've developed the next new thing, it's time to relaunch your brand.

» **Holidays and observances:** Certain days, weeks, and even months provide great brand launch opportunities, and I'm not just talking about Halloween, Thanksgiving, Christmas, Hanukkah, and Kwanzaa. We also celebrate National Pet Appreciation Day, National Doughnut Day, National Yoga Day, National Coloring Book Day; Termite Awareness Week, Work at Home Moms Week, International Clown Week (no kidding); National Black History Month, National Back to School Month, and Mad for Plaid Month. Here's a list of holidays just in the first week of January:

   National Bloody Mary Day (January 1)

   National Buffet Day (January 2)

   National Cream Puff Day (January 2)

   Fruitcake Toss Day (January 3)

   National Chocolate Covered Cherry Day (January 3)

   National Spaghetti Day (January 4)

   National Whipped Cream Day (January 5)

   Apple Tree Day (January 6)

   National Bean Day (January 6)

   National Shortbread Day (January 6)

   National Tempura Day (January 7)

To find holidays and observances relevant to your brand, search the web for the product/service type that best represents your brand followed by "holidays and observances" or search for "holidays and observances" and browse through the lists that turn up. You can also look up the best season for your product through Google.

When you're launching on a holiday or observance, be sure to use hashtags to spread the word, such as #TeacherAppreciationWeek. Hashtags extend your reach in increase shareability.

Creating a launch calendar

When you have a comprehensive to-do list and a launch date, you're ready to schedule launch activities, assign them to the responsible person (or people), and backdate them. *Backdating* is the practice of setting milestones on dates earlier than the date a project needs to be completed so that time is available to complete the project. If one of your activities is to deliver in-store demonstrations, you set the dates for those demonstrations and then set earlier dates to allow time to prepare for them.

You can use project-planning or collaboration software such as Google Workspace (https://workspace.google.com), an online calendar such as Google Calendar (https://calendar.google.com), a traditional day planner or 12-month calendar, or a table to create your launch calendar. Be sure to include the following details:

>> A descriptive name for each activity or project.

>> The date on which each project is to be completed or each activity is to be performed, along with any milestones leading up to that date.

>> The person or people responsible for each project/activity. Obviously, this detail isn't necessary if you're doing everything yourself.

If you have your own marketing team or strategic partnerships with other brands, strongly consider using a cloud-based calendar, project-management, or collaboration software so that everyone on your team has access to the same information.

Preparing incentives for initial customers

A great way to encourage your target audiences to participate in your brand launch is to offer an incentive, such as the following:

>> Swag, such as free branded T-shirts, baseball caps, keychains, refrigerator magnets, pens, or water bottles. If you're opening a new gym, you can offer a free bag with a branded water bottle and gym towel, a protein bar, and a coupon for a free month's membership.

TIP

Several online businesses specialize in manufacturing and selling branded promotional merchandise, such as Swag.com (https://swag.com) and DiscountMugs (https://www.discountmugs.com). You can also order swag in more general marketplaces, such as Etsy (https://www.etsy.com) and Zazzle (https://www.zazzle.com). Search the site for something along the lines of "promotional items with logo."

>> A product sample or free trial, such as a sample of an all-natural skin rejuvenation cream you developed or a free subscription to a monthly investment newsletter.

>> A coupon or a discount card or code that's available exclusively to a certain number of your first customers. If you're selling gym memberships online, you could offer a free one-month trial to anyone who enters the code JOESGYMVIP at checkout. All e-commerce sites (including Amazon.com, Shopify, and eBay) include a feature for creating discount codes; search your site's help system for details.

>> Sweepstakes and prizes. You can enter customers into a drawing for a chance to win $100 in free merchandise for making a minimum purchase of $20, for example.

>> A bonus product with purchase. You might give a free branded compact mirror with a purchase of $100 worth of beauty products, for example.

Imagine what you would want if you were one of your brand's customers. What would be valuable enough to you to make an initial purchase and tell all your friends about this great promotional offer?

Choosing metrics for success and establishing your benchmarks

Before launching your brand, identify which metrics to use to measure the success or impact of each activity and your overall brand launch. If you're relaunching a brand, include prelaunch benchmarks for each metric to compare your brand's prelaunch status with its postlaunch status. You may even want to compare your postlaunch metrics with your prelaunch benchmarks at certain intervals, such as one week, two weeks, and four weeks after launch.

Here are a few metrics you may want to track:

>> **Social media impressions:** *Impressions* are the number of times your brand is mentioned on social media. If influencers are participating in your launch, track the social media impressions generated by their posts. Tracking social media impressions is a great way to gauge *brand awareness* — the degree to which a brand is recognized among a target group.

>> **Website traffic:** Use Google Analytics (https://analytics.withgoogle.com) or a similar website data collection and analysis tool to track the impact of your launch on the number of visits to your website.

>> **Press coverage:** Set up a Google news alert for your brand name to receive email alerts whenever your brand is mentioned in the news. To set up an alert, go to https://www.google.com/alerts, type your brand name in the box near the top of the page, and click the Create Alert button.

TIP

If you reached out to any specific media outlets or journalists, follow up after your launch to see whether they posted anything. If so, get the link to the post so you can share it on your website, blog, and social media accounts. You may also want to take a screen shot of the piece to use in your marketing efforts. See "Tapping the Power of the Press to Launch Your Brand" later in this chapter for more about working with the press.

>> **Sales:** Track the number of products sold, new customers, new memberships or subscriptions, and any other metrics that reflect sales relevant to your brand. To measure online product sales, you can export a report directly from your e-commerce provider; check its help system for details.

These metrics provide a good general indication of your brand launch success. More difficult metrics to track include brand consideration, perceived quality, and brand loyalty. See Chapter 4 for more about monitoring these and other metrics.

Budgeting for your launch

Using the to-do list you created (refer to "Creating a to-do list" earlier in this chapter), create a budget for your brand launch. I recommend using a spreadsheet application or a budget template in the personal or business finance program you use so it can handle the calculations for you.

Here are some of the expenses you may want to include in your budget:

>> **Assistant compensation:** Expense for hiring an assistant or outsourcing some of the work to a virtual assistant

- » **Marketing materials:** Signs, posters, banners, brochures, postcards, business cards, and flyers — mostly printed materials but also their digital equivalents in some instances

- » **Mass media ads:** Advertisements in newspapers and magazines and on TV and radio

- » **Pay-per-click advertising:** Search engine ads, social media ads, promoted posts, and so on

- » **Content marketing:** Video, podcasts, white papers, e-books, case studies, infographics, webinars, blogging and guest blogging, newsletters, and so on

- » **Public relations:** Press releases and media kit

- » **Email marketing:** Email marketing service provider fees, campaigns for capturing email addresses, and design costs

- » **Promotional items (swag):** Branded T-shirts, baseball caps, keychains, refrigerator magnets, pens, water bottles, and other trinkets you plan to give away

- » **Website/blog development:** Expense for any changes for your brand launch if not already accounted for in your overall branding budget

- » **In-person events:** Pop-up store, swag (if not accounted for already), signage, staffing, and venue

- » **Influencer:** Compensation, influencer marketing platform fees, and the cost of shipping to the influencer (in some instances)

- » **Industry event fees:** Booths at trade shows, conferences, and expos

- » **Launch party:** Venue, food, beverages, music, and fun stuff (video, mascot, prize drawing)

TIP

If you're building partnerships with other brands that have deeper pockets, consider asking them to sponsor your launch party.

Launching your brand internally

Perhaps the most important phase of any brand launch is the internal brand launch, when you reveal your brand to everyone in your organization. A successful internal launch generates the organizationwide buy-in necessary for a successful external launch.

REMEMBER

Branding isn't just about marketing; it goes much deeper. Every customer encounter is an opportunity to promote or demote your brand in the minds of potential customers, so everyone in your organization must embrace your brand's mission, vision, and values, and follow its policies and procedures.

Your internal launch should be fun and engaging, but it needs to get down to business too. The purpose is to build support and enthusiasm for the brand while overcoming any internal resistance to it. Sometime during the business portion of your internal launch, take the following steps:

1. **Make a case for the value of branding (see Chapter 1).**

2. **Review your brand's mission, vision, and values (see Chapter 3).**

3. **Reveal your brand identity.**

   Show your logo and slogan, and explain what they represent.

4. **Introduce your brand promise.**

   Your brand promise reflects what you promise to deliver to customers. It's why customers will choose your brand over other options (and customers *always* have other options).

5. **Give every member of your team a quality branded gift.**

   Gifts may include polo shirts with your brand's logo, pens, notebooks, and so on. Gifts don't have to be expensive, but they should be high-quality items reflecting the quality you expect from everyone in your organization.

6. **Ask everyone in your organization to embrace the brand and become brand ambassadors.**

   Emphasize the importance of not just talking the talk, but also walking the walk. Everything employees do at work and even away from work, everything they say about the brand, and everything they post about it on their social media accounts must reinforce the brand's identity and promise in a positive way.

TIP

After your internal launch, you may want to follow up with a soft launch or soft opening exclusively for VIP customers, strategic partners, and members of the press. Another option is a friends-and-family night for everyone who participated in creating the brand and will support it moving forward.

Tapping the Power of the Press to Launch Your Brand

The press is powerful, but it's also needy: It thrives or dies on the news it reports. Every journalist loves a great story. If you can deliver a compelling brand story, reporters and their readers will eat it up. You'll get lots of free press and additional content to talk about, blog about, and post to your social media accounts.

In this section, I explain how to attract members of the press and get them excited about your brand, but first you must tackle the question of whether to outsource press contact to a public relations (PR) firm or consultant or handle that job internally.

TIP

Most people trust the press implicitly, so when a reporter does a story on your brand, you gain a little of that credibility. Use it. On your web page or blog, create a "Featured in . . ." section or page with all the articles, audio, and video published about your brand, along with quotes. When prospective customers visit your site, they'll be impressed by the coverage and find your brand trustworthy.

Deciding whether to hire a PR firm

A PR firm or consultant can be a powerful asset when you're trying to get press coverage because they have (or at least should have) solid relationships with members of the press and know how to pitch a story. A skilled PR firm or consultant can get you relevant press coverage for your target demographic, assist you in your launch campaign, and save you considerable time.

Unfortunately, they can cost you a considerable amount of money too. As with most things in marketing, you have a choice to make: Do you want to spend the time or the money? If you're a small-time operation, you probably have no choice but to do the work yourself. If you're a midsize operation, hiring a PR firm may be the best choice. And if you're a large firm, you may have the resources to hire a dedicated PR person or team.

If you don't have any glowing references for a PR firm or consultant to contact, start by researching brands in the same industry as yours, and visit their websites to find out who they use as their press contact.

WARNING

PR firms traditionally work on a contract for a minimum time before the contract can be terminated. (All contracts can be negotiated, of course.) Just be sure to read the contract thoroughly, understand everything in it, and have the funds available to cover the minimum term. Consult your attorney if anything is unclear.

If you decide to serve as your own PR specialist, keep reading for additional guidance.

Creating a hit list for press and influencers

When you're acting as your own PR person, your first order of business is creating a list of journalists and influencers you want to reach out to. You want a long list, of course, but limit it to relevant people — those who serve the audiences you're targeting.

Start your list with journalists and influencers you already have in mind, such as journalists from magazines and blogs you read, and active, influential members of the social media communities you belong to. Then add to the list as you encounter more people who meet your criteria. Searching the web for magazines, blogs, and newsletters that people in your audience are likely to read may also turn up some useful leads.

When you're preparing to launch your brand, create a hit list for the journalists and influencers you want to contact so you can keep track of your communications (see Figure 10-1).

Outlet	Role	Name	Email	Instagram	LinkedIn	Date Sent	Status	Follow Up
Faves	Senior Contrib	Sammi Robert	sr@faves.com	@sammir379	https://www.link	7.15.22	Told to circ	8.3.22
Lashes	Editor	Cindy Smith	csmith@lashe	@csmith931	https://www.link	7.16.22	Send more	8.5.22
Bling	Contributor	Meg Tyrell	mtyrell@blin	@maggiet32	https://www.link	7.16.22	Draft article	8.20.22
Vague	Fashion Edito	Sarah Parson	sparson@vag	@sarahparson	https://www.link	7.17.22	Interview	8.22.22
Trendsetter	Fashion News	Emily Grant	egrant@trend	@emilygrant2397	https://www.link	7.18.22	Podcast int	8.31.22

FIGURE 10-1:
A sample hit list.

Creating a brand launch press release

Organizations and people send out press releases to announce anything newsworthy that members of the press may want to write about. A press release is a necessity for any brand launch. You want as much free press as you can get (ideally, mostly positive), and sending out a press release is one of the best ways to get it.

THE HOT MESS ICE ROLLER

When Lauryn Bosstick launched her first product, The Skinny Confidential Hot Mess Ice Roller ("a preventive skin care tool that uses the power of cold therapy to contour, tighten, and de-puff the skin"), she rallied the press, as well as the community that developed around her brand, to generate buzz for her product launch.

She sent PR boxes to the press, influencers, her podcast guests, medical experts, and friends. Each box contained a Hot Mess Ice Roller, additional self-care products, a book written by the founder, and details about the product. By providing the information and products that recipients would need for a full experience, she enabled them to create content for their respective communities that went beyond product promotion to the sharing of self-care tips.

In return, the product received authentic reviews from people in her circle, and Bosstick was able to build trust among fans and the customer base she was targeting.

In Chapter 8, I provide some basic guidelines for writing a press release. In this section, I offer additional suggestions specifically for brand launch press releases.

Structuring your press release

When creating your press release, include the seven essential elements below:

1. *Headline:* Come up with a compelling headline so that nobody reading the press release will even think about putting it down before reading the first paragraph.

2. *Summary and key details:* Pack the first paragraph with all the key details, answering the 5W questions (Who? What? When? Where? Why?). Be sure to include the date and location of the launch, regardless of whether you're launching at one or more physical locations or totally online.

3. *Features and benefits:* In the second paragraph, expand on the features and benefits of what you're selling in a way that showcases your brand's identity and promise. Here, you're making the case for what makes your brand special or highlighting a problem and presenting your brand as a unique solution.

4. *Expert/insider opinions:* In the third paragraph, include what others who matter (industry experts, your organization's leaders, or early adopters) have stated about your brand. Include compelling quotes that reporters can use in their pieces.

5. *Closing:* In the fourth paragraph, briefly encapsulate the key points you covered. If you're announcing a product or service brand, specify where and when the products or services will be generally available.

6. *Call to action:* Your final paragraph is your call to action, which may be a web address or a link to a web page where reporters can go to obtain additional information. It can also be a request to call your PR contact for more information.

7. *Contact information:* Include the name, email address, and phone number of the person to contact for more information.

Don't write your press release like a sales letter. Pretend that you're talking to a reporter about an upcoming newsworthy event: your brand launch.

FROM PR AGENCY TO FASHION BRAND

Mayfair Group, a PR and branding agency that pivoted to merchandise, recently launched its own clothing line. By the end of its first year, it had generated several million dollars in revenue. That's impressive for a young company, but many businesses are multimillion-dollar companies. What's compelling about the brand's story is that it achieved these numbers after transitioning from a PR agency to a fashion brand.

Mayfair Group made the most of its brand story by weaving it into the title of an article about the company in *Forbes* magazine: "How The Mayfair Group Pivoted From Agency To Multimillion-Dollar Fashion Brand, Thanks To Positive Messaging And Empathy."

As you can see, this headline has a unique angle while succinctly conveying what the brand is about, its accomplishment, and why that accomplishment is so impressive.

Coming up with headlines that convert

A press release is worthless if nobody reads it. Most press releases land in the cluttered Inboxes of overworked journalists. You need to give them a compelling reason to open your press release and read it. The key is to get creative with the Subject line of your email message and the headline in your press release. Here are a few examples of compelling headlines:

> Why Dollar Shave Club Co-Founder Michael Dubin No Longer Believes in DTC
> — Dollar Shave Club
>
> This Out-of-Home Campaign Wants to Make You Think About How You're Feeling
> — MadHappy
>
> NYC's Trendiest Salon Launched the Coolest Summer Nail Art
> — ChillHouse

Improving Your Campaign's Chances of Going Viral

Every business on the planet wants its brand launch to go viral and bring in a rush of customers, followers, and brand ambassadors. You can't do that with traditional marketing — highlighting the features and benefits of what you're selling and trying to convince your audience that what you offer is better, faster, or cheaper than what's already available. You do it by creating content that people feel overwhelmingly compelled to share with everyone they know.

"What kind of content is that?" you ask. It's the kind of content that meets one of the following three criteria:

>> Funny

>> Inspiring

>> Exciting

REMEMBER

Viral marketing isn't about the products or services you offer. It's about what your audience will find funny, fantastic, or outrageous. Here are a few examples:

>> **Oreo's Dunk in the Dark:** When the New Orleans Superdome experienced a 30-minute power outage during the 2013 Super Bowl, Oreo tweeted "Power out? No problem" followed by a photo of an Oreo cookie faintly glowing the darkness (https://twitter.com/Oreo/status/298246571718483968). Twitter users couldn't believe the speed and cleverness of the ad and quickly retweeted it.

>> **Dollar Shave Club: Our Blades are F**ing Great:** To promote its shaving blade subscription service, in 2012, the Dollar Shave Club posted a hilarious YouTube video featuring its founder explaining what makes the company's blades and service so special. But the video isn't so much about the blades as it is about making the audience laugh. To date, it has received more than 27 million views.

>> **Wendy's Chicken Nugget Retweet Challenge:** In 2017, Twitter user Carter Wilkerson posted a tweet asking Wendy's how many tweets he would need to get himself free chicken nuggets for a year. Wendy's responded, "18 million." Wilkerson retweeted the answer, asking other Twitter users to help him meet that goal. That tweet became the most-retweeted of all time. He didn't quite meet his goal, but Wendy's rewarded him for his efforts.

Here are a few suggestions for creating a viral marketing campaign:

>> Be clever and quick-witted.

>> Look for opportunities to play off content that others have posted.

>> Use catchy, memorable titles for all your content.

>> Practice proven search engine optimization (SEO) techniques (see Chapter 8).

>> Include something that's sharable — funny, fantastic, or outrageous content; a fun challenge; an incredible deal; or a simple, innovative solution that nobody ever considered.

>> Make it easily shareable. Include share buttons whenever possible for everything you post.

>> Make it viewable and readable for any screen size. You have a much greater chance of having your content go viral if it's accessible to everyone.

TIP

To get a sense of what works and what doesn't, what interests your audience and what turns them off, track the social media shares for everything you post. You can find plenty of tools online for tracking shares, such as Khoros (https://khoros.com) and Sprout Social (https://sproutsocial.com).

3

Building a Strong Brand Presence

Connect with customers face-to-face via pop-up shops, retail stores, marketing events, and booths at conferences and workshops.

Get the word out through podcasts, blog posts, and online video and monetize that content to create additional revenue streams.

Tap the power of social media to market your brand on popular online hangouts including Facebook, Instagram, TikTok, and Twitter, without doing any heavy-duty (and expensive) advertising.

Strengthen brand identity and reach via email marketing. Build an email list, compose effective messages, choose an email marketing platform, and execute your first email marketing campaign the right way.

Get started and get the most bang for your buck with paid advertising. Discover how to work with online advertising providers and with ad agencies and track results so you know what's working and what's not.

Strengthen brand loyalty by building a community around your brand. Create safe spaces on social media, stimulate engagement, and empower your brand's community.

Chapter **11**

Creating In-Person Experiences

oliticians know that to earn enough votes to win an election, they need to "press the flesh" — meet and greet their constituents, shake hands, and kiss a few babies (at least before the latest pandemic). Face-to-face, in-person encounters create an intimate emotional connection unmatched by any other form of political campaigning.

The same is true of brands. After all, would you be more likely to hire a financial adviser you never met based solely on what you read on the person's website or one you met at a financial management seminar? Would you be more likely to buy a $50,000 boat you saw online or one you sat in at your local marina or at your city's annual boat, sport, and travel show?

In this chapter, I explain how to create opportunities for existing and prospective customers to engage with your brand up close and personal.

Creating a Pop-Up Shop

Pop-up shops are small retail stores that open for a relatively short period of time, typically to take advantage of seasonal demand or fads. You've no doubt encountered shopping kiosks at your local mall, at your favorite spring-break destination, or in your town around Halloween (costume shops). A pop-up shop provides retailers a short-term sales opportunity or a lower-risk way to test a retail space or product line before going all in and leasing or building a more permanent space.

Pop-up shops also provide a great way to test or promote a new business or brand. You enter into a short-term lease with an existing location, set up your space, stock the shelves, advertise your grand opening, and start selling. Even having a pop-up shop at a popular weekend festival can help people connect with your brand in real life.

Scoping out your options

You have several options for creating a pop-up shop experience for customers. You can set up shop in an existing space, create a new space, or host a virtual pop-up shop online.

Using an existing building

Short-term commercial leases are often available in shopping malls and strip malls, business districts, office buildings, and large hotels. In some areas, you can even rent mobile marketing trucks. Depending on what you have in mind, leasing an existing space is usually more affordable than building a space.

SHARING SPACE

Teressa Foglia (https://teressafoglia.com) is a modern milliner. She makes and sells high-quality handcrafted made-to-order hats. She opened her first Teressa Foglia Hat Studio + Shop, which she refers to as her Hatmosphere, in New York City in December 2017. Now she has locations in California (Malibu, Playa Vista, Laguna Beach, Palm Springs) and New York (Nolita), where customers can shop her selection, meet for custom hat fittings, host an event, or feature their own independent brand products via pop-up displays.

By allowing other female-owned and sustainable (environmentally friendly) brands to market their products in her space, Foglia attracts new clients and extends her brand's reach while demonstrating her commitment to the environment and to helping other entrepreneurial artisans get their start.

TIP

You may be able to use an existing space for free or negotiate a lower price if your shop will offer something of value to the owner of the space. If the owner has a restaurant next door, for example, and you'll be increasing foot traffic, which benefits the restaurant, the owner may cut you a deal.

Building a temporary retail space

In some cases, you can rent space, but you have to bring your own "building" — a kiosk, tent, pop-up truck, or makeshift partition that defines your retail space. You've probably seen branded kiosks in the thoroughfares of large malls or large tents erected in parking lots around the Fourth of July to sell fireworks. You can build temporary retail spaces yourself or buy ready-made units from suppliers such as Cart-King (https://cart-king.com).

Hosting a virtual pop-up shop

Creating a pop-up shop doesn't necessarily entail running a temporary bricks-and-mortar business. If you can't reach your target market with a physical location for any reason (distance or budget constraints, pandemic lockdowns, and so on), you can create a similar brand experience online via any of the following virtual venues:

>> Social media tools such as IG Live or Facebook Live

>> Video chat platforms such as Zoom

>> Social-shopping networks, such as talkshoplive

HOSTING A SOCIAL MEDIA POP-UP SHOP

Instagram, Facebook, and other social media platforms enable you to livestream video, which is perfect for hosting a virtual pop-up shop. (See Chapter 13 for details about using social media to promote your brand.)

The only real challenge, in addition to performing live, is having something in place that enables audience members to place orders. Here are two solutions:

>> During your presentation, pin a website link to your live stream. Check the social media platform's help system to find out whether it has this feature and how to use it.

>> Have viewers post a comment if they're interested in placing an order or want more information about what you're selling.

RUNNING A VIRTUAL POP-UP SHOP THROUGH VIDEO CHAT

For a more exclusive virtual pop-up-shop experience, consider using a videoconferencing platform, such as Zoom. With Zoom, you can send an invitation to journalists, influencers, and others, and then log on when the date and time rolls around to deliver your live presentation.

Offer an exclusive deal to participants to increase participation.

USING A SOCIAL-SHOPPING NETWORK

Social-shopping networks such as talkshoplive (https://talkshop.live) are perhaps the best alternatives to a bricks-and-mortar pop-up shop. These networks are very similar to the Home Shopping Network, which markets products directly to consumers via television. You need to apply to get your show on one of these networks, and the company takes a percentage of any sales.

Planning a physical pop-up shop

When you're launching a physical pop-up shop, you're creating a physical location, which is a big deal. To increase your chances of success, plan carefully by following these steps:

1. **Define your objectives.**

   Are you looking to extend your brand's reach, increase brand awareness, test new products, or see what having a physical location is like? Clarifying your objectives enables you to make better decisions. If you're using a pop-up shop to capitalize on increased sales related to a specific holiday, for example, you may need more storage than if you're using a shop to test a new product or increase brand awareness.

   See Chapter 4 for more about branding goals, and be sure that what you're planning to accomplish with your pop-up shop aligns with the overall goals you set for your brand.

2. **Set your budget.**

   Determine the maximum amount of money you can afford to spend on a pop-up store. You'll need enough money to cover rent (and possibly utilities), inventory, signage, décor, promotional items (such as goodie bags), and perhaps finger food and beverages for your grand opening.

   If you're planning to profit from your pop-up shop (or at least not lose money), you can use your budget as your break-even point to determine how much merchandise you must sell to break even on your investment.

3. **Choose a location, and lease a venue.**

   Choose a city or town and a location in that city or town (such as a shopping mall or a booth at an open market), contact venues for info about leasing opportunities, and book the available venue that holds the most promise for your brand. Be sure to consider the location and hours of operation carefully to ensure convenient access for your customers and clientele.

TIP

   Concierge services such as Storefront (https://www.thestorefront.com) and Splacer (https://www.splacer.co) can help you locate pop-up shop venues in major cities around the world.

WARNING

   Check with your landlord and with the municipality to make sure that no construction projects are scheduled nearby on or close to the dates you'll be renting the space. Any nearby road closures or other big construction projects could negatively affect foot traffic.

4. **Put some thought into your venue's layout and design, and order your décor.**

   Follow your brand style guide (see Chapter 6) to ensure that your design is consistent with the guidelines you established.

5. **Arrange to have a point-of-sale (POS) system in place if customers will be making purchases.**

   You can find numerous POS system providers online, such as Lightspeed (https://www.lightspeedhq.com) and Clover (https://www.clover.com).

6. **Check with your business insurance provider to see whether you need additional coverage.**

   Your current policy (assuming that you have one) may not cover some of the issues that may arise when conducting business in a temporary leased space.

7. **Obtain any permits or licenses you need to do business in the chosen location.**

   The company or person leasing you the space should be able to tell you which licenses or permits you need and where to get them.

8. **Choose your metrics for success, and figure out how you're going to collect and analyze data for those metrics.**

   Are you going to measure success by foot traffic, sales, number of new customers, or interest in a new product? Your metrics need to align with the objectives you set in Step 1, and you need to have a system for collecting data in place.

Promoting your pop-up shop

As soon as you have plans in place for creating a pop-up shop, you can and should begin to promote it, especially if you're planning a very short-term operation. Here are some effective ways to get the word out:

>> Post about it on your blog (see Chapter 12).

>> Use social media before and for the duration of your pop-up operation (see Chapter 13).

>> Send out an email blast to your existing customers and everyone else in your list of contacts (see Chapter 14).

>> If you have a newsletter, use it to promote your pop-up shop.

>> Provide incentives for showing up, such as a free product or a discount.

>> Host special events within your space during the run of your pop-up shop. (See "Taking Advantage of Marketing Event Opportunities" later in this chapter for details.)

>> Collaborate with the press and with any influencers you have to spread the word. (See Chapter 10 for more about working with the press and Chapter 13 for details on collaborating with influencers.)

Consider hosting a special open house exclusively for journalists and influencers to create some buzz before your grand opening.

>> Use paid advertising (see Chapter 15).

When promoting your pop-up shop online, encourage sharing of your posts and messages, which is the best way to spread the word organically through your customer base and their networks.

Getting your physical pop-up shop up and running

As you promote your pop-up shop, you can begin the process of getting your shop up and running as soon as the space is available. Follow these steps:

1. **Decorate your space in a fashion that's consistent with your brand guidelines.**

If you need furniture or other furnishings, you may be able to rent them for less than the cost of buying them. Search the web for furniture rental or home staging services near your pop-up shop.

2. **Set up your product displays.**

   Companies such as Displays2Go (https://www.displays2go.com) specialize in shelving and signage for pop-up shops and other short-term retail events.

3. **Stock your store with the merchandise you plan to sell.**

4. **Hire and train staff, if necessary.**

   Be sure your training includes information about what your brand stands for.

5. **Set up your POS system for accepting payments.**

6. **Test everything, including lights, any sound system you plan to use, and your POS system.**

Getting Your Products into Stores

If you're primarily a manufacturer, one way to create in-person experiences with your brand is to get your product into stores. With this approach, your in-person experience is with the store's owner or buyer, but retail outlets also provide an opportunity for shoppers to experience your brand firsthand. Getting your product into stores can also result in a big boost in sales and revenue, of course.

In this section, I lead you through the process of getting your products into stores.

TIP

Approach local shops, small chains, and regional buyers before pitching to large national or international chains. Starting small enables you to test the waters and work out the kinks in a lower-risk environment. Regardless of how much you prepare, you're likely to encounter surprises and setbacks. Learning from small mistakes is always better than learning from big ones.

REMEMBER

Generally, major retailers will demand that your business be structured as a legal entity and have an employer identification number (EIN); see Chapter 2 for details. Many of these retailers won't consider working with businesses that operate as sole proprietorships.

Laying the groundwork

Wholesale is risky, so be prepared for both failure and success. If you load up on inventory, and then your sales tank, you stand to lose a lot of money. Likewise, if you're low on inventory and can't scale up production fast enough, you'll lose sales and revenue, and you'll disappoint your retail partners. Take the following steps to prepare your brand for wholesale opportunities:

1. **Set your sales, revenue, and branding goals so that you'll have a clear metric for measuring your retail success.**

2. **Consider the costs involved in the process.**

   Make sure to include the cost of preparing and sending out samples and possible travel to meet with store owners or their buyers.

3. **Ensure that you have a system in place to scale your business quickly.**

   Discuss your plans with your suppliers and line up additional suppliers, if necessary.

4. **Estimate your manufacturing, packaging, and shipping costs and the price you need to charge the shop to earn the desired profit.**

5. **Arrange for financing to fund the manufacture or purchase of the quantities of product you expect to sell (see Chapter 2).**

6. **Decide where you're going to store inventory and how you're going to ship it.**

Identifying stores to launch in

One of the first steps toward getting your products into stores is figuring out which stores would be the right fit. Look for stores that meet the following criteria:

>> Serves the same clientele as you. (See Chapter 5 for details about sizing up your customers.)

>> Shares your values (see Chapter 3).

>> Is likely to charge the price point you need to earn the desired profit. If you're selling top-of-the-line products, you don't want to be in stores that charge bargain-basement prices.

>> Provides an opportunity for you to offer something unique that will stand out from comparable products that the store carries.

Creating a line sheet

A *line sheet* is a document that contains key details about your brand that store owners or their buyers reference when deciding whether to purchase your brand. Include the following information on your line sheet:

>> Wholesale price — at least 50 percent off your manufacturer's suggested retail price

>> Minimum order quantity — the smallest quantity of items that the store must purchase to get the wholesale discount

>> Professional-grade product photos

>> Production and shipping times (how quickly you can deliver the goods)

Preparing samples

The store's owner, manager, or buyer will want to see product samples before deciding to carry your product, so be sure to bring samples to your meeting, or send samples along with your line sheet if you're making your pitch remotely. You can use samples of existing products; they don't have to be samples of the products you envision specifically for the store.

TIP

The goal is to impress, so pay attention to even the smallest details when presenting samples. Make sure that they're brand-new and arrive in pristine condition. Be meticulous with your packaging. Include a branded thank-you note or card.

Developing your pitch

When you're trying to get your products into stores, you need to be persuasive. You must show how your brand enhances the store's brand, appeals to its existing customer base (and possibly expands that base), and will help boost sales and revenue. When developing your pitch, make sure to highlight the following:

>> **Your brand's platform:** Highlight your brand's popularity in the form of existing sales and revenue numbers, press coverage, social media followers and fans, website engagement, and so on. Your brand's platform demonstrates your commitment and the potential of the brand to sell in stores.

>> **Your brand's point of differentiation:** Like consumers, store owners and their buyers want to see that your brand is different from and better than what they already sell. See Chapter 3 for details about positioning and defining your brand as something special.

>> **Your knowledge and expertise:** If you're selling something that requires specialized knowledge and expertise to make or use, demonstrate that knowledge and expertise in your pitch, and suggest ways to use it in the store's marketing. You might offer to contribute to the store's newsletter or blog, appear as a guest on its podcast, or help to develop other marketing materials.

>> **An explanation of how your brand can strengthen the store's brand:** Highlight your brand's values, showing how they align with those of the store, how they're similar to the values of the clientele you serve, or how your brand can extend the reach of the store's brand to a new market segment.

REMEMBER

Your pitch isn't about your brand. It's about theirs. When developing your pitch, focus on how your brand can benefit the store's brand. What do you bring to the table — a community, unique designs, a proprietary product, or locally made goods? You don't need to be as large as the retailer you're pursuing; you just need to come up with a convincing value proposition.

Negotiating an agreement

As soon as you persuade a retailer to carry your product in its stores, negotiations begin. This stage of the process requires some finesse. You want to negotiate an agreement that results in maximum profit for you without pricing yourself out of the deal or appearing to be too difficult to work with. During negotiations, keep the following important points in mind:

>> Approach the negotiation as a partnership instead of as individual businesses working solely for their own best interests.

>> Negotiate a wholesale price and quantity discounts that make the partnership work for both you and the retailer.

>> Consider the possibility that your product won't sell as well as you hope, and be sure that the contract contains language to address this possibility. You don't want the retailer to be able to submit a huge order and then return all unsold products for a full refund.

>> Beware of any language in the contract that penalizes you for supply-chain disruptions beyond your control.

>> Consider lowering your wholesale price or offering more attractive quality discounts for better product placement or promotions in the stores.

>> Use the value that your business and brand offer both the retailer and consumers to negotiate a better deal. Don't agree to prices or other terms that could hurt your brand just to avoid losing the deal. Sometimes, you need to walk away.

WARNING

Double-check the numbers to ensure that any deal you agree to has the potential to generate the profits you need to make the venture for you and your brand.

Choosing and working with a manufacturer

Unless you manufacture the product yourself, you'll need to team up with a manufacturer to produce the product and deliver it to retailers. Choose a manufacturer that has a track record of making quality products and delivering them on time to retailers.

GETTING GIRL GANG THE LABEL INTO NORDSTROM

Our clothing brand, Girl Gang the Label, launched in Nordstrom for its winter 2019 collection. We collaborated on a licensed product line with the *Peanuts* brand, using our flagship saying "Support Your Local Girl Gang" and incorporating the female *Peanuts* characters. Until that point, we had never launched into a major retailer or multiple stores, so much of what we were doing was new to us.

Because we were collaborating with a licensee, we had to submit all our preliminary designs to them for approval. When our partners at *Peanuts* signed off on your design concepts, we moved forward to develop computer-aided-design versions of our concepts. We used these designs to show exact measurements and placements on different sizes of products, as shown here:

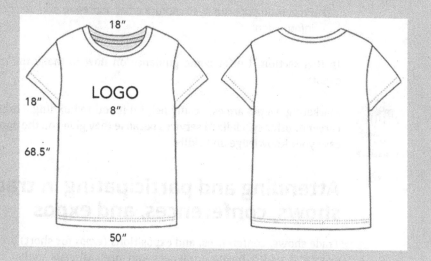

REMEMBER

Just as you must negotiate a contract with retailers, you must negotiate with your manufacturer to ensure that it can make and deliver your product in line with your budget and timeline.

TIP

Your retailer may have a list of preferred manufacturers that it will be happy to share it with you.

Taking Advantage of Marketing Event Opportunities

A *marketing event* is any opportunity you have to get your brand in front of people. It can range from hosting an open house for your business's grand opening to delivering a presentation at a conference to hosting free seminars to demonstrating your products or services. Marketing events can enhance your brand in the following ways:

>> Extend brand reach

>> Strengthen brand awareness

>> Build credibility and trust

>> Serve as a source for developing marketing content, such as blog and social media posts

>> Enable you to network with others in your industry

>> Provide an opportunity to capture email addresses and other contact information

In this section, I offer some guidance on how to make the most of marketing events.

REMEMBER

Marketing events are especially helpful if you're building a brand to further your career or offer specialized services because they give you the opportunity to showcase your knowledge and skills.

Attending and participating in trade shows, conferences, and expos

Trade shows, conferences, and expositions (*expos* for short) are industry-specific events at which business owners and professionals gather to network, share information, and promote their products and services. If you have a business-to-business (B2B) brand, these events can give you a lot of exposure to potential customers and clients; if you have a business-to-consumer (B2C) brand, they give you the opportunity to introduce your products to store owners and buyers.

Here's how trade shows, conferences, and expos differ:

>> A *trade show* is a gathering where businesses sell and trade items. You can participate as an attendee or set up a booth (for an additional fee) to promote your products or services.

>> A *conference* is a gathering where people involved in a particular industry network, exchange information, and talk shop. This event isn't so much about marketing and selling as it is about learning. If you're an expert in a certain field, however, a conference provides a great opportunity to showcase your specialized knowledge and skills to strengthen your personal brand's credibility and trust.

>> An *expo* is a gathering at which the leading businesses in a particular industry showcase their latest products and services to the press and to enthusiasts. An expo is very similar to a trade show, in that you can participate as an attendee or set up a booth for an additional fee.

If you're involved in an industry, you probably already know which trade shows, conferences, and expos are the best; they're the ones everyone goes to and talks about. If you're new to the industry, you can find the best industry events by networking with others in your industry; reading the leading industry journal; or searching the web for the name of your industry followed by "trade show," "conference," or "expo" and then researching the events that appear.

TIP

Before an industry event, set goals, and think about ways to promote your brand in the best way possible. Try to find out who's attending and whom you'd like to meet. Decide whether you want to participate as an attendee or presenter and whether having a booth would be worth the cost. Review the event's schedule, and decide which sessions you want to attend. Scope out the event map, and trace a route to all the booths you want to visit. You can waste a lot of time at these events if you don't plan.

Hosting seminars in your area of expertise

Seminars (or workshops) are popular ways to market products and services. B2B businesses often host seminars to bring other business owners and professionals up to speed on new technologies, procedures, and solutions in a given industry. A medical equipment company might conduct a seminar for doctors on how to use a new machine for laser surgery, for example. B2C businesses often use seminars to promote their products and services. An attorney might host a seminar on estate planning, for example, or a heating and air conditioning company might host a seminar on insulating a home properly.

The biggest challenge is preparing and conducting the seminar, which varies considerably by topic and is far beyond the scope of this book. Planning and running a seminar is fairly straightforward. Follow these steps:

1. **Choose an event format: in person or online (a webinar).**

2. **Create a budget.**

   For an in-person seminar, your budget might include the cost of a venue and any equipment you need to buy or rent, training materials such as manuals, compensation for outside speakers or presenters, food and beverages, marketing costs, and attendance fees (if any).

3. **Choose a date.**

   If you plan to have presenters other than you, choose a date that works for them.

4. **Estimate the number of attendees.**

5. **Choose a location to record your webinar or a venue to host an in-person seminar.**

6. **Promote your seminar, and manage registrations.**

7. **Prepare everything you need to conduct the seminar.**

   This list might include name tags; training manuals; handouts; your presentation; and any equipment, such as a computer, projection screen, and projector.

8. **Keep participants informed.**

   Initially, you may want to send a seminar orientation package containing the address and directions to the venue, places to stay, what to bring, and so on. When you get closer to the date of the seminar, be sure to send reminders.

   If you're using outside presenters, be sure to confirm with them at least one week before the seminar.

9. **The day or night before the seminar, make sure that everything you need to conduct the seminar is set up and working.**

Hosting other events

An event doesn't need to be as formal as a trade show, conference, or seminar; it can simply be an open house, a meet-and-greet, or a small get-together of like-minded people. With a small budget to cover food, beverages, and marketing materials, you can host informal events to extend your brand's reach and increase brand awareness in a more personal way. All you have to do is line up a venue and catering service (or do the catering yourself) and promote the heck out of the event.

REMEMBER

Be sure to have a system in place for collecting contact information from attendees. You may have a registration book where attendees can enter their names, email addresses, and phone numbers, or have a drawing for a prize that requires this information (or a business card) for each entry.

Landing event sponsorships

Events can get costly and break the budgets of small brands. One way to offset the costs is to recruit sponsors to donate money, products, or services in exchange for the opportunity to get *their* brands in front of *your* customers. Product donations or discounts on valued services are great for adding to swag bags and offering people incentives to attend your event.

When pitching potential event sponsors, highlight how the event can benefit their brands. The following details may help persuade them to participate:

>> The number of people you're inviting

>> The number of people you're expecting

>> How the sponsor's brand will be promoted at the event and in marketing leading up to the event

>> Your event's social reach — your brand's number of followers/fans on social media platforms and the reach of any influencers you use (see Chapter 13)

>> A list of any other brands that you're inviting or that have agreed to participate

IN THIS CHAPTER

» **Understanding what content marketing is all about**

» **Hosting a podcast to promote your brand**

» **Blogging to boost brand recognition**

» **Creating and posting branded video clips**

» **Using your content to generate additional revenue**

Chapter **12**

Blogging, Podcasting, and YouTubing

To build and launch a brand successfully, you practically need to create your own media production company, complete with the equivalent of online news, radio, and television. Fortunately, all the tools required to promote your brand in text, audio, and video are readily available online and mostly free. By using these tools effectively to deliver quality content, you can build brand recognition fast without spending a penny on advertising. Better yet, you may be able to monetize the content you produce by using it to sell advertising, merchandise, or both.

In this chapter, I bring you up to speed on the basics of podcasting, blogging, and creating and posting branded video, and I share several techniques and tips I've discovered when using these media to promote my own businesses and brands and monetize my content. But first, I introduce you to the concept of content marketing.

REMEMBER

Creating and posting valuable content regularly in any form is challenging and time-consuming, but it can be a fun way to build your brand while connecting with existing and prospective customers.

Appreciating the Value of Content Marketing

Content marketing is creating and sharing material (such as blog posts, social media posts, white papers, podcasts, and video) that doesn't explicitly advertise a brand but stimulates interest in its products and services. With content marketing, you generate interest in your brand, engage your audience, and interact with them on an ongoing basis to transform prospects into customers and customers into brand ambassadors.

You can also use content marketing as a way to generate revenue streams. You'll already be using the content to sell your products and services, of course, but you can also use it to generate additional revenue. You can use it to cash in on advertising opportunities; earn sales commissions as another company's affiliate; and even sell merchandise, such as T-shirts, hats, and travel mugs. Near the end of this chapter, I dig a little deeper into the topic of monetizing content.

REMEMBER

Your content should always be useful to your audience. When creating content, focus on delivering information that's relevant, valuable, engaging, and entertaining for existing and prospective customers.

Promoting Your Brand Via Podcasting

A *podcast* is a series of digital spoken-word audio recordings distributed via the Internet. Listeners can download the recordings to their smartphones or other personal electronic devices and listen to them at their leisure or tune in to livestream podcasts.

In this section, I lead you through the process of getting set up to create podcasts, recording your podcasts, and making them available on the Internet. I also dip into related topics, such as recruiting guests for your podcast.

REMEMBER

Podcasts are a popular medium for use in content marketing, but you can also build an entire business around a podcast — sort of like having your own talk-radio show. You can even join podcast networks to extend your reach to larger audiences. The advertising revenue space associated with podcasts has experienced explosive growth over the past couple of years, and podcast platforms are optioning exclusive deals with popular podcasters for big bucks.

TIP

Before you even think about recording a single podcast episode, listen to popular podcasts to observe how successful podcasters ply their trade. For more detailed guidance than what I provide in this section, check out *Podcasting For Dummies*, 4th Edition, by Tee Morris and Chuck Tomasi (John Wiley & Sons, Inc.).

Naming your podcast

Every podcast needs a catchy name. For branding purposes, come up with a name that reflects your brand and the products or services you offer. If you own a bait-and-tackle shop called The Whopper Tail, that name would be a great name for your podcast. A key factor in successful branding is consistency. If *The Whopper Tail* is already taken, maybe you could call your podcast *Something Fishy*.

TIP

I like to work backward when selecting a name for a podcast. Write a description of what the show's going to be about and then pick words out of your description. We came up with *Girl Gang the Podcast* after writing a mission statement for our brand that included "Support Your Local Girl Gang" as our slogan. We pulled *Girl Gang* from our copy and added *the Podcast*, and we were ready to roll.

If you are your brand, and you're creating a variety show with no specific genre in mind, consider naming the show after yourself. Hey, if it works for Ellen and Oprah, it should work for you too.

Gearing up to podcast

One of the great aspects of podcasting is that you can do it on a shoestring budget. All you need are an Internet-enabled device with a microphone and speakers (or headphones) and a podcasting platform to record and host your podcast. If you have a smartphone with an app for recording and uploading podcasts, you have all you need to get started.

On the other hand, if you're aiming to create professional-quality podcasts with multiple guests, the sky's the limit. You can build your own recording studio with high-end mics, boom arms and shock mounts, studio headphones, audio mixers, and your own digital audio workstation.

In the following sections, I provide detailed guidance on choosing the basic podcasting equipment you'll need.

Answering a few preliminary questions

Before you go shopping for podcasting equipment, answer the following questions:

» **Are you flying solo, or do you plan to have guests?** If you're flying solo, you can get by with a smartphone or a computer with a single microphone. If you plan to have guests, you'll want a microphone for each person on the podcast.

» **What quality are you aiming for?** Generally, as long as listeners can hear what you and your guests are saying, that's good enough. Most people tune in for the quality of content, not the quality of the sound, although sound quality can be distracting if it's really poor. If you want higher-quality audio, you need higher-quality equipment.

» **What's your budget?** You can spend a lot on recording equipment and can even build your own recording studio, but you can start a podcast for less than $100 — much less if you already have a smartphone.

» **How much of the work do you want to do yourself?** Podcasting requires some time, effort, and expertise. At bare minimum, a podcast requires copywriting, recording, and editing. You can do everything yourself or outsource part or all of the work.

REMEMBER

You can get started with whatever equipment you can afford and acquire better recording equipment as your podcast grows in popularity.

Choosing a microphone and accessories

A quality microphone goes a long way toward producing a quality recording. When choosing a microphone and accessories, I recommend the following:

» **Dynamic (versus condenser) microphone:** A *dynamic microphone* is best for most people and most situations in which you'll be recording podcasts. These mics are more durable, versatile, and forgiving. They're also less sensitive, so they don't pick up as much background noise as condenser mics do.

» **USB microphone for recording yourself or XLR for recording yourself and guests:** The benefit of a USB microphone is that it plugs into a standard USB port on a computer. An XLR microphone plugs into a professional audio recording device or mixer, allowing you to scale your podcast to include guests.

>> **Cardioid microphone:** A *cardioid microphone* is more sensitive to sound in front of the microphone and less sensitive to sound in back of it, so it's less susceptible to picking up background noise.

>> **Pop filter:** A *pop filter* is foam inside or outside the microphone that prevents the *p* sound from making annoying pops when you're recording.

>> **Shock mount:** A *shock mount* filters out low-frequency vibrations, such as the sound of a coffee mug sliding across the table on which the microphone sits.

>> **Switches or dials to customize the sound and mute the mic when someone else is talking:** Being able to adjust the mic to improve sound quality or muffle noise is a plus.

Adding headphones to your setup

When creating a podcast, headphones are optional, but they're an option you should seriously consider. When you're doing a podcast, you should hear how you sound to others so that you can adjust how you're talking on the fly. The only way to hear how you sound to others is to listen to yourself through headphones. Any guests you have on your podcast should wear headphones too.

When choosing headphones, look for the following characteristics:

>> **Flat frequency response** to ensure that you're hearing the audio accurately, without any filtering.

>> **Full-size headphones versus earbuds (over the ear versus in the ear)** to filter out noise from the environment more effectively.

>> **Comfort** ensures that you and your guests can wear the headphones for the duration of the podcast without having to adjust them constantly.

>> **Wired or wireless** is a preference. I don't like to deal with cables, but if you go with wireless headphones, be sure that your batteries are charged before starting a podcast.

Choosing and prepping a recording space

The space in which you record your podcast can make or break your sound quality. To improve sound quality, take the following steps:

1. **Choose a quiet place.**

   You don't want to hear dogs barking, neighbors partying, or planes flying over in the middle of your recording session. A basement may be best.

2. **Choose a big room over a small room.**

   Generally, the bigger the room, the better, but successful podcasts have been recorded in even the tiniest of spaces.

3. **Fill the space with soft objects.**

   Carpeting, blankets, mattresses, pillows, sofas, and stuffed animals can all help prevent echoes.

4. **At the very least, stick some foam in the corners of the room.**

   The corners are the worst source of echoes. If you have the means to do so, stick some foam to the walls as well, or hang blankets on them.

Choosing recording software and a podcasting host

In addition to hardware (a recording space and gear), you need software to record and edit your podcast, as well as a podcasting host, where your podcast will live on the Internet. A couple of services provide a combination:

» **Anchor** (https://anchor.fm) is an all-in-one podcasting platform from Spotify that enables you to create, distribute, and monetize podcasts for free. It includes free, unlimited hosting; automatic distribution to all major listening apps; analytics to find out who's listening to your podcasts and which ones they like best; and various options for monetizing your podcasts.

» **Podbean** (https://www.podbean.com) is one of the best options for recording podcasts on a smartphone and uploading them to the Internet. It includes Podcast Studio for recording and editing, unlimited podcasting, performance analytics, the ability to interact with listeners, and PodAds to monetize podcasts with paid advertising.

Another option is to use software dedicated to recording and editing your podcasts and then upload your recordings to a podcast host or distributor. Here are a few podcast recording/editing programs:

» **Adobe Audition** (https://www.adobe.com/products/audition.html) is a professional audio workstation for recording, editing, mixing, and exporting audio content to upload to any podcast hosting service.

» **Audacity** (https://www.audacityteam.org/download) is free open-source software for recording, editing, and exporting audio content. You can download a version for macOS, Windows, or Linux.

>> **GarageBand** (https://www.apple.com/mac/garageband) is Apple's full-featured music-creation studio that's also a great solution for recording, editing, and exporting spoken word audio for podcasts. It comes preloaded on Macs, iPhones, and iPads.

>> **Riverside.fm** (https://riverside.fm) is a subscription-based podcast recording platform that enables local audio recording of interviews conducted remotely. It's a great tool if you plan to interview people who can't make it in to your recording studio.

>> **Logic Pro** (https://www.apple.com/logic-pro) is a high-end digital audio workstation application for macOS. Consider it to be a step up from GarageBand, but it may be overkill for recording podcasts.

>> **TwistedWave** (https://twistedwave.com) is a simple yet powerful audio recording and editing program for Macs, iPhones, and iPads. A cloud-based version is also available; you can run it on any Internet-enabled device in a web browser.

After recording your podcast and saving it or exporting it as an audio file (either MP3, M4A, MP4, or WAV), you upload the file to a podcast host to make your podcast available to listeners and to promote your podcast and track its performance. Your host will also get your podcasts into all the directories where listeners look for podcasts, such as iTunes, Spotify, and Google Podcasts. Here are some popular podcast hosts:

>> **Buzzsprout** (https://www.buzzsprout.com) offers a free plan and features easy uploads, a podcast player that you can easily embed in your website, analytics to track podcast performance, and the ability to add episode chapter markers to your podcasts.

>> **Libsyn** (https://libsyn.com) offers affordable podcast hosting, distribution, analytics, and monetization.

>> **SoundCloud** (https://soundcloud.com) is the world's largest free online audio distribution platform and music sharing platform. SoundCloud enables you to upload, promote, share, and monetize your podcasts; and engage with your listeners.

>> **Simplecast** (https://simplecast.com) bills itself as "the first and last word in podcast management and analytics." It features one-click podcast uploads, multiple web and podcast players, advanced analytics, collaboration tools, and the ability to Recast (schedule and share your podcasts on your social media accounts).

>> **Spotify for Podcasters** (https://podcasters.spotify.com/) has about 300 million listeners in about 100 markets worldwide, so it's one of the best platforms in terms of distribution. It also features a dashboard that provides insight into your podcast's performance among listeners.

I use Adobe Audition to record and edit my podcast and Buzzsprout to host it.

Recording, editing, and uploading a podcast

The process for recording, editing, and uploading a podcast varies a great deal based on the tools and services you use; the number of people involved; and whether you plan to interview guests remotely. It can be as simple as running the Anchor app on your smartphone, tapping the Record button, speaking into your phone, and then choosing the option to upload your recording. Or it can be as complex as recording and editing separate tracks, mixing audio, fine-tuning the sound, and then uploading your recording to multiple podcasting platforms.

In this section, I guide you through the overall process, which will give you a good idea of what's involved.

Outlining your podcast episode

To keep yourself and your guests from drifting off topic, outline your podcast episode or at least create a list of bullet points describing what you're going to cover. If you plan to interview guests, include a brief introduction or biography of each guest and a list of questions. If you have a cohost or guests, share your notes and questions with them so they can prepare for the recording session.

You don't need to write a detailed script, although that's certainly an option. You just need a collection of notes to prevent yourself from rambling, which is a big turn-off to listeners.

Writing an intro and outro

Write and record an intro and outro to insert at the beginning and end of your podcast. You can use the same intro and outro for every episode or use something fresh for each episode. Using a unique intro and outro for each episode has the advantage of allowing you to showcase highlights of each episode at the beginning and add a teaser for the next episode at the end. Starting each episode with highlights provides listeners a preview, so they can decide whether a particular episode interests them before they make a commitment to listen to the whole thing.

Try to limit your intro and outro to 60 seconds or less combined; for example, 25 seconds for the intro and 35 seconds for the outro. Use the intro as an opportunity to introduce new listeners to your show and the outro to encourage listeners to come back for your next episode. You can include in both your intro and outro one or more calls to action — something to keep listeners connected to your brand outside the episode. For *Girl Gang the Podcast*, we let listeners know about our clothing brand and online magazine so that they can maintain engagement with the brand and we can monetize our podcast with the merchandise we offer.

Here's our standard intro for our podcast:

> Welcome to Girl Gang. I'm your host, Amy Will, the founder of Girl Gang. This podcast is brought to you by girlgangthelabel.com. Head to our website after the show to browse our directory of female-owned businesses and enjoy exclusive discounts from them. Read our online magazine, *The Edit,* for interviews with female creatives, plus tips, tools, and rituals to level up your own career. Shop our line of merchandise, including our signature "support your local girl gang" collection. For every item sold, we team up with a charity to support women's education, health, and empowerment. Shop today and use code GIRLGANG to receive 20 percent off at girlgangthelabel.com. Show us you're listening by tagging us on Instagram @girlgangthelabel.com. Thank you so much for tuning in!

If you don't have your own online store, you can replace the discount code with an advertisement or promotion from a sponsor.

Here's our outro for our podcast:

> Thank you so much for tuning in. If you liked this episode, please take a moment to leave us a review. It helps us out so much. Remember to head to girlgangthelabel.com to redeem your 20 percent discount with code GIRLGANG. Take a moment to remind the females in your life that they inspire you, and support your local girl gang.

The outro provides an opportunity to highlight a product or service and leave a lasting impression about your organization's or podcast's mission. At its core, *Girl Gang the Podcast* is about empowering women; that's why we end with a call to action to reach out to an inspirational female.

If you'd like to add music to your intro or outro (or both), you can find royalty-free music and other audio starting at $1 at sites such as Envato Market (https://audiojungle.net) and Storyblocks (https://www.storyblocks.com/audio).

Scheduling your podcasts

One of your goals as a podcaster is to build a following — to stay engaged with existing listeners while attracting new ones. To do that, you need to podcast regularly, usually at least once a week. Scheduling podcasts helps you achieve that goal and prepare for upcoming podcasts, especially if you need to line up guests ahead of time. Another benefit of a schedule is that it encourages you to add variety.

Use a calendar or a scheduling form, such as the one shown in Figure 12-1, to schedule your podcast. Specify the title of the podcast, the date, and any guests you plan to have (as discussed in the next section).

Episode	Guest Name	Title / Company	Description Complete	Release Date
1	Teressa Foglia	Owner / Teressa Foglia	On today's episode...	1.1.2021
2	Laura Berg	Owner / Nourish Sweat Soul	On today's episode...	1.8.2021
3	Jessica Olson	Co-Owner / Wren Amber Clothing	On today's episode...	1.15.2021

Featuring guests on your podcast

Interviewing interesting, well-known people on your podcast is a great way to lighten your workload, keep your podcast fresh, and build branding synergies with others in the same or ancillary markets. The challenge comes in persuading busy people to take the time to be guests on your show.

TIP

Prepare a simple, direct pitch to persuade others to participate as guests on your podcast. Explain how your show aligns with their interests and furthers their goals. Keep the pitch short (two brief paragraphs, max), and include the following details:

>> Your podcast title and a blurb about it — think elevator pitch

>> The name, title, and organization of any notable past guests

>> Why your listeners would benefit from hearing what your guest has to say

Following is a sample guest pitch for my podcast:

Hi,

My name is Amy Will, and I am the host of *Girl Gang the Podcast*, a podcast focusing on highlighting female founders and creatives. I would love the opportunity to interview you about your career path and highlight your brand, Tattooed Chef. As your brand is focused on sustainable sourcing, quality products, and a unique business model, I know our guests would love your story.

Past guests include an editor at British *Vogue*, the founder of Y7 Studios, and the executive director of video and social media at BuzzFeed. Our podcast was also featured as one of the best podcasts of 2020 by *Marie Claire*.

If you'd like to continue the conversation about being a guest or have any available days coming up, feel free to reach out at amy@girlgangthelabel.com.

Sincerely,

Amy

Recording a podcast

Not much is involved in recording a podcast. You connect your microphones and headsets to your recording device, turn them on, make sure that they're selected as the input and output devices in your recording software, tap the Record button, and start your show. When you're done, tap the Stop button.

What requires some effort and expertise is using your microphone(s) the right way to get the highest-quality audio possible and, of course, talking like a professional. Here are a few suggestions that can help you sharpen your skills with a mic:

>> If you have a cohost or guests, record each person on a separate track so that you can edit their audio individually. (Check your recording software's help system to find out how to record on separate tracks.)

>> Stay close to the mic when speaking — about the width of two to four fingers.

>> Back off from the mic when others are speaking so you won't record your breathing.

>> Avoid extremes when speaking louder or softer.

>> Experiment with the positioning your microphone *on axis* (pointing directly at your mouth) and *off axis* (positioned at an angle to your mouth). If your voice sounds too high-pitched, try angling the mic more (off axis) so it picks up less of the high frequencies. If your voice sounds too low, position the mic on axis so it picks up more of the high frequencies.

REMEMBER

Practice makes perfect. Don't worry if the audio doesn't sound quite right. As you become accustomed to podcasting and to your equipment, you'll naturally make adjustments that improve the audio quality.

Editing your podcast

You don't necessarily need to edit a podcast before uploading it to your podcast host, but you can do some basic edits to improve its quality without getting too in the weeds. The editing process varies depending on the software you use, but general editing techniques remain the same across all software:

» **Cut any audio you're not going to use.** Why edit what you're not going to include in your podcast?

» **Listen to your podcast once all the way through without editing anything, and create a punch list as you listen.** A *punch list* is a complete record of everything you need to fix.

» **Edit individual tracks.** If you have multiple tracks (you and a cohost or guests, for example), edit them individually to tone down any loud bursts and raise the volume of any audio that's too soft.

» **Use fading to hide the blemishes.** If you have an abrupt transition or noise that you can't edit out, fade out the audio where the problem starts and fade in where it ends.

TIP

If you're not comfortable editing your podcast, you can hire an editor on Fiverr.com or Upwork.com, or use a service such as Resonate (https://resonaterecordings.com) or We Edit Podcasts (https://www.weeditpodcasts.com). Before hiring an editor, conduct your own background check; look at ratings and testimonials, and listen to samples of their work.

Exporting and uploading your podcast

When you're done editing your podcast, export it in the file format your podcast host recommends — usually MP3 (smaller files, lower quality) or WAV (larger files, higher quality). Check your host's help system for any additional recommendations regarding the file format and audio quality. After exporting your recording to a file, you can log in to your podcast host and follow its procedure for uploading the file.

TIP

Consider uploading a batch of podcast episodes and then publishing them according to your schedule. Most podcast hosts provide options to publish your podcasts immediately, leave them unpublished, or schedule them for release at a later date. I prefer uploading several episodes at a time and scheduling them for release because it helps me deliver a steady flow of content to my listeners.

After you upload your audio file, your podcast host prompts you to enter a title and description, choose appropriate categories for indexing it, add tags, and select or upload art to serve as a visual for your podcast or a specific episode. You may have the option to add more information, such as guest names, your email or website address, and other details.

TIP

If you have a website (see Chapter 7), I strongly recommend that you embed your podcast in your site. Most podcast hosts have players that you can embed in web pages or blog posts.

Blogging to Promote Your Brand

A *blog* (short for *web log*) is like a publicly accessible online journal in that it contains regular entries — usually daily or weekly. Unlike a personal journal, however, blogs are often used as an informal and subtle way to promote brands, products, services, and causes. They're great tools for individuals and businesses to establish themselves as thought leaders in their industry. They serve as an easy means to post fresh, relevant content, and they allow readers to post comments, which increases engagement. As a blog grows in popularity, it becomes very attractive to search engines, so it can be a great tool for drawing traffic to a site.

In this section, I introduce you to blogging basics.

Choosing a blogging platform

A *blogging platform* is software hosted online that simplifies the process of publishing content on the web and enables readers to comment on it. Several blogging platforms are available, including the following:

>> **WordPress** (https://wordpress.org) is the most popular platform for creating websites, blogs, or a combination of the two. It's designed for simplicity, so you can focus on sharing your story, insights, products, and services. Because so many people use WordPress, you can find plenty of support for it online, along with lots of themes and plugins to enhance your site's appearance and functionality.

>> **Wix** (https://www.wix.com) is a drag-and-drop website and blog-creation suite for creating and managing professional-grade sites. It includes Ascend for connecting with customers and managing workflows, Wix Stores for selling products and getting paid online, Wix Logo Maker, Wix Blog, Wix Video Maker, and hundreds of other tools.

>> **Squarespace** (https://www.squarespace.com) is a good option if you're an online retailer and already have your store hosted on Squarespace. Your blog can serve as an extension of your store. Squarespace makes it easy to embed product listings in your blog posts.

>> **Shopify** (https://www.shopify.com) is another e-commerce platform that can host both your online store and your blog. If you have a Shopify account, it includes a default blog named News. You can keep that blog or create your own with a custom name.

See Chapter 7 for more detailed guidance on setting up a website, online store, blog, or a combination of all three.

Naming your blog

As with your podcast, your blog needs a catchy name that reflects your brand and the products and services you offer. In fact, if you already have a podcast, you should strongly consider using the same or a similar name for your blog. (See the earlier section "Naming your podcast.")

In the process of naming your blog, decide on its purpose and focus. If you're using it to establish yourself as an expert in a certain field and build trust, you'll want your entries to demonstrate your knowledge and expertise in your field. If you're selling organic honey and related products, your posts may center on bee-keeping, the health benefits of honey, the varieties of honey, and how honey is produced. If you're promoting your own brand of clothing, you'll want to blog about what's hot and what's not in the fashion biz.

REMEMBER

Consistency is crucial to building a strong brand. Everything from the title of your blog to the content you post on it should reflect your brand and its mission.

Composing blog entries

Composing blog entries requires some creativity and writing talent. First, you must come up with ideas for topics to write about; then you need to write the post. (Doing research may also be necessary.) Which task is harder is a toss-up; coming up with topic ideas can sometimes be the bigger challenge.

In the following sections, I present two approaches for coming up with topic ideas and offer a little guidance on writing engaging, informative, and entertaining blog entries.

Building topics around keywords

TIP

If you're to succeed as a blogger, search engines need to recognize your blog as being a leading source for content related to your blog's subject area, so consider creating a list of keywords and developing topics around those keywords. See Chapter 8 for more about keywords and other ways to implement a search engine optimization (SEO) strategy.

After you have a list of relevant keywords, you're ready to start composing blog entries around those keywords. On my Girl Gang blog, I use the keywords "female owned," "small business," and "women empowerment." Using these keywords, I could construct a blog post titled "Best Female-Owned Small Businesses to Support in Los Angeles." This title narrows the focus of my research and writing.

Using blog formats to come up with ideas

You may be able to find inspiration for topic ideas by looking at different blog formats, such as these:

- » **Narrative:** You can simply tell a story about yourself or someone you know.

- » **Q&A:** Think about questions customers often ask, and compose answers to those questions.

- » **Problem/solution:** Consider a problem that needs to be solved, and present a solution for it. If a product or service you sell solves the problem, all the better!

- » **Survey:** Ask your readers what they think, which is a great way to increase engagement on your blog. Plug-ins are available for most blogs to add a survey to a post quickly and easily.

- » **Roundup:** Showcase a selection of items. The roundup format would be perfect for my "Best Female-Owned Small Businesses to Support in Los Angeles" entry described earlier. I could choose five female-owned businesses to research and write about, allowing me to include my third keyword, "women empowerment," in the post.

   I actually wrote this post, which covered a store on Melrose called House of Intuition — a crystal shop that sells sage, tarot cards, intention candles, and other spiritual/magical merchandise. I showcased an item in the store that symbolized female empowerment, which provided a perfect opportunity for including that keyword in the post.

- » **Comparison and contrast:** Compare and contrast two or more things, such as the way you do something versus the way your competition does it, and explain why your way is better.

Writing blog entries

Writing engaging, informative, and even transformational blog entries is more art than science. Although I can't possibly provide all the guidance you need to become a great writer, I can offer the following suggestions:

>> **Write with your readers in mind.** When writing, imagine you're presenting your content to someone sitting right in front of you. Imagine how they'd respond to what you're writing.

>> **Adhere to your brand style guidelines.** See Chapters 6 and 8 for details.

>> **Keep it short.** 1,000 words max. People are busy and tend to have short attention spans.

>> **State the main point of your entry in the first sentence.** Use the rest of the post to support or develop your main point.

>> **Break up the text.** Write short paragraphs, and use lists and headings to create plenty of white space. Long paragraphs don't play well online.

>> **Be clear.** Read and reread everything you write for clarity. If something isn't crystal-clear to you, it won't be clear to your readers.

>> **Get feedback before you publish your post.** Have someone edit your post and provide feedback on content, organization, spelling, and grammar. Preferably recruit someone who's good with spelling and grammar.

Posting blog entries

After composing a blog entry, posting it is as easy as typing a document in a word processor or desktop publishing program. In fact, you can type your post in a word processor or text editor and then copy and paste it into a post. In WordPress, the steps for posting a new blog entry go like this:

1. **Log into your WordPress dashboard.**

   (Go to your blog's login page, such as girlgangthelabel.com/blog/wp-login.php, and enter your username or email address and password.)

2. **Select Posts and then select Add New in the navigation bar on the left side of the screen.**

   The Add a New Post page appears, as shown in Figure 12-2.

3. **Type a title for your new post in text box at the top of the page.**

4. **Click in the content area, and type your post.**

   Use the toolbar above the content area to format your text and add media, such as images.

5. **Select categories and add tags to help search engines index your post properly.**

6. **Click the Publish button.**

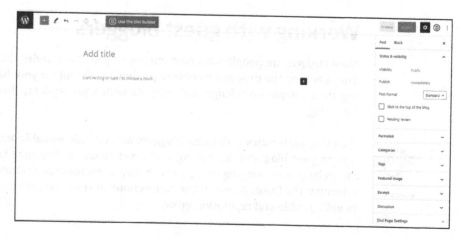

FIGURE 12-2:
The Add a New
Post page.

For details on posting entries with the blogging platform you use, consult its help system.

Engaging with your readers

One great thing about blogging is that you can get readers to write a lot of your content for you by encouraging them to comment on your posts and on the comments other readers post. If you can spark a lively discussion around a blog entry, its search-engine ranking will soar as search engines recognize the interest the post is generating.

Here are a few ways to increase engagement on your blog:

>> **Post great content.** Include entries that may be somewhat controversial or thought-provoking.

>> **Ask readers to weigh in.** At the end of an entry, you might write something like "I'd like to know what you think. Please post a comment below."

>> **Pose a challenge.** Ask readers to solve a problem or perform a difficult task and then post a comment about their experience.

>> **Monitor and respond to comments.** Your blogging platform's dashboard should have an option to view comments, which simplifies the process of reviewing and responding to comments. Responding to a comment is especially important if a reader specifically requests a response from you; responding shows that you're listening and that you care.

Working with guest bloggers

Guest bloggers are people who post entries to your blog under their own names. They save you the time and trouble of producing content for your blog while sharing their unique knowledge and insights with your readers, thereby enriching your blog.

REMEMBER

Pursue opportunities with guest bloggers who can add valuable and relevant content to your blog and are willing and eager to do so. You may be able to trade favors by guest-blogging on a partner's blog to increase your brand's reach while returning the favor. As you make connections in your market's community, your brand's profile and reputation grow.

Spreading the word about your blog

As you post valuable content to your blog, you increase the likelihood that it will be discovered by search engines and then readers who are interested in the content you've published. But why wait? You can speed this discovery process by spreading the word about your blog and encouraging your readers to share your blog entries with their friends, family members, and colleagues. Here are a few ways to spread the word about your blog:

>> Blast an email message to all your contacts announcing your blog, providing a link to it, and asking them what they think of it.

>> Add your blog address to all your social media profiles.

>> Post about your blog on all your social media accounts.

>> If you have a stand-alone website or online store, link from it to your blog.

>> Register your blog on directories such as Blogarama (https://www.blogarama.com), Blogging Fusion (https://bloggingfusion.com), and Blogville (https://blogville.us).

>> Add share buttons to your blog that enable readers to share your blog posts with others via email and their social media accounts quickly and easily. The process for adding share buttons to a blog varies by platform, but it's usually as easy as installing a third-party plug-in or app. Check your blogging platform's help system for details.

Building Brand Recognition with Online Videos

Creating and posting videos online is very similar to podcasting but with the addition of video. You can even create video podcasts and conduct webinars by using online videoconferencing and collaboration platforms, such as Zoom (https://zoom.us) and Skype (https://www.skype.com).

In this section, however, I focus on one tried-and-true method of using online video to build brand recognition: recording and uploading videos to YouTube, one of the most popular video sharing and social media platforms on the planet. YouTubers, who create and post video, upload more than 100 hours of video per minute, and users watch more than 1 billion hours of video every day.

As a YouTuber, you can upload your video to YouTube and then embed that video content in your social media posts, website, and blog. You can also quickly and easily monetize your content by allowing YouTube to include advertising with your video.

In this section, I bring you up to speed on using YouTube to promote your brand. To go beyond the basics and become a YouTube pro, check out *YouTube Channels For Dummies*, 2nd Edition, by Rob Ciampa, Theresa Go, Matt Ciampa, and Rich Murphy (John Wiley & Sons, Inc.).

Recognizing the different genres you can use to promote your brand

You can find all sorts of videos on YouTube, but to promote your brand, consider the following video content types:

>> Announcements of special events, new products, and so on

>> Anything really funny, even commercials

>> Behind-the-scenes footage

>> Case studies

>> Competitions or contests

>> Interviews with interesting people

>> Livestreams from events

>> Meet-the-team profiles

- **»** Presentations or webinars
- **»** Product or service demos
- **»** Testimonials
- **»** Tutorials

Recording a video

Recording videos for YouTube is very similar to recording audio content for podcasts. You can go low-end, using any device that can record digital video — your smartphone, a computer equipped with a digital video camera, or a GoPro, for example — or you can go high-end with fancy video production equipment, as though you're filming a Hollywood movie.

At the low end, anyone can record a video. You open the camera app on your smartphone, switch to video mode, tap the Record button, and start filming, as shown in Figure 12-3. When you're finished recording, tap the Stop button. You end up with a digital video file that you can upload to YouTube as is or edit with the help of video editing software, as explained in the next section.

Recording Video With Smartphone

FIGURE 12-3:
You can record
video on your
smartphone.

TIP

Here are a few tips for recording quality video:

- **»** If your camera or app has a stabilization feature, turn it on.
- **»** Use a tripod when possible, and when filming yourself speaking to your audience, position the camera at about eye level.

>> If you're using your smartphone's camera, rotate your phone 90 degrees and film horizontally. On YouTube, video is shown in landscape mode.

>> When filming yourself speaking to your audience, be sure to look at the camera.

Editing your video

Editing a video usually involves chopping excess footage from the beginning, end, or somewhere in the middle of the video, but you may also want to splice two or more videos together; adjust the brightness or contrast; stabilize a shaky video; add an audio track; or make other changes. You can edit your video before uploading it to YouTube or upload it first and use the video editor in YouTube Studio (https://studio.youtube.com).

TIP

If you record video on your smartphone, you can select the video on your smartphone and then select the edit option to access some basic editing tools, which may be all you need.

For more and better video editing tools, you can use Microsoft's Video Editor, which is built into Windows; iMovie, which is included on macOS, iOS, and iPadOS devices; or a third-party video editor, such as Adobe Spark (https://www.adobe.com/express/feature/video/editor).

Video editing is beyond the scope of this book and differs among video editing applications. Check the help system of the application you're using for details. For more guidance, check out *Filmmaking For Dummies*, 3rd Edition, by Bryan Michael Stoller (John Wiley & Sons, Inc.).

When you're done editing your video, save it as an MPEG-2 or MPEG-4 file — the two video file formats YouTube prefers. YouTube has a long list of guidelines that cover file format, audiovisual duration, frame rate, aspect ratio, resolution, and more. Consult YouTube's help system for details.

Uploading videos to YouTube

Uploading a video to YouTube is a snap, but the process varies depending on the device you're using. If you're using a smartphone, the process goes like this:

1. **Select the video you want to upload, tap Share, and choose to share the video to the YouTube app.**

   The YouTube app opens the video.

2. In the bar below the video, drag the vertical bars on the left and right ends to crop footage at the beginning or end of the video.

3. Enter a title and description of the video in the designated fields.

4. Select whether to make the video public (anyone can watch it), unlisted (anyone who has the link to it can watch it), or private (only people you specify can watch it).

5. Tap the Next button.

6. Choose the option to specify whether the video is suitable for kids, and specify any age restrictions for viewing the video.

7. Tap the Upload button.

   Your phone uploads the video to your YouTube account.

If you're uploading videos from a laptop, desktop, or tablet computer (as opposed to a smartphone) log into YouTube at https://www.youtube.com, click the Create icon (the video-camera icon with the plus sign in it in the top-right corner of the page), click Upload Video, and follow the onscreen prompts to complete the process.

TIP

After uploading a video to YouTube, you can embed it in a web page or blog post. Open the video in YouTube, click Share (below the video), click Embed, and click Copy to copy the embed code. Then paste the code into the HTML version of the page or post in which you want the video to appear.

Creating a branded thumbnail

After you upload a video, YouTube uses one of its frames to create a *thumbnail* — a snapshot that represents your video on YouTube. Thumbnails are the first things people see when they're browsing for videos, and they often determine whether a person chooses to watch a video. Instead of letting YouTube choose your video's thumbnail, create a custom, branded thumbnail of your own — something that pops!

You can use just about any graphics software to create a thumbnail. You can even find dedicated YouTube thumbnail creators online, such as Adobe Spark's free YouTube thumbnail maker (https://www.adobe.com/express/create/thumbnail/youtube).

Here are a few guidelines for creating YouTube thumbnails:

» Create a thumbnail that accurately depicts the video's content.

» Follow the recommended dimensions (1280 pixels wide by 720 pixels high).

- » Use as high a resolution as possible, but keep the file size below 2 MB.

- » Save your thumbnail as a JPG or PNG file.

- » Make good use of your brand's color scheme. (See Chapter 6 for more about brand guidelines.)

- » Create an image that'll look good large or small; many people will be viewing it on their smartphones.

- » If you include text, keep it short, and make sure that it's easy to read when viewed on a device of any size.

- » Steer clear of any nudity, sexually provocative content, hate speech, violence, or potentially harmful or dangerous content.

Creating a branded YouTube channel

YouTube enables you, as an individual or business, to have your very own YouTube channel, so members of your audience can quickly and easily access all the videos you uploaded. Your personal channel is linked to your Google account and uses your YouTube user name as its name, though you can edit it. With a Google Business account, you can create custom branded channels.

REMEMBER

Another advantage of a Google Business account is that you can grant others access to your account (so team members can manage it) without having to share your login information.

First, you need to create a Business account on Google. Go to Google (https://www.google.com), click the Sign In button in the top-right corner of the page, click Use Another Account, and then click Create Account. If you're already signed in, click your profile picture in the top-right corner of the page, click Add Another Account, click Create Account, and select To Manage My Business. Follow the onscreen prompts to create your Google Business account. Now you're ready to create a branded channel:

1. **Log in to YouTube, using the username and password for your Google Business account.**

2. **Click your profile picture or icon in the top-right corner of the page, and choose Create a Channel.**

    If you already created your first channel, instead click Settings, click Add or Manage Your Channel(s), then Create a New Channel. The Choose How to Create Your Channel box appears, prompting you to specify whether you want to use your name or a custom name for your channel.

3. **Under Use a Custom Name, click the Select button.**

YouTube prompts you to type a name for your channel. Make sure that the name reflects your brand and the video content you'll be posting on your channel.

4. **Select the check box next to the "I understand" legal statement, and click Create.**

A confirmation box appears, congratulating you on creating a new channel.

5. **Follow the onscreen prompts to complete the process by entering details about your channel.**

During this process, you get to upload a profile picture, type a description of your channel, and add links to your sites and social media profiles.

6. **Click Save and Continue.**

You return to the YouTube home page, which prompts you to upload a video to get started, but hold off on that.

7. **Click your profile image in the top-right corner of the page, choose Settings, and click Channel Status and Features.**

8. **Click the Verify button (top left), and follow the onscreen prompts to verify your channel.**

When your site is verified, you're returned to the Status and Features page, where you can enable additional features for your channel.

9. **Enable all the channel features you want to use, such as Monetization and Custom Thumbnails.**

10. **Click Return to YouTube Studio in the top-right corner of the page, click your new channel's icon in the top-left corner of the page, and click the Customize Channel button.**

Your channel's customization page appears.

11. **Use the available options to customize your channel, including adding a branded banner.**

As you make changes to your channel, they're saved automatically.

12. **When you're done making changes, click the YouTube Studio button below the branded banner you added, and choose Settings in the menu bar on the left side of the screen.**

The Settings dialog box appears.

13. Enter additional information for your channel, including keywords, your geographical location, a branded watermark, and an indication of whether your channel is made for kids.

14. When you're done entering settings for your channel, click the Save button.

Monetizing Your Content

Podcasting, blogging, and video can be very effective in promoting your brand, which indirectly increases sales and revenue, but you can also use this content to generate revenue more directly. Here are a few ways to monetize your content:

>> **Sell advertising.** When you upload podcasts or videos, you can enable an option to monetize your content or include advertising, and the company that hosts your content (such as YouTube) will automatically include advertisements with it and pay you for it. If you have your own blog or website, you can easily add advertising to it with the help of services such as Google AdSense (https://www.google.com/adsense/start). You just create an AdSense account and then copy and paste one piece of code into your website or blog that shows ads on your site tailored to its layout.

>> **Create and sell merchandise.** Creating a strong brand via content marketing can drive demand for branded merchandise, such as T-shirts, hats, coffee mugs, stickers, keychains, and other clothing and accessories. Your merchandise may have your brand name and logo, a catchphrase, or a design that aligns with your content's overall theme.

>> **Charge for livestream events.** Livestream events are just what they sound like: live performances streamed over the Internet in real time to whoever happens to tune in. You can monetize livestream events by selling advertising space, requesting donations, charging a fee (like selling tickets to a concert), offering pay-per-view, or getting a sponsor.

MERCHANDISE VERSUS BRANDED PRODUCTS

Girl Gang the Podcast has been monetized since its inception. I started with the podcast, which I monetized by selling merchandise. Instead of taking on outside advertisers, at the end of each show, I encourage listeners to purchase one of my Support Your Local Girl Gang items. As soon as I saw how popular that merchandise was, I launched my own clothing label to sell on my website and collaborated with retailers including Nordstrom and The Beverly Hills Hotel to create limited-edition collections.

I distinguish my merchandise from my clothing brand. *Merchandise* is any generic product stamped or printed with something special. They're like the items that bands sell at concerts and on their websites. This same merchandising model has been adopted by podcasters, YouTubers, and other creatives and performers. On the other hand, a *clothing brand* is a collection of specially designed apparel with its own label.

I often encourage novice entrepreneurs to start with merchandise, because it's more affordable and less risky. It enables you to test your idea without investing a lot of time, energy, and money up front. With a clothing line, you have to find a reliable and trustworthy manufacturer, comply with government regulations, and pay up front for goods. If you're simply looking to create a revenue stream from content creation, I recommend starting with merchandise and transitioning to a clothing line as a phase-two rollout if the merchandise is successful.

IN THIS CHAPTER

» **Creating branding strategies for top social media sites**

» **Optimizing engagement on social media**

» **Using visuals to your advantage**

» **Recruiting and working with influencers to promote your brand**

» **Streamlining operations with social media management software**

Chapter **13**

Promoting Your Brand via Social Media

Social media is all the rage, but if this is the first time you're hearing the term, welcome to the 21st century. *Social media* consists of forms of online communication that enable users to create communities in which they share information, ideas, messages, and other content. The Internet is home to numerous social media platforms, including Facebook, Instagram, Pinterest, YouTube, Twitter, and TikTok.

Although the emphasis is on social as opposed to commercial activities, social media platforms are powerful tools for promoting businesses, products, services, and brands. In a matter of minutes, you can set up a social media account for your brand and start engaging with members of the community to boost brand awareness and engagement. Do things right, and your content can go viral, spreading across social media platforms to reach millions or even billions of prospective customers.

In this chapter, I introduce you to the top social media sites and present effective branding strategies for each. I explain how to optimize engagement on social media through the use of text content and visuals, team up with social media influencers to promote your brand, and save time with social media management software.

WARNING

The challenge for businesses and brands is maintaining social engagement. If you try to hard-sell on social media, you're liable to get shunned in the community or even have your account suspended or terminated. Imagine having your Uncle Fred show up at your birthday party only to pitch nutritional supplements and natural cleaning products to all your guests. It's like that.

REMEMBER

Social media marketing is a topic I can't possibly do justice to in a single chapter. For a deeper dive, check out *Social Media Marketing For Dummies*, 2nd Edition, by Shiv Singh and Stephanie Diamond, or *Social Media Marketing All-in-One For Dummies*, 3rd Edition, by Michelle Krasniak, Jan Zimmerman, and Deborah Ng (both John Wiley & Sons, Inc.). These books explore the full capabilities of social media and deliver the guidance you need to scale your social media marketing efforts.

Getting Started with Branding on Social Media

Social media is often where prospective customers first encounter a brand, so it provides with a golden opportunity to make a great first impression. You can showcase your products and services, share your brand's mission and values, and engage with prospective customers in a relaxed social setting, all while reinforcing brand identity through your brand's logo, colors, and other assets.

Different social media platforms provide different ways to promote a brand. On Facebook, for example, you can create a brand page complete with your logo and brand story, and engage with fans of your brand. My girlgangthelabel profile on Instagram (see Figure 13-1) contains my brand's logo and color scheme, along with links to stories I created (sort of like photo albums): Girl Gang, Podcast, Quotes, Discounts, The Edit, and Questions.

REMEMBER

Every social media profile you create provides an opportunity to showcase your brand identity and extend your brand's reach.

In this section, I go into detail about creating brand strategies for different social media platforms.

Instagram Story Highlights

girlgangthelabel [Edit Profile] ⚙

857 posts   41.5k followers   5,629 following

GIRL GANG™
Community
#SUPPORTYOURLOCALGIRLGANG
🎙 Girl Gang the Podcast
✉ hello@girlgangthelabel.com
⬇ shop merch ⬇
girlgangthelabel.com

GIRL GANG   PODCAST   QUOTES   DISCOUNTS   THE EDIT   QUESTIONS

FIGURE 13-1:
Instagram story
highlights.

Scoping out popular platforms

Dozens of social media platforms are available, but they're not equally effective for all brands. Explore and evaluate your options, and choose one or more platforms that best serve your branding goals (see Chapter 4). In this section, I introduce some of the most popular social media platforms, all of which you should consider.

REMEMBER

You don't need to be active on all platforms to execute a successful social media brand strategy. You can start with one platform. What's most important is that you have a strategy, execute it, and maintain continuous engagement — meaning that you post content regularly and engage with your followers, fans, and others. You'll get more bang for your time and effort by committing to one platform than you will by making sporadic efforts on multiple platforms.

TIP

If you choose to focus your efforts on only one or two social media platforms, you should still create an account on every platform covered here and claim your brand's handle before someone else has a chance to claim it. (Your *handle* is your user name or business or brand name, and it should reflect your brand's identity.) You might start with one platform and expand to others, in which case you'll want a branded handle on each of those platforms. For every brand I create, I claim handles on all the platforms I might eventually use, even though I choose to be active on only a select few.

Deciding the right social media platforms for you

The first step in formulating a social media branding strategy is evaluating the leading social media platforms. Then choose the ones that are likely to be best for your brand. But first, you need to figure out the criteria for choosing which platforms are most promising for your brand. Follow these steps:

1. **Define your customer avatar, as explained in Chapter 5.**

Your *customer avatars* are detailed descriptions of your ideal customers, including their demographics, goals, interests, pain points, role in the purchasing process, where they go for information, and where they choose to socialize online.

2. **Identify your branding goals, as explained in Chapter 4.**

Typical branding goals include building brand recognition and awareness, creating an emotional connection with customers, differentiating your brand, building credibility and trust, and driving sales.

When you have a clear understanding of the consumer and your branding goals, you're ready to evaluate social media platforms to determine the best fit for your brand.

FACEBOOK

One of Facebook's main attractions for brands is the size and diversity of its user base, with more than 2 billion active users per month of all genders, ethnicities, socioeconomic status, education levels, political affiliations . . . and the list goes on. Nearly 75 percent of all Facebook users visit the site daily.

Facebook is also business- and brand-friendly, offering the following features:

» **Business or brand pages:** You can create a business or brand page for free and use it to post announcements; run surveys; schedule live events; share information, photos, and videos; and so on.

» **Facebook Group:** You can created a branded group to build a community around your business, brand, or even a unique product or service you offer. (See Chapter 16 for more about building a community around your brand.)

» **Paid targeted advertising:** Facebook ads are a great way to extend your brand's reach and target your sales to specific markets. See Chapter 15 for guidance on how to promote your brand with paid advertising.

» **Ecommerce integrations:** If you sell products online, you can list them for sale on Facebook, giving your Facebook customers the ability to purchase your products with a single click.

- » **One-on-one customer engagement through Facebook Messenger:** As a business or brand, you can interact with customers directly through Messenger to announce new products, provide shipping updates, and issue other notifications.

- » **Facebook pixels:** A *Facebook pixel* is a piece of computer code you place on your website that collects data to track conversions from Facebook ads. With the data and analytics available from pixels, you can optimize your Facebook ads and remarket to people who've shown interest in your brand.

TWITTER

Twitter is a microblog that limits posts to 280 characters. It's a great platform to showcase your brand's voice, connect directly with your customers and prospects, expand your brand's reach, and build brand loyalty. The biggest benefits of Twitter are the following:

- » Real-time engagement with customers and prospects.

- » The ability to drive traffic to your website, blog, or online store.

- » The ability to deliver basic customer service quickly and easily by replying to tweets from customers.

- » The ability to notify customers and prospects quickly and easily about new products, website updates, live events, and so on. You can notify followers in real time about anything related to your brand and clear the air if your brand receives any negative publicity.

YouTube

For some brands, YouTube is a key component of social media marketing and may even serve as the primary means of delivering their product or service. If you build a business around posting informative or entertaining videos on YouTube, those videos are your product, enabling you to generate some impressive revenue.

Most brands, however, use YouTube to strengthen brand identity, expand the brand's reach, deliver some level of customer service, and sell products and services. Here are some great ways to use YouTube for the purpose of building and launching a brand:

- » Post product demos.

- » Position yourself as a thought leader in your industry or field.

- » Post tutorials on assembling, using, or repairing a product.

>> Interview known and respected members of the market you serve to attract attention and build trust for your brand.

>> Share funny or otherwise interesting and engaging content, such as a quirky advertisement.

See Chapter 12 for guidance on creating and posting videos on YouTube and creating a branded YouTube channel.

INSTAGRAM

Instagram is great for reaching teenagers and young adults but not so good for targeting high-net-worth, highly educated professionals or older people. Engaging with users on Instagram and holding their attention for more than a few seconds can be a challenge, because users tend to flip past images that don't catch their interest.

Even with those limitations, Instagram is attractive for branding purposes and has several features that can be very effective:

>> **Instagram stories:** With the stories feature, you can share multiple photos and videos taken throughout the day (optionally adding overlays of doodles and stickers to add some fun). From the time you stop adding photos and videos to a story, it remains on your profile for only 24 hours, but you can preserve a story by adding a highlight for it on your main page.

>> **Instagram feed:** A feed consists of the photos and videos you post and is more selective than what you post in a story. Your feed is where most people will go to find out more about your brand, so it's a great place to tell your brand story visually. (See Chapter 8 for more about writing a brand story.) You can optimize each post with hashtags and share buttons to reach more people.

TIP

Be sure to create an Instagram business account, which adds a View Insights tab to your home page, allowing you to evaluate the performance of each photo and video you post.

>> **IG Live:** IG Live enables you to stream live video either by yourself or with another Instagram member. If you conduct interviews as part of your content strategy, IG Live comes in very handy. The only drawback is that you can't do retakes. If you mess up, your mistakes are streamed live.

>> **IGTV:** IGTV is Instagram's version of YouTube. This feature enables you to post long-form video (more than a minute) by uploading video to your Instagram account or using the IGTV app on your Android or iOS device.

>> **Instagram Reels:** Reels are 15–30 second videos that you can enhance with a variety of tools, including Effects, Time, Speed, and Align. This feature is great for introducing a brand, business, product, or service and for just keeping in touch with people who love your brand.

REMEMBER

For additional guidance on using Instagram to promote your brand or business, check out *Instagram For Business For Dummies*, 2nd Edition, by Jennifer Herman, Eric Butow, and Corey Walker (Wiley).

PINTEREST

Pinterest is a search engine than a traditional social media platform. Users often search Pinterest for ideas, such as "how to decorate my studio apartment" or "women's short hairstyles," making it a great place to market fashion, home décor, cookware, health and fitness products, hair and beauty products, and more. If your target market is women, Pinterest should definitely be on your list of social media platforms to consider, but plenty of men use Pinterest too.

Along with having its own built-in search engine, Pinterest is search-engine friendly. As you post content on Pinterest, it's commonly picked up by Google, Yahoo!, DuckDuckGo, and other search engines, so it's very useful for extending a brand's reach.

TIP

As you develop content to post on Pinterest, think about how it might be picked up and shared by other users, who create boards to express their moods, interests, and ideas. As you create content, be sure to make it board-worthy. If you're building a brand around wedding products, for example, make sure that the images you post will be picked up and look good on the boards of users who are planning their weddings.

TikTok

TikTok is an app that enables users to share 15-second videos. This social media platform is one to consider if you're developing a personal brand around a specific marketable talent, especially if you're targeting a young, hip crowd. It's also useful for showcasing a business, product, or service. According to Wallaroo Media, 60% of TikTok users are between the ages of 16 and 24, so TikTok's primary audience is younger than some of the audiences of other platforms.

TIP

When creating TikTok videos, aim for razzle-dazzle. Deliver something uproariously funny, deeply moving, awesomely beautiful, incredibly challenging, or mind-blowing — something TikTok users will feel compelled to share with everyone they know.

LinkedIn

LinkedIn is social networking platform for businesses and professionals, which makes it a great place for business-to-business brands and personal brands for consultants and other professionals who have skills and knowledge of value to businesses. If your brand fills the bill, create a LinkedIn account, and start networking to build brand recognition and awareness.

TIP

The secret to branding success on LinkedIn is being unique and generous. Create an original profile that's designed to impress, get connected to thought leaders in your target industry, join relevant LinkedIn Groups, and share what you know. Strive to make others on LinkedIn more successful than they already are. Help them overcome challenges and solve problems.

WARNING

Don't go on LinkedIn and start sending out invitations to everyone LinkedIn suggests to you. People generally won't connect with you unless they think the connection will benefit them in some way. If you offer valuable content on LinkedIn, users will be sending *you* requests to connect.

Choosing different metrics for different platforms

Whenever you implement a marketing campaign, you should use metrics and analytics to gauge its success and figure out what's working and what's not. Take the same approach when building a brand presence on any social media platform. The only tricky part is choosing the metrics that most accurately reflect performance and success, such as the following:

>> Number of followers, friends, or fans is always a key metric, but having lots of followers on Facebook or Instagram is more important than having lots of followers on Pinterest, because the number of times your brand appears on users' Pinterest boards is more important.

>> Number of shares for specific content is always important, because shares reflect not only how impressed users are by the content you posted, but also how effective your word-of-mouth advertising is — a good gauge of organic marketing.

>> Content metrics, such as percentages of photos, infographics, audio, video, and text you post or original content versus shared content, can vary from one platform to another. Instagram is highly visual, for example, so certain content metrics may not apply.

>> Audience metrics such as gender, ethnicity, age, and education and income levels may be more important on more-diverse platforms such as Facebook and Twitter than on less-diverse platforms such as TikTok.

These are just a few examples of some of the social media marketing metrics you may want to consider: engagement metrics (clicks, likes, shares, comments, and mentions); competitor metrics (comparative engagement metrics); social traffic (traffic from different platforms to your website or online store); and conversion rates (incoming traffic converted to sales).

Most social media platforms feature metrics and analytics for business users, but a good social media management platform is likely to provide more robust analytics. See "Saving Time and Effort with Social Media Management Tools" later in this chapter for more about social media management platforms.

Following the Rules of the Road

Online marketing best practices vary depending on whether you're marketing on your own properties (your website, blog, or online store) or on community properties (social media sites). When you're building and launching a brand on social media, you need to be more transparent, engaging, humble, and generous. In the following sections, I offer guidance on how to fit in while standing out.

REMEMBER

Social media is *social* — no commercial activity, no business activity (except on LinkedIn), and definitely no hard-selling. As a rule, create and share content that your followers will enjoy and find useful, not content that merely promotes your brand. To keep your followers and attract new ones, focus on serving your audience's needs and preferences, not your own. If you want to attract customers, be attractive.

Optimizing your social media profile

Nearly all social media platforms enable users to create and maintain a business or brand account, profile, or page. Take full advantage of what each platform offers by fleshing out your brand's profile or page, as follows:

>> Add your brand's logo.

>> If given an option, follow your branding guidelines (see Chapter 6) to specify the colors and fonts that reinforce your brand's identity.

>> Include the address of your brand's website, blog, or online store.

>> Include your brand story or a description of your brand or business.

>> Add a call to action, if you have that an option. A Facebook Business page, for example, enables you to add a call to action that directs visitors to do something, such as visit your website or call your store.

TIP

Consider using Linktree (`https://linktr.ee`) to create a customizable landing page for your brand that contains links to all the valuable content you want to share. Figure 13-2 shows the Linktree landing page I created for my Girl Gang the Label brand. You can add the address of your Linktree landing page to your social media profiles on Instagram, TikTok, Facebook, YouTube, Twitter, LinkedIn, and so on. With a Linktree landing page, you can update important links without having make the changes separately on all your social media accounts.

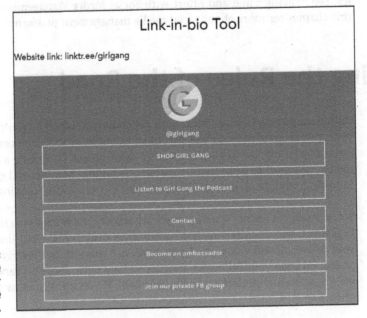

FIGURE 13-2:
My Linktree landing page for Girl Gang the Label.

Posting regularly

Branding on social media requires more than creating a brand or business page or account, adding a profile, and posting relevant content occasionally or sporadically. For optimum results, post something relevant and interesting at least twice a week; otherwise, your friends, followers, and fans will quickly forget about your brand. Steady visibility is key.

To keep yourself on track, create an editorial schedule one or two months out, listing the dates of your future posts and their content. Consider creating a weekly feature centered on a specific day of the week. At Girl Gang, I highlight female-owned businesses on "Female Founder Friday." Our audience knows that at the end of each week, they can tune in for stories and insights from female entrepreneurs.

TIP

Start thinking about regular content you can create and promote. If you have a monthly newsletter, you can post a teaser on social media with a call to action to sign up for your newsletter for more information. In addition to increasing engagement, a newsletter provides the means to capture customer email addresses and other contact info for direct marketing campaigns.

Monitoring and responding to posts

Not monitoring and responding to posts on your social media sites is like throwing a party and then ignoring your guests and letting the event get out of hand. You need to keep an eye on what's going on and engage with visitors for two important reasons:

» If anyone's posting comments that are offensive or abusive, you need to remove their comments and report them so that their accounts can be suspended or canceled.

» If anyone asks a question, expresses a concern, posts a positive or negative comment about your brand, or posts anything else that warrants a response, you need to know about it and respond. People want to know that you listen, understand, and care about what they think.

REMEMBER

You're better off committing to one social media platform and doing it right than setting up shop on multiple platforms and neglecting them.

TIP

Before posting a response to someone's comment, consider how your response will reflect on your brand. Make sure that the tone of your response is consistent with your brand and that the content is respectful and courteous.

Choosing your friends carefully

On social media, you're often judged by the company you keep, so associate only with people, businesses, and brands that align with your brand's mission and values.

REMEMBER

By remaining consistent to your brand's mission and values, you make your brand attractive and open to associations and partnerships with other brands and businesses. Protect your reputation, or you'll lose out on such opportunities.

Harnessing the Power of Photos and Video

On some social media platforms, text is almost taboo. YouTube and TikTok are exclusively video, and Instagram and Pinterest are huge photo libraries. The only social media venues that support much text-based content are Facebook, Twitter, and LinkedIn, and even on those platforms, users like to see pictures and videos. In short, if you want to build and launch a brand on social media, you need to know your way around a camera . . . or hire someone who does.

Taking your own photos on a budget

Anyone with a decent smartphone can take respectable photos these days, and uploading them to social media sites has never been easier. If you don't know where to start, begin by collecting photos from other brands you like, and figure out what you like about them. Do all the photos have people in them? Are the images dark or bright? Are the photos still shots of products, or do they show products in use? Answers to questions like these will help you decide on the *composition* (setting) and lighting for your photos.

Photography is a complex topic far beyond the scope of this book. You can find plenty of guidance on the topic in *Digital Photography For Dummies*, 7th Edition, by Julie Adair King (Wiley), along with countless online tutorials on taking everything from product photos to personal branding photos.

TIP

Start taking photos, and get feedback from friends, relatives, and associates. If you wait until you know everything and you're able to take professional-looking photos, you'll be waiting forever. Here are a few tips I can offer from experience:

» Use a tripod whenever possible to ensure clear focus. You can fix nearly anything in a digital photo by using photo editing software as long as the photo isn't blurry. (Try taking photos with and without flash.)

» Make sure that the location and context support the brand's image and values, especially everything in the background.

» Pay attention to lighting and shadows. Use natural light for the best results. If you're taking photos outdoors, morning or early evening is best unless you're going for super-bright sunshine.

» For *flat lays* (photos of a product on a flat surface), incorporate items aligned with things your customer avatar would enjoy. If you have a swimwear line, for example, place sunscreen and sunglasses in the picture.

» Take lots of photos to improve your chances of getting the perfect one.

>> Use photo editing software to improve the quality of your photos. Free applications such as Canva's online photo editor (https://www.canva.com/photo-editor) make it easy to filter, resize, crop, and edit photos for free.

Recording and posting video content

Video is one of the most effective media for building brand recognition and identity. In fact, videos generate more likes, comments, and discussion than static photos or text. They also provide the means to diversify the content you offer.

You don't need a movie studio to shoot your own video for branding purposes. A smartphone with a decent camera should do the trick. You can use the video editing software that comes installed on every Apple and Windows PC to edit the video and even layer audio on top of it. Then you can upload your video to your social media account.

See Chapter 12 for more about shooting video and posting it on YouTube. The process is similar across all social media platforms. If the platform has a mobile app (as most platforms do), you can use it to upload video directly from your phone to your account.

TIP

Shoot all video in landscape mode unless you're posting it to Instagram, which optimizes the video to be viewed in portrait mode on smartphones.

When posting video, be sure to add a title, description, keywords, and tags, and choose a category if the platform provides a field for adding it. The more descriptive text you can add to the video, the better, because search engines use that text to determine how to index the video.

Hiring content creators

If you can't get the photo or video quality you need by doing it yourself, or if you prefer to outsource this chore, hire a professional photographer or videographer. Here's how to go about finding the right candidate for the job:

1. **Ask you friends, colleagues, and associates whether they know any good photographers near you, or search sites such as Craigslist, Upwork, or even Instagram for candidates.**

2. **Vet the candidates by checking out their photos and videos and by contacting their references.**

   Faking talent online is easy, so make sure that the person you hire has a track record of producing quality photos and video, preferably for the social media platforms you intend to use.

3. **Whittle down your list of candidates based on their rates and the quality of their work.**

4. **Contract the top candidate on your list.**

   Make sure that your contract covers the following:

   - Both parties' contact info.
   - Rate/price.
   - Deadline/timeline.
   - Ownership of content produced. (Normally, the photographer/videographer retains the copyright and grants you use rights, but this aspect is negotiable.)
   - Statement of who's responsible for obtaining signed model and property releases so that you have legal permission to show the model and location.
   - Details on postproduction editing and any additional costs associated with it.
   - Cancellation policy.

WARNING

Have your attorney prepare the contract or review the vendor's contract before signing anything.

Teaming Up with Influencers

Influencer marketing is a form of social media marketing involving product placement and recommendations from people whose opinions many other people know and trust. This type of marketing is a great way to increase brand exposure and reach. Just imagine the exposure your brand would get if an Instagram user with more than 50,000 followers started posting about it!

REMEMBER

The key to successful influencer marketing is choosing people who are active on social media and who have a large audience that's likely to be interested in your brand. If you're selling clothing made from recycled materials, for example, getting an endorsement from an influential environmentalist or group could be very helpful.

Before you start recruiting candidates, you have two choices to make: micro influencer versus macro influencer and paid versus organic.

Micro influencer versus macro influencer

Influencers are often divided into two categories: *micro influencers*, who have 10,000 to 100,000 followers, and *macro influencers*, who have more than 100,000 followers. Macro influencers are more likely than micro influencers to charge for their services, and they're likely to charge more, but they're not necessarily the more effective of the two. A micro influencer with a smaller audience of highly engaged and motivated followers may be the better choice.

When evaluating influencers, consider more than cost and number of followers. Also consider the level of engagement, which is reflected in how followers respond to the influencer's posts, such as the number of likes, shares, and comments. Depending on the level of engagement, an account with a smaller following may actually reach more people.

Paid influencer versus organic influencer

Another distinction among influencers is paid versus organic. Per-post rates for paid influencers generally are based on the influencer's number of followers and the social media platform, and they range from single-digit dollar amounts to tens of thousands of dollars.

Organic (unpaid) influencer campaigns, however, can be just as successful for a tiny fraction of the cost — sometimes just a polite request, some swag (such as a branded T-shirt), or a complementary product.

Send a free product or a sample to an influencer, along with a brief handwritten note (including your social media handle) asking the influencer to post a product review. When you give a free product, you can't demand specific terms regarding the post, as you can with paid influencers, but if you get your product in the hands of influencers and they love it, chances are good that they'll post about it.

Saving Time and Effort with Social Media Management Tools

If you're building brand identity on several social media platforms, posting regularly, monitoring comments, and responding to comments can become a full-time job. Some large organizations have teams of people dedicated to the task, but if you're a small business (You, Inc.), you're doing everything yourself.

To maintain engagement through your social media accounts, I recommend that you use a social media management tool — software that enables you to create an editorial calendar, post content automatically according to a schedule, distribute content to social media platforms, monitor engagement (comments, shares, likes, and so on), and post comments.

In the following sections, I introduce some popular and affordable social media management platforms, most of which offer a free trial period.

Planoly

Planoly (https://www.planoly.com) enables you to plan and schedule content to post on Instagram, Pinterest, Facebook, and Twitter. If you're sharing your social media management workload with members of a team, you can create multiple logins and even manage campaigns for multiple brands (for an additional cost) from a single account. One of Planoly's coolest features is sellit, which enables you to turn any social platform into a storefront and sell items directly on the platform instead of linking to a separate website or online store.

Hootsuite

Hootsuite (https://www.hootsuite.com) is a social media management platform that enables you to schedule posts across all your social media accounts, access all your brand images directly from the Hootsuite dashboard, monitor social conversations and brand mentions, respond quickly to comments and (with the help of analytics) see what's working and what's not.

Tailwind

Tailwind (https://www.tailwindapp.com) bills itself as a smart marketing assistant exclusively for Facebook, Instagram, and Pinterest that enables you to automate your designs, schedule posts, and analyze engagement data. One of its most useful features transforms your photos into various branded designs suitable for posting on Facebook, Instagram, and Pinterest. It can also help you team up with influencers on these platforms.

TIP

Pinterest works best when you create a schedule and post pins regularly. (A *pin* is a single item posted on Pinterest, typically consisting of a photo and caption, compared with a *board*, which is a collection of related pins.) Tailwind makes it easier to batch pins and set up auto posting for your account.

Buffer

Buffer (`https://buffer.com`) is a simple social media management tool that enables you to plan and coordinate campaigns on most popular social media platforms. You can use Buffer to monitor your social media accounts from a single interface and instantly respond to brand mentions and comments. The software also offers analytics that provide valuable insight into campaign performance.

Chapter **14**

Email Marketing

mail marketing combines the power of direct-mail marketing and the Internet, enabling you to send an email blast to thousands of recipients with a click. If you've ever wondered why you receive so much spam, that's because email marketing works. In one study conducted by the Direct Marketing Association in the United Kingdom, every dollar spent on email marketing generated an average return on investment of $38.

Every brand should include email marketing as one of its regular promotional activities. You can use it to lead people through the sales process, drive traffic to your blog or social media accounts, distribute an electronic newsletter, announce new products and services, offer customers suggestions on how to get the most out of the products or services they ordered, and more. You can even segment your email distribution to target users by demographic, by where they are in the sales process, or by nearly any other criteria.

Email marketing, however, is only as effective as you make it. In this chapter, I explain how to do it right so that your email campaigns strengthen the bond between your customers and your brand.

REMEMBER

For a complete guide to email marketing, check out *Digital Marketing For Dummies*, 2nd Edition, by Ryan Diess (John Wiley & Sons, Inc.).

Becoming a Trusted Sender

Nobody likes spam, and most people have some sort of spam filter built into their email client to automatically route any spammy-looking email messages to their spam or junk folder, so they won't even see it. For your email marketing messages to be effective, they must show up in the recipient's inbox, and that'll happen only if you're a trusted sender — someone who hasn't been identified as a spam source.

Here are some suggestions for becoming a trusted sender and preventing your outgoing messages from being blacklisted (flagged as spam):

REMEMBER

>> Don't buy email lists. If you purchase email addresses, you'll get some that are valid and some that aren't. Also, owners of most email addresses you purchase will know they did not sign up for your list and will mark you as spam.

Include in your mailing list only people who choose to be in it. Otherwise, recipients will be more likely to report your email as spam, which will get you blacklisted. I share some ideas for getting people to opt in to your email list in "Building a Quality Email List" later in this chapter.

>> Avoid typing anything in your message or message description that's spammy, including the following:

- ALL CAPS

- Exclamation points, dollar signs, and words such as *free* and *bargain*

- Phrases such as *increase traffic* and *lose weight fast*

>> Add an unsubscribe link to the bottom of every outgoing message so that recipients can opt out quickly and easily. It's better that they opt out than report you as a spammer.

WARNING

In the United States, federal antispam laws require you to give people a way to unsubscribe from your list in every email message you send.

>> Deliver content that people find useful and is less likely to be reported as spam.

>> Segment your contacts and remove unengaged contacts — recipients who aren't opening your email messages or responding in any way. If you keep sending messages to people who aren't interested in it, you're more likely to get reported as a spammer. Read about tracking metrics related to your email campaigns in "Tracking Results: Email Metrics" later in this chapter.

>> Send bulk email from an email marketing service, such as Mailchimp (https://mailchimp.com), Constant Contact (https://www.constantcontact.com), or HubSpot (https://www.hubspot.com). These services can help you maintain compliance with spam rules and regulations and keep you from getting blacklisted.

Hosting providers commonly feature shared email servers, so if anyone on the server is identified as a spammer, everyone using that server gets blacklisted. If you're using your hosting provider's email server (as opposed to a dedicated email marketing platform), check with your hosting provider for additional ways to keep your email address from being blacklisted or to get it removed from blacklists.

TIP

To see whether your domain has been blacklisted, visit MXToolbox (https://mxtoolbox.com), type your domain name in the search box, and click Blacklist Check. The site checks your domain against nearly 100 spam blacklists and indicates whether it appears on any of the lists. If your domain is blacklisted, the site indicates the reason. The MXToolbox delivery system can help you fix any issues that are causing your address to be blacklisted and monitor your email address for any future problems.

Defining Your Objectives

Before you launch any new branding initiative, you should have a clear objective in mind. An objective provides direction and enables you to gauge your success. Following are some common objectives for email marketing campaigns:

>> **Upselling and cross-selling:** Whenever a customer shows interest in a product or service you're selling, you have an opportunity to increase the total order amount through upselling, cross-selling, or both. *Upselling* involves encouraging the customer to buy a more expensive version of a product, such as the X21 deluxe smartphone instead of the X21 standard edition. *Cross-selling* involves persuading the customer to buy related products, such as a wireless charger and a protective case for that X21 deluxe smartphone.

>> **Increasing brand awareness:** You can use email marketing to keep your brand in the minds of customers and increase their understanding of what it offers and stands for. To increase brand awareness, send existing and prospective customers information they'll find valuable regularly — once a week.

WARNING

Don't get into any heavy sales pitches via email or send email too frequently (more than once a week). Approach email marketing the same way you'd write to a friend to provide helpful information and guidance.

>> **Finding out more about your customers:** Engage your customers in a conversation about their interests and the challenges or problems they face. In addition to demonstrating that you value their opinion and genuinely care about them, conversations like these can serve as valuable sources of insight and innovation. You can be far more effective serving people when you know what they need and want.

REMEMBER

- **Soliciting customer reviews and ratings:** Customer reviews and ratings can make or break a brand. Positive reviews and high ratings increase trust and break down the barriers that make people hesitant to place an order. On the other hand, negative reviews and low ratings can drive potential customers to competing brands. When you have a satisfied customer, don't be afraid to request a review or rating.

  Negative reviews and low ratings aren't necessarily bad for business. They can be valuable, though painful, learning experiences. In addition, you can turn a negative into a positive by following up with the customer to resolve the issue that prompted the negative feedback. By going above and beyond to satisfy the customer, you may inspire them to remove or change their review or rating. They may even sing the praises of your brand's customer service.

- **Issuing announcements:** Email is a great tool for keeping customers posted about important changes or events related to your brand, such as an upcoming webinar or podcast, a change in leadership, an exclusive sale, or an in-person event. One reason why people register to receive email from businesses is that they want to be the first to hear any news.

- **Introducing a new product or service:** Whenever you introduce a new product or service, send an email blast to everyone on your email list. Even better, offer them an exclusive discount or free trial. Give your recipients a reason to spread the word about your brand (and not unsubscribe from your mailing list).

- **Promoting your website or social media offerings:** If you're launching a new website or blog or establishing a presence on a new social media platform, let everyone on your mailing list know. Send them an invitation to visit and to post a question or comment.

- **Delivering customer service:** With email, you can take a more proactive approach to customer service by delivering information that enables customers to make the most of your products and services and by letting them know about any issues (such as product recalls) before they find out from other sources.

- **Reducing the number of abandoned shopping carts:** If you have an online store, and shoppers are frequently adding items to their shopping cart but leaving without buying anything, consider setting up an automated messaging system that reminds customers of the items in their cart. They're close to making a purchase; they may just need a little nudge.

- **Distributing invitations to special events:** If you're hosting a physical or virtual event, email is a great way to send invitations; collect information about who's attending; and distribute details, such as the date, the time, the location, places to stay, and a schedule or itinerary.

Building a Quality Email List

Search the web for "buy email lists," and you'll find dozens of businesses that specialize in gathering email addresses and selling them to companies. Sounds like a great idea, right? Why go through the trouble of collecting email addresses when you can buy them for a few cents each? Some companies even offer specialized lists, such as consumer lists, business lists, and lists of people and families who recently moved into a specific market.

The big drawback to buying email lists is that the people on the list haven't agreed to receive email from you. As a result, they're more likely to flag any email messages coming from you as spam, which could get you blacklisted, bringing your email marketing campaign to a screeching halt. Many marketing email servers, such as Mailchimp, prohibit the use of purchased email lists for this very reason.

To create a quality email list of your own, persuade people to opt in to receiving email messages from you. Here are a few suggestions for doing just that:

>> Include a call to action at the end of every blog post and on all web pages, encouraging people to sign up to receive email messages. At the end of a post, you might say something like this: "To be the first to find out about our latest designs, sign up for email notices."

>> Create pop-ups on your website and blog prompting visitors to sign up to receive email messages. Most website and blogging platforms have pop-up generators available as plug-ins. If you use an email marketing platform, it may provide a form you can use on your site to collect email addresses. See "Exploring Email Marketing Platforms (Free and Paid)" later in this chapter for details.

TIP

Tie your pop-ups to certain behaviors or events. If a visitor looks at three pages on your site, for example, have a message such as this one pop up: "You seem interested in what we offer. Would you like to subscribe to our e-newsletter?" Or if a person tries to leave your site, you might have pop-up says "Leaving so soon? We can keep you looped in via your inbox."

>> Be creative in your call-to-action options. Instead of offering a basic Yes or Subscribe option, for example, use something like Access Our Exclusive Offers or Download Our Free e-Book, with fields for the person's name and email address.

TIP

Consider taking a humorous approach to your call-to-action options (assuming that humor fits with your brand's personality). Instead of Yes and No options, you may want to use something like Yeah, Sign Me Up! and Are You Kidding Me?

>> Recruit subscribers through your social media accounts. People who choose to follow you on a social media platform are more likely than others to want content from you delivered to their inboxes.

>> Include an invitation to subscribe to email notifications on all written communications with customers, such as customer service email messages.

>> Bring a signup sheet to all live events, and encourage people to provide their names, email addresses, and other contact info. You may even want to sponsor a drawing and have people write their email address on the back of their tickets so that you can notify the winner (and grow your mailing list). See Chapter 11 for more about using in-person events to promote your brand.

TIP

Consider removing email addresses from your mailing list when people on the list stop engaging with your brand. Why? Because they're increasingly more likely to report any messages coming from you as spam. In addition, if they haven't opened or responded to an email message from you for several months, they're probably not interested in your brand. Focus your efforts on motivated customers.

Composing Effective Email Messages

The success of any email message or campaign hinges on the quality of its content. You need to offer something that appeals to the target audience and is written in an engaging, error-free way. You must pay close attention to everything from the Subject line to the message itself and the way you present it in words and images. In this section, I guide you through the process.

REMEMBER

At some point in the course of your education, you probably encountered the four essential elements of good writing. If you didn't, or if you need a refresher, here they are. Be sure you're clear about them before you start writing, and keep them in mind as you compose your email messages:

>> **Audience:** Imagine the people you're addressing sitting across from you. Identify their interests, needs, desires, challenges, and personalities. Why did they opt to receive email messages from you? What do they hope and expect to gain in exchange for giving you access to their inbox? See "Sizing up your audience" later in this chapter for details.

>> **Purpose:** Define the purpose of your message or email campaign. Is your purpose to sell, entertain, inform or educate, or drive traffic to your website or blog? Refer to the earlier section "Defining Your Objectives."

>> **Tone:** Choose the attitude, emotion, or personality you want to covey through your writing. Are you serious, lighthearted, concerned, assertive, or nostalgic?

What emotion do you want your audience to feel? See Chapter 6 for more about tone.

>> **Content:** Describe the content type. Are you announcing an upcoming event or a new product, delivering news about your industry or business, following up with a customer about a concern or complaint, offering a discount, or requesting participation in a survey?

REMEMBER

Content is the raw material. Audience, purpose, and tone influence how that content is expressed (see Figure 14-1).

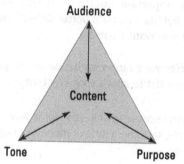

FIGURE 14-1:
Audience,
purpose, and
tone influence
how content is
presented.

Sizing up your audience

Before writing anything, you must determine who your audience is. You're likely to write very differently depending on whether your audience is young or old, male or female, consumers or people in business, those seeking entertainment or those trying to overcome a difficult challenge. Imagine that you're a TV executive. Who's your audience, and why are those people tuning into your station? These are also known as your customer avatars, which we discuss in detail in Chapter 5. Conducting an effective email campaign is all about meeting or exceeding your audience's expectations.

The challenge of sizing up your audience is compounded when your audience is fragmented in some way. My husband targets his Color Me Book brand to both consumers and to business owners who want to use the custom coloring books to promote their brands, for example. He takes a much different approach depending on whether we're writing to consumers or to business owners. Consumers are usually buying a Color Me Book as a gift for a loved one, whereas business owners are using them as a marketing tool and want to know how effective they are for that purpose. Your audience may be fragmented in other ways as well, including demographics, where they are in making a purchase decision, their specific interests and needs, and whether they're influencers.

TIP

As you collect email addresses, organize recipients into groups so that you can easily send targeted email messages to people in different groups. If you're using a dedicated email marketing platform, it may provide additional tools for targeting specific segments of your audience.

Offering something of value

People need a good reason to let you add them to your email list, to open and read the email messages when they arrive in their inbox and to respond favorably to your call to action. Before a person does just about anything, they consciously or subconsciously answer the all-important question "What's in it for me?" Are people that self-centered? You betcha. So you'd better deliver something valuable enough to get them to do what you want them to.

Make a list of what you can offer your target audience to compel them to follow your call to action. Here's a short list to spark your creativity:

>> Valuable information that can improve their lives in some way — make their lives easier or more enjoyable, save them time or money, or help them overcome a specific challenge

>> Announcements of upcoming events (online or in-person) that may interest them

>> News and insights (who doesn't like being the first to know something?)

>> Previews of new products or services

>> Gift ideas

>> Tips for getting more out of the products or services they bought

>> Information about contests or drawings

>> Case studies or success stories — examples of how other customers benefit from the products and services you offer

>> Product videos

>> New-product updates and releases

>> Deals, discounts, and freebies

>> A survey or poll

>> Links to blog or social media posts that may interest them

>> An advice column

>> Free resources, such as e-books or newsletters

HIGHLIGHTING INDUSTRY EXPERTS

Creating scheduled content and features can keep readers engaged and grow your email list as subscribers share your content with their contacts. I seek inspiration from columns and feature stories in my favorite magazines. I particularly enjoy articles that showcase interesting people, so when I'm planning my email campaigns, I try to include at least one interview with a relevant expert every month.

Most likely, your readers will enjoy content that's aligned with your brand identity — why they chose to follow your brand. If you have an eco-friendly clothing line, you can interview an expert in sustainability for a feature in your email newsletter that includes tips on living a more eco-friendly lifestyle.

Creating From and Subject lines that grab people's attention

One of the most important metrics in any email marketing campaign is its *open rate* — the percentage of recipients who open the message. (Read more about email metrics in "Tracking Results: Email Metrics" later in this chapter.) You can launch an awesome email campaign, but it will fall flat if nobody opens the message. The first things people see when they receive an email message are the From and Subject lines, so do what little you can to make those items compelling.

The first order of business is changing the entry in the From line to your brand name. On dedicated email marketing platforms, changing the From line is easy; you do it when you're creating your email campaign. In personal email clients, you may be able to make the change through the client's account or profile settings. Check your email client's help system or online support for specific instructions.

Entering a Subject line is easy. Just type a brief phrase that's likely to entice the recipient to open and read the message. Here are a few example Subject lines to get your creative juices flowing:

>> Top 10 Fashion Secrets

>> Top 20 Kayak Adventures in the United States

>> Work Less, Earn More

>> Be Your Family's MVP

>> Join Our 5-Day Challenge

>> When's the Last Time You . . .?

>> Stop Working So Hard!

TIP

Depending on your target audience, consider adding a relevant emoji to the beginning or end of your Subject line to make it stand out. You can copy and paste an emoji from a site such as Emojipedia (https://emojipedia.org) or use a shortcut key combination on a Mac or Windows PC. On a Mac, click the Subject line and press Control+⌘+space bar. On a Windows PC, press the Windows key and either the period or semicolon key.

WARNING

Don't overuse emojis, ALL CAPS, dollar signs, or exclamation points, all of which can make your subject stand out in a bad way.

Writing a clear call to action

The purpose of every email message you send is to persuade the recipient to respond favorably in some way — to order a product or service, download an eBook, take a survey, claim a discount, you name it. At the end of every email message, include a clear call to action, telling the person what you want them to do, even if it's something relatively passive, such as "Keep an eye out for next week's email, when we'll present 52 uses for our new product."

Writing a clear call to action at this point in the process may seem to be premature, but I recommend writing with the end in mind. This approach clarifies the purpose of the email, inspiring you to write a message that builds up to the call to action.

REMEMBER

If you're not good about asking for what you want, get good at it. People can't read minds. If you tell people exactly what you need or want them to do, you significantly increase the odds that they'll do it.

Write your call to action as a command, starting with a strong, descriptive verb such as *buy, order, subscribe, support, volunteer, download, claim,* or *register.* Make sure that your value proposition is enticing enough to get recipients to follow your call to action. Here are a few examples to get you thinking in the right direction:

>> Buy now and get 50% off.

>> Spend your next vacation with us.

>> Snuggle up to our pillows and sheets.

>> Lose inches, gain muscle.

>> Breathe easy, eliminate allergies for good.

>> Enroll now to start your journey.

>> Join the world's top-selling language app.

>> Subscribe to our weekly tips for digital nomads.

>> Stop overpaying for insurance.

>> Eliminate distractions.

REMEMBER

In most cases, present your call to action as a live link or button or as a text message followed by a link or button. In some cases, plain text may be more fitting.

Composing your message

I have one piece of advice for writing compelling email messages: Make them good, or keep them short. People have short attention spans these days. They're constantly being driven to be more productive, and they don't want their day interrupted by anything that's not interesting, informative, helpful, hilarious, or entertaining.

Here are some additional pointers for writing email messages that compel recipients to follow your call to action:

>> **Address readers personally.** Use each person's name (if you know it) at the beginning of every email message. The sweetest sound in the world to most people is the sound of their name. According to a study by Bluecore, personalizing email messages increases click-through rates by as much as 139 percent. (The *click-through rate* is the percentage of recipients who click something in your email message to respond to your call to action.)

>> **Be succinct.** If you have something really engaging to say, feel free to provide more detail. Otherwise, get to the point in as few words as possible.

>> **Inject some energy and personality.** Your brand has a personality, as explained in Chapter 6, so let it show through in your email marketing. Nobody likes to read flat, lifeless writing. Adopt a more conversational, lively tone.

>> **Keep it light.** Use headings, brief paragraphs, and lists to make your message easier to skim.

>> **Use FOMO (fear of missing out) to your advantage.** People don't want to miss out on a good thing, so use scarcity and urgency to compel them to act now.

Researching emails in your industry

Become a student of email marketing. Get your name on the email lists of your competitors and other brands in your industry. Store great marketing messages in a folder, and use them for inspiration.

Instead of subscribing to receive email and then having to unsubscribe later, head to Milled.com (https://milled.com), where you can research email marketing campaigns from thousands of retailers and brands on demand. Use the search box near the top of the opening page to find popular brands; then click a brand in the search results or scroll down to view marketing emails that are the best match. These examples are great for getting inspiration, finding ways to stand out, and seeing how other brands engage with their subscribers.

Including images

Including images in your email messages makes them more visually appealing and increases click-through rates significantly. According to a study of more than 5,000 email campaigns conducted by Vero, those with images had, on average, a 42 percent higher click-through rate than those without images. Mailchimp conducted a similar study of 5 billion campaigns and had nearly the same results. Specifically, email messages with more than ten images performed best.

When incorporating images into your email campaigns, keep the following suggestions in mind:

>> **Use images to create context.** Show products and services in natural settings to illustrate their functionality. If you sell swimming pools, for example, include images of people enjoying their pools.

>> **Adhere to your branding guidelines.** Your branding guidelines specify colors, along with sizing and quality standards for images. See Chapter 6 for details.

>> **Be sensitive to image size, resolution, file size, and file format.**

- *Image size:* Generally speaking, aim for image widths of 600 to 800 pixels. Anything smaller is likely to look blurry on a wide display, and anything larger may get cut off in the email viewer. Larger images often mean bigger files, which can slow the transmission speed of email messages.

- *Resolution:* Save a copy of the original image (so you don't overwrite the original) at 72 dots per inch (dpi), which is good enough quality for onscreen viewing but reduces the file size.

TIP

- *File size:* Try to limit the size of each image to 5 megabytes (MB).

  If your image consists of two or more layers, flatten the layers before saving the image to reduce its file size.

- *File format:* Use GIF, JPG, or PNG. PNG offers the highest quality of the three but results in the largest files.

» **Use relevant images.** Your Subject line, message, call to action, and any images you use should align.

» **Make your images clickable.** If your call-to-action button doesn't appear on the recipient's page, the person should be able to click an image to go to your website, blog, or *landing page* (a single web page to which the user is directed).

» **Test the email message before sending it.** Send the message to yourself, view it on different devices (such as desktop and tablet computers and smartphones), check its quality, and make adjustments if necessary.

A/B testing email copy

A/B testing is a user-experience research method that involves testing two versions of something on randomly selected users to see which version is more successful. You can use A/B testing on a small sample of recipients before distributing your message more broadly, or you can send one message to half the people on your list and the other message to the other half. Either way, you can track metrics such as open rates and click-through rates to find out which message is more effective. See "Tracking Results: Email Metrics" later in this chapter for details.

EMAIL MARKETING FROM STYLE ME GHD

Home décor and furniture company Style Me GHD (https://stylemeghd.com) uses email marketing to showcase its inventory of furniture and home accessories. The company's emails feature photos of room themes and interior designs to spark the imagination and encourage customers to rearrange (and replace) their furniture and furnishings.

Real estate agents use similar techniques to stage a home, helping prospective buyers envision just how pleasant their lives could be if they decide to move in. Style Me GHD takes this approach to showcase its products, enabling customers to see products in context and imagine the possibilities. By curating products for email subscribers, the company saves them time and energy in creating their dream space.

When conducting A/B testing on marketing email, you can change one or more of the following elements:

>> From line

>> Subject line

>> Value proposition (what you're offering)

>> Personalization (add, remove, or modify)

>> Message

>> Images

>> Timing

In other words, you can change just about everything *except* your call to action, because success is measured by how effective the message is in persuading the recipient to follow the call to action. (Changing one element at a time is usually best, because if you change more than one thing, you won't know which change was responsible for making the message more or less effective.)

REMEMBER

A/B testing enables you to find out what works and what doesn't for different audience segments. Keep a record of results to guide future email campaigns.

Exploring Email Marketing Platforms (Free and Paid)

If you're going to do email marketing, I strongly recommend using a dedicated email marketing platform instead of just sending email through a traditional email client, such as Gmail or whatever your Internet service provider offers. Dedicated email marketing platforms offer the following benefits:

>> **Customizable email templates to simplify design:** All you do is select the desired colors and fonts and supply your own images.

>> **Automated mailing list management:** When people subscribe, their email addresses are added to your list, and when they unsubscribe, they're removed from the list.

>> **Simplified compliance with antispam laws:** Your email marketing platform helps you abide by the rules and can prevent you from getting blacklisted. See the earlier section "Becoming a Trusted Sender."

- » **Support:** Most email marketing platforms have articles, tutorials, and tech support staff to answer questions, address any issues you encounter, and help you find out more about email marketing.

- » **Analytics:** Email marketing platforms keep track of important metrics, such as open, click-through, and conversion rates, so you can easily see what's working and what's not. See the next section for details.

- » **Free trials:** When you're getting started, most platforms are free. Mailchimp, for example, gives you a free account as long as your email list has fewer than 2,000 addresses and you send fewer than 12,000 email messages per month.

Here are a few popular email marketing platforms to check out:

- » **Mailchimp** (https://mailchimp.com) is user-friendly, packed with powerful features, and has app integrations for major e-commerce platforms. They have a free plan and upgrades depending on the size of your mailing list and the volume of email messages you send.

- » **Constant Contact** (https://www.constantcontact.com/) is very similar to MailChimp but focuses on enabling you to manage all your points of contact with customers online. You can create branded emails, sell products, build a website, and manage your social media accounts from this platform.

- » **HubSpot** (https://www.hubspot.com) is more of a customer relationship management platform that has an email marketing component. It includes Marketing Hub, Sales Hub, Service Hub, CMS Hub (for content management), and Operations Hub.

- » **ConvertKit** (https://convertkit.com) is an integrated package for managing all points of contact with customers. It features landing pages, email sign-up forms, email marketing, and e-commerce integrations so you can sell products on a variety of platforms.

Tracking Results: Email Metrics

Tracking the results of your campaign provides insight into what's working, what's not, what you should do more of, and what you need to change. Here are the most important email marketing metrics you need to track through the platform you choose for sending your emails:

- » **Bounce rate:** The percentage of intended recipients who didn't receive the email message. This number may indicate that you need to remove some email addresses from your mailing list.

>> **Open rate:** The percentage of recipients who open a specific message.

>> **Click-through rate:** The percentage of recipients who click a link in response to your call to action.

>> **Conversion rate:** The percentage of recipients who follow through on your call to action. If your call to action is to buy a specific product, for example, the percentage of recipients who ordered the product is the conversion rate.

>> **Return on investment (ROI):** The profit gained by the email campaign minus the money spent on the campaign divided by the money spent. If you spent $10 on a campaign that generated $2,500, your ROI would be ($2,500 – $10) / $10 = 2,400 percent.

>> **Unsubscribe rate:** The percentage of recipients who opened the message and clicked the link to be removed from your mailing list. A high unsubscribe rate may indicate a problem with your mailing list or your messaging. You're either sending the right message to the wrong people or the wrong message to the right people.

>> **Forward/share rate:** The percentage of recipients who forwarded your message to someone they know. A high forward/share rate is great, because it shows that you're expanding your brand's reach beyond the contacts you already have.

Chapter **15**

Boosting Brand Awareness with Paid Advertising

When you're promoting a brand, you can get people's attention in various ways. You can earn it by building an awesome brand that inspires your customers to sing its praises. You can own it by building popular media channels, such as a website, blog, Facebook page, YouTube channel, or podcast. Or you can pay for it by creating ads and having them appear in a variety of media, including newspapers and magazines, TV and radio, other people's websites and blogs, and social media. If you have deep pockets, paid advertising can deliver excellent results with little investment of your time and effort, and that's just one of its benefits.

In this chapter, I lead you through the process of weighing the pros and cons of paid advertising, bring you up to speed on your advertising options, offer guidance on working with an advertising agency, and explain the importance of using metrics and benchmarks to evaluate the success of your advertising campaigns.

Weighing the Pros and Cons of Paid Advertising

Marketing can be divided into two categories:

>> **Organic marketing** involves direct contact with customers. You deliver content to them via web content, blog posts, email, newsletters, whitepapers, online videos, podcasts, and so on; engage with them via social media; and interact with them in more traditional ways, such as sales, customer service, and tech support. Organic marketing is free (to some degree), but it generally takes months to have a measurable impact.

>> **Paid advertising** involves connecting with customers through a third party that delivers advertisements to your target audience. Ads are delivered via various media channels, including TV, radio, search engines, websites, blogs, newspapers, and magazines. You can also pay social media influencers to promote your brand. Paid advertising can get expensive, but its impact is immediate.

Paid advertising can help you reach a wider audience than one you've built organically. With algorithms changing constantly on social media platforms, extending your reach organically is increasingly challenging. Having 100,000 followers on Instagram, for example, doesn't mean that 100,000 people are going to see the content you're posting. In fact, only about 10 percent of your followers will see any given post.

TIP

Consider using organic and paid marketing in tandem — paid marketing to get a short-term burst of interest in your brand and organic marketing to build a following over the long term.

In the following sections, I take a deeper dive into the pros and cons of paid advertising so you can decide for yourself whether it's the right approach for you and your brand.

Pros

Paid advertising has several advantages over organic marketing, including the following:

>> **It's quick and easy.** You design and develop an ad, submit it, and pay the going rate to have it distributed to the media of your choice.

>> **You see returns rapidly.** You receive your return on investment quickly as customers encounter the ad and perform the call to action or don't. Either way, you'll know soon after running the ad how effective it is.

>> **Paid advertising enables you to target a narrow audience.** You can choose media based on demographics and interests or even, in some cases, on consumers' behaviors and purchase histories.

>> **Paid advertising has a long track record of success.** Advertising in traditional media and online has proved to be effective in reaching both broad and targeted audiences.

REMEMBER

You can use paid advertising in two ways: to promote your product/service or to promote your content, such as by driving traffic to your website or blog, or encouraging people to sign up for your newsletter.

Cons

As with most things, paid advertising isn't ideal. It has several disadvantages compared with organic marketing, including the following:

>> **Paid advertising can be expensive.** In the world of advertising, you generally get what you pay for. According to Statista, in 2019, the average cost of a 30-second commercial aired during television programming in the United States was $104,700. Even a modest pay-per-click advertising campaign on Google can cost thousands of dollars.

>> **It has less chance of going viral.** Unlike organic marketing efforts, which can be shared easily, paid ads often don't go viral. As soon as you stop paying to have the ad displayed, the benefit ends. Organic marketing, on the other hand, has a much longer shelf life.

>> **Its effect can be diluted if the audience sees it too often.** Over time, even if the ad continues to run, its impact gradually declines.

Getting Started with Paid Advertising

When you decide to add paid advertising to your marketing arsenal, you have plenty of decisions to make. Your first choice is the media you want to use — newspapers, magazines, TV, radio, social media, other people's websites or blogs, and so on. Then you need to narrow your choice to specific options.

In this section, I encourage you to explore your options, and I offer some general guidance on how to choose the best option(s) for promoting your brand. I also provide some tips for implementing each option.

REMEMBER

When you're buying media space or time, you often need to make trade-offs between reach and frequency:

>> **Reach** is the number of unique customers exposed to an ad. Reach is important for increasing brand awareness.

>> **Frequency** is the number of times each customer is exposed to an ad. Increased frequency typically equates to increased conversions.

When you're operating with a limited budget, consider limiting your reach and increasing your frequency.

REMEMBER

In some cases, you may not be choosing media channels that reach the consumers of your product or service; you may be choosing channels that reach the people who influence those consumers. If you're selling test-prep products and training for high-school students, for example, you want to choose channels that are more likely to reach their parents.

Tapping the power of search engine marketing and pay-per-click advertising

Search engine marketing (SEM) and pay-per-click (PPC) advertising are very similar. I highlight the differences in the following sections.

Search engine marketing

SEM comprises both organic marketing and paid advertising (PPC):

>> **Organic:** SEM is organic when a link to your website, blog, or online store naturally appears in search results; you're not paying anyone for that placement. The only way to increase your site's organic search engine ranking is to engage in search engine optimization (SEO), as discussed in Chapter 8.

>> **PPC:** SEM is PPC when you pay to have a clickable ad appear in a prominent location in the search results. You've probably noticed that when you conduct a search on Google, some of the search results at the top of the page are flagged as ads, whereas those farther down the page (organic results) are not.

Pay-per-click advertising

PPC has no organic component and isn't limited to search engines. Your ads may appear in search results, on social media channels, or on other people's or organizations' websites or blogs. Every major search engine offers PPC advertising, including Google (https://ads.google.com) and Yahoo! (create a free Yahoo! account and sign up for its Ad or Ad Groups to create ads on Yahoo!). Bing and Duck Duck Go both offer PPC through Microsoft Advertising (https://about.ads.microsoft.com/en-us).

The process of creating a PPC marketing campaign differs among providers but generally follows this pattern:

1. Set up an account, which involves specifying your desired payment method.

2. Create and name your campaign. You can have multiple campaigns running at the same time.

3. Choose a goal for your campaign. Do you want to increase sales, generate leads, drive traffic to your website, or increase brand awareness and reach?

   TIP

   If none of the goals applies to you, you can opt out of selecting a goal and choose to run your campaign without guidance.

4. Select a campaign type. Google Ads, for example, enables you to choose Search Network, Display Network, Shopping, Video, or Universal App (see Figure 15-1).

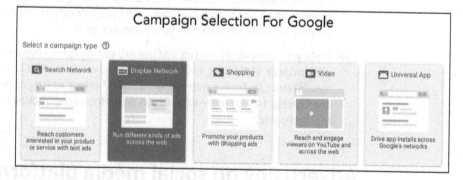

FIGURE 15-1: Google Ads PPC campaign types.

5. Specify the audience you want to target.

6. Create your ad, using the tools provided by the platform.

7. Set your budget — the total amount of money you're willing to spend on the campaign.

8. Choose the keywords you want to bid on. The keywords you choose help the search engine determine how relevant your ad is to what a user is searching for at any time.

9. Specify your maximum bid for each keyword. Your bid determines how likely your ad is to appear whenever someone searches for that word or something related to it.

TIP

Here are a few tips for creating an effective PPC campaign:

>> Choose an ad platform that will display your ad to your target customers. If you're marketing to an audience that's probably concerned about search engines such as Google collecting and sharing their data, Duck Duck Go would be the better choice.

>> Carefully research keywords, as explained in Chapter 8. Keywords need to be popular and relevant so that your ad will appear on the screens of people who are likely to act on it.

>> Optimize your ad for mobile platforms, and if your ad is sending people to your website or blog, make sure that those sites are optimized for mobile too. If you're not optimizing for mobile devices, you're missing out on half the market — maybe more, because people check their mobile devices far more frequently than they do their desktops or laptops.

>> Before creating a new campaign, specify your primary goal for the campaign. Do you want to increase traffic to your website or blog, increase sales, increase brand awareness and reach, create mutually beneficial partnerships, or promote an app? Some platforms guide you through the process of creating effective ads based on your campaign goal.

>> Track your campaign's metrics and use A/B testing to improve each ad's performance. (*A/B testing* involves creating two versions of an ad or targeting two different audiences with the same ad and seeing which performs better; see Chapter 14.) For more information on metrics, see "Tracking Results" later in this chapter.

Advertising on social media platforms

Like SEM, social media marketing encompasses both PPC and organic marketing — publishing and sharing great content and engaging with followers and fans. In Chapter 13, I focus on the organic marketing aspect of social media. My focus here is on the paid advertising opportunities on social media platforms.

Every major social media platform features some form of paid advertising, including Facebook (https://www.facebook.com/business/ads), Instagram (https://business.instagram.com/advertising), LinkedIn (https://business.linkedin.com/marketing-solutions/ads), YouTube (https://www.youtube.com/ads), and Twitter (https://ads.twitter.com).

Each social media platform has its own approach to creating and launching a digital advertising campaign. In the following sections, I offer guidance on using paid advertising on Instagram and Facebook so that you have a general understanding of the process.

Promoting your Instagram posts

Assuming that you have an Instagram business account, you can promote your posts to extend your reach. You can switch a personal account to a business (professional) account by taking the following steps:

1. **Click the Settings icon, select Account, and choose Switch to Professional Account.**

2. **Choose the category that best describes your business.**

3. **Select Business.**

   You have an Instagram business account. See Chapter 13 for general guidance on using Instagram.

By converting to a business account, you unlock two important features: View Insights and Promote. Whenever you post a photo on Instagram, you see two options: View Insights or Post.

Click View Insights to access the following information:

>> **Accounts reached:** This number represents the total number of Instagram users who were able to view your post, broken down by followers and nonfollowers.

>> **Content interactions:** This number includes likes, comments, messages, shares, saves, and replies. Each interaction someone has with your post is *engagement*, which is an important metric to track.

>> **Total followers:** This metric reflects trends across your followers when you have at least 100 followers. Insights include growth (number of followers gained or lost), top locations of followers, followers' age range, and the times they're most active on Instagram.

You can improve these numbers by creating a sponsored post. To promote an existing Instagram post, follow these steps:

1. **Go to your profile.**

2. **Tap the post you'd like to promote.**

3. **Below the post's image, tap Promote.**

4. **Enter your promotion preferences (including goal, audience, duration, and budget), and tap Next.**

5. **If you're prompted to link to a Facebook account (because Facebook owns Instagram), you can do so now or tap Skip.**

   If you tap Skip, you won't be prompted again to link to a Facebook account.

6. **Tap Create Promotion.**

   Your ad is submitted to Instagram for approval and begins running as soon as it's approved.

You can also promote a new post by toggling on the Create a Promotion option before sharing the post.

Creating and running a Facebook ad

To create a Facebook ad, you first need to create a Facebook page for your business and set up a valid payment method. (Search Facebook's help system to find out more about creating a page and setting up a payment method.) Then you can use Facebook's Ads Manager to create an ad by following these steps:

1. **Log in to Facebook, navigate to your business page, click Ad Center (near the top), click All Ads (under Create Ad, on the left), and click Ads Manager.**

2. **Click Create a New Ad Campaign, and enter a name for the campaign.**

   An ad campaign can contain one or more ads (an *ad set*).

3. **Choose an objective for your ad campaign, such as Send People to Your Website, Boost Your Posts, Promote Your Page, or Reach People Near Your Business.**

   Your choice enables Facebook to present the options that are likely to be most effective for you.

4. **Enter the details Facebook prompts you to enter and click the Create Ad section.**

5. **Choose your audience.**

   Facebook displays a map with numerous options for specifying an audience: location, age, gender, language, interests, behaviors, connections, and so on.

   Save your audience settings to use for future campaigns.

TIP

6. **Set your budget.**

   You can set a daily or lifetime budget. With a daily budget, Facebook paces your ad spend over the entire day. With a lifetime budget, it paces your spending over the duration of the campaign.

REMEMBER

   The minimum daily budget is $1 and must be double your cost per click bid so that you can have at least two ads during the chosen period.

7. **Create your ad, using Facebook's tools.**

   This process depends on the objective you chose in step 3, your design preferences, and other factors.

   Be sure to adhere to Facebook's guidelines pertaining to image dimensions and character count, which are available through the help system.

REMEMBER

8. **Specify how you'd like to display your ad: Desktop Newsfeed, Mobile Newsfeed, or Desktop Right Column.**

   Your choice depends primarily on the device you think your audience will be using most often when they see your ad.

9. **Choose Place Your Order to launch your campaign.**

As soon as your ad is running, you can begin to track metrics related to it. Head back to Ad Center (see step 1), click All Ads, and click the ad you want to track. See the later section "Tracking Results" for more information about the metrics Facebook allows you to track.

Advertising through popular podcasts

You can incorporate paid advertisements into podcasts by creating a script for a podcast or paying the host to create content that promotes your brand. In this section, I offer guidance on how to find podcasters and work with them to optimize results. (See Chapter 12 for more about podcasting.)

REMEMBER

Audio advertising contains no visual element, so it isn't the best fit if your product relies heavily on visuals or is difficult to promote with audio alone.

Finding a suitable podcaster

The best way to find a podcaster to promote your brand is to check out podcasts on major hosts, such as iTunes and Spotify. Look at the list of podcasts that are charting in your industry to see which ones may be the best fit. This information is public on all major platforms. When you find a podcast that seems to be suitable, check the podcaster's profile or the show's page notes for contact information.

TIP

If you don't have the time or focus to listen to hundreds of podcasts to find a podcaster who's open to promoting your brand, consider using a matchmaker service such as PodcastOne (https://www.podcastone.com) or PodBean (https://www.podbean.com). On each site, go to the Advertise or Reach Out to Us section to contact a representative about advertising opportunities.

Optimizing your podcast advertising results

TIP

Here are some insights that will help you get the most bang for your buck when partnering with podcasters:

>> When choosing a podcast, consider the demographics of its listeners, and make sure that they align with your customer base.

>> Check the podcast's reach — the total number of active listeners. You can ask the podcast or referral network for listenership stats.

>> Ask about your ad's length and placement. How long will your ad be, and at what point in the podcast will it play — intro (preroll), middle (midroll), or outro (postroll)? The *preroll* is the beginning of the show; the *midroll* of the show is an advertisement break; and the *postroll* is the end of the show. The difference in advertisement placements is the likelihood of listeners playing your ad or skipping it. You can incorporate more than one ad into an episode. Midrolls have a higher chance of conversion, but they're usually more expensive. Evaluate your budget and goals before choosing.

>> Ask whether your ad will be the only one on the show (which would be ideal). If it won't be the only ad, how many others will there be?

>> Collaborate closely with the podcaster to develop a script for your ad that's true to your brand and suitable for the content of the podcast.

Paying influencers and other talent to promote your brand

One of the newest and most popular forms of paid advertising involves the use of social media *influencers* — people who have large followings and are able to sway people's opinions. The key to successful influencer marketing is picking the right person (within your budget). When you're looking for the right influencer, consider the following qualities:

>> **Relevance:** Choose an influencer who connects with the audience you want to reach. If you're building a brand around cookware, for example, you may want to consider a popular chef.

>> **Reach:** Reach is a measure of the person's audience — friends, followers, and fans. Generally, the greater the reach, the greater the cost.

>> **Engagement:** Engagement is a measure of the degree of interaction between the influencer and their followers, as indicated by the number of likes, shares, comments, and so on. A good engagement rate varies from platform to platform. Anything higher than 1 percent is good on Twitter, for example, whereas Instagram would require a rating above 7 percent.

>> **Personality, mission, and values:** Choose an influencer who aligns with your brand's personality, mission, and values. If your brand is all about having fun in the great outdoors while preserving and restoring natural habitats, choose someone who's fun and committed to conservation.

>> **Connections with other influencers:** Generally, an influencer who has connections to many other influencers is better than one who has only a few, but also consider who these influencers are. Do they align with your brand's personality, mission, and values?

>> **Platform(s):** The influencer you choose should have a strong presence on the social media platform(s) favored by your target audience. If you're trying to appeal to people who tend to get their information from YouTube, for example, you'll want to choose an influential and well-connected YouTuber.

>> **Content quality and alignment:** Check out the content the influencer has posted in the past. Does it meet your quality standards? Does it reflect your brand's personality and support its mission and values? Does it resonate with your brand story?

>> **Soft skills:** Soft skills include communication and collaboration, a pleasant demeanor, and a strong track record of delivering quality content on time.

>> **Cost (including any agent fees):** Costs vary considerably and are based primarily on most of the preceding criteria, especially reach, engagement, and platform. When you're choosing among multiple candidates, you choice comes down to what you can afford.

MICROINFLUENCER CAMPAIGNS

For my Girl Gang the Label brand, we pay microinfluencers (influencers who have a smaller number of followers who are highly engaged) to work with our brand and promote our clothing. I look for people who already wear our products or are interested in the industry we're in — in this case, female empowerment brands.

After I've identified micro influencers we want to pay and activate campaigns with, I put together an overall budget and divide it among the various influencers we're working with. I offer to pay them for their time as well as provide them free products and a unique discount code that they can share if they'd like.

The great thing about running campaigns like this one is that you can spread your budget across multiple creators rather than work with one premium influencer who may exceed your budget. I have the most success with influencers who align with my customer avatars and are paid for their time.

WARNING

Don't let lack of money discourage you from engaging in influencer marketing, which doesn't need to break your budget. You can become your own influencer, or you may be able to recruit a great influencer who's willing to work for free products or services and an opportunity to use your product or service to increase their influence and further their career. Finding the right influencer to partner with is all about making connections, starting conversations, and negotiating mutually beneficial arrangements.

See Chapter 13 for more about teaming up with influencers.

Running TV and radio ads

TV and to a lesser extent radio traditionally have been the go-to media channels for reaching large, diverse audiences and delivering results quickly. They can be expensive, however. You pay production costs to create high-quality ads and then pay the media channels to run them. In addition, you need to run the ads often; the audience needs to be exposed to the ad repeatedly for it to have much impact.

REMEMBER

If you decide to add TV or radio ads to your marketing plan, give careful consideration to the networks your target audience is likely to watch/listen to and the times of day they're likely to tune in.

I strongly recommend that you hire a skilled media production business or consultant to produce your ad. A homemade ad will come across as a cheap, do-it-yourself project that will reflect poorly on your brand. You can find plenty of TV and radio commercial production businesses by searching online for "TV commercial production" or "radio ad production." Most of these companies have samples posted on their sites, so you can check out their work. Some production companies not only help you produce quality commercials, but also help you choose the right media channels for distribution.

Another way to track down TV and radio commercial production companies is to contact the person in charge of selling advertising time on the network or station and ask them for recommendations. You can usually obtain their contact information by visiting the network's or station's website, scrolling to the bottom, and clicking the Advertise with Us or Contact Us link.

TIP

As in any advertising medium, consistency is key when you're trying to extend your brand's reach and strengthen its identity. Consistency applies to the look and feel of the ads, the music or other audio, the presentation (action, dialogue, testimonial, voice-over, and so on), characters or people in the ads (such as the spokesperson), and so on. If you're doing several different broadcast ads for the same brand, consistency is even more important.

Advertising in print media

Print media are paper publications, including books, newspapers, magazines, journals, and newsletters. I recommend not doing much advertising in print media unless, of course, everyone in your target market reads a certain publication that sells advertising space. When creating a print ad, you have three areas of focus:

>> **Headline:** Write a succinct, attention-grabbing headline.

>> **Design:** Develop an attractive design using your brand's logo, color scheme, and font and other graphic elements to convey your brand identity and any other visual message you want to send. See Chapter 6 for details about developing a logo and color scheme and choosing a font.

>> **Copy:** Write additional content that highlights the benefits of your brand and presents the desired call to action — what you want the person viewing the ad to think or do in response to it. Note that some print ads contain no copy, relying solely on the headline and graphics to communicate the message.

Working with Advertising Agencies

If you have deep pockets and a desire for an ambitious, comprehensive, and well-coordinated marketing campaign, consider teaming up with an advertising agency. Advertising agencies offer several benefits, including the following:

>> **Experience:** Advertising agencies have numerous clients in a variety of industries, so they already know what works and what doesn't. When you're doing the work yourself, you're learning by trial and error.

>> **Expertise:** Agencies know all the strategies, tactics, tools, and technologies available and can create a comprehensive marketing plan that cherry-picks what's best for promoting your brand.

>> **Relationships with media outlets:** Agencies have an inside track to journalists and others who can promote your brand effectively.

>> **Time and focus:** Agencies' sole focus is promoting your brand. When you're doing the work yourself, you have to divide your time and attention among all the tasks involved in building and launching your brand and managing your business.

Even if you don't have deep pockets, you can benefit from other people's marketing and advertising expertise by hiring skilled freelancers. You can search the web for people who do advertising on specific platforms, such as Facebook and Instagram, or search a general freelancer marketplace, such as Upwork (https://www.upwork.com).

Knowing when to outsource

I think that consulting an advertising agency or expert is a good idea, even if you do it only once, so you can observe what they do to promote a brand. The decision to outsource some or all of your marketing to an outside firm or person, however, generally boils down to budget and need. If you have the money to hire a firm, and you don't have the time and expertise to do the work yourself, or if you start to do the work yourself and feel that you're in over your head, the choice is obvious: Hire a professional. If you don't have the money to hire an expert, the choice is also obvious: You must do the job yourself.

TIP

If you're running a mom-and-pop operation, consider starting a small, highly focused advertising campaign on your own. As you grow and build capital in your business, consider investing in professional services. You can start by interviewing several candidates to find out what they would do to promote your brand (which is another great way to pick the brains of experts). Better yet, schedule a one- or two-hour workshop to see what sorts of ideas they come up with, which is a great way to evaluate their creativity and how well you work with them.

Choosing the right advertising agency for your brand

You can find tens of thousands of advertising agencies simply by searching the web for "advertising agency," and you can narrow your search to local agencies by specifying your location. You can also ask for referrals from business owners you know or by posting a request for referrals in a business-oriented discussion forum. Another option is to identify advertisements you like and then contact the businesses that ran the ads to find out who created them.

When you have a few candidates, use the following criteria to evaluate them and make your choice:

>> Experience in your industry
>> Expertise (deep knowledge of advertising strategies and the latest techniques, tools, and technologies)
>> Creativity
>> Personality (would you look forward to collaborating with them?)
>> Cost

Tracking Results

Whether you're working with an advertising agency or working as your own advertising agency, be sure to track results so that you know what's working and what's not and can evaluate the impact of any changes you make to improve your campaign's performance. Follow these steps to track results:

1. **Choose the metrics you want to use to measure the success of your campaign.**

    Metrics vary based on each campaign's goals and include sales volume, website visits, click-through rate, engagement, and number of leads generated.

2. **Identify the current benchmark for each metric, if available.**

These values establish a baseline for evaluating the success of your campaign. One benchmark might be weekly sales volume or number of new website visitors daily.

3. **Set a goal for each metric — values you can use to determine whether the campaign is successful.**

   Another option is to use return on investment as your goal. You might set a goal of increasing revenue by $2 for every $1 spent on advertising.

Some metrics can be difficult to track, especially when you're running print (newspaper and magazine) or broadcast ads (TV and radio). If you're doing PPC, you can access a dashboard through your PPC provider to track common metrics, such as total clicks, cost per click, and so on.

Common PPC metrics include the following:

» **Impressions:** The number of times the ad has been displayed. The people your ad is reaching don't need to click or respond to the advertisement to have it count as an impression. You're not charged for impressions.

» **Clicks:** The number of times the ad has been clicked, even if it doesn't result in a sale, captured lead, or other desired action. You're charged for every click.

» **Cost:** The amount of money you've invested so far on the selected campaign, which is calculated by multiplying the number of clicks by the cost per click.

» **Conversions:** The number of times a click has resulted in a customer's buying something from you, visiting your website, subscribing to your newsletter, downloading your e-book, or doing whatever else your call to action prompted them to do. Conversion rate is a great metric for evaluating the success of a campaign.

» **Click-through rate:** (The number of clicks per impressions multiplied by 100. If your ad was displayed 250 times (250 impressions) and was clicked 100 times, your click-through rate is 40 percent: 100/250 = 0.4 and 0.4 x 100 = 40%.

Consider your first campaign to be a dry run. Then examine the campaign's metrics to see whether they spark any ideas for improving those metrics.

TIP

Create an A/B test for ad campaigns. Continue experimenting until you're getting the desired results.

Chapter **16**

Building a Vibrant Community around Your Brand

What if I were to tell you that you can build a strong brand without spending a single penny on advertising, marketing, or public relations (PR)? You'd probably think I was pulling your leg, but it's true: You *can* build a strong brand solely through word-of-mouth advertising. You do it by building an enthusiastic and active community around your brand.

Now, that's easier said than done. Anyone can create a Google ad, but building a community is a huge challenge, involving networking, communications, relationship building, and sometimes social activism. (After all, people generally rally around a common interest or cause.) Your brand must be the catalyst that brings community members together and inspires them to become brand evangelists, spreading the word about your brand to grow and strengthen the community.

How do you do *that*? Well, you're about to find out.

Starting with a Sense of Purpose

Purpose is like a magnet that pulls people together, points them in the same direction, and enables people to play a part in something that's bigger than themselves.

When I created my Girl Gang the Label brand, I wasn't interested so much in selling merchandise as I was in building a thriving community around female empowerment. I knew in the back or my mind that success in building community would eventually translate into profitable ventures; whenever people unite behind a common cause, wealth-building opportunities tend to pop up. But generating revenue wasn't and isn't the brand's primary purpose. Its purpose is to empower women.

REMEMBER

A community that has a higher purpose is far more resilient and scalable than a community built around a product, service, or business. The brand's purpose serves as the focal point of the community, enabling the brand to branch out in different directions, as long as all those directions are consistent with its purpose. Because the Girl Gang community is committed to empowering women, I can grow the brand with any number of products and services aligned with that mission.

To build a community around your brand, come up with a clear sense of purpose — something you're passionate about and believe that you can get people excited about. Your brand's purpose is its mission. When you're formulating your brand's mission or vision statement, as discussed in Chapter 3, you're defining its purpose. Here are a few examples:

Coca-Cola: Refresh the world. Make a difference.

Nike: Bring inspiration and innovation to every athlete in the world.

Starbucks: Inspire and nurture the human spirit — one person, one cup, and one neighborhood at a time.

Disney: Entertain, inform and inspire people around the globe through the power of unparalleled storytelling, reflecting the iconic brands, creative minds and innovative technologies that make ours the world's premier entertainment company.

Zappos: Deliver happiness.

Formulating a community-building strategy

Having a strong sense of purpose and instilling that sense of purpose in others are two very different things. To build a community around your brand, you need to figure out how to bridge that gap — how you're going to motivate people to rally around your brand's purpose. You need a community-building strategy.

Take the following steps to begin formulating a strategy for building community around your brand's purpose:

1. **Describe the impact you want your brand to have on the community your brand will serve.**

   How do you want your brand to influence people's thoughts and behaviors? I envision a community, for example, in which women support one another and collaborate in ways that empower them to achieve ever-increasing levels of self-fulfillment and joy.

2. **Identify the characteristics of your brand that make it uniquely qualified to fulfill its mission.**

   Characteristics may include your brand's name, identity/personality, mission, and core values (see Chapter 3); the products/services you offer; your brand's points of differentiation (what makes your brand different and better); the education, experience, and interests of the people in your organization; and so on. What you're looking for is anything you can use to demonstrate your brand's alignment with and commitment to its higher purpose.

3. **Start a list of what you can do to start building a community around your brand's purpose.**

   Here are a few examples:

   - Start with your inner circle — your team (if you have one), family members, and friends. Every community starts small.

   - Increase your presence on social media with an emphasis on making your brand's higher purpose a bigger part of what you do.

   - Get people actively involved. Recruit others to participate and contribute to the cause. Encourage them to share their stories about how they promoted the cause. When people have some skin in the game, they begin to feel a greater sense of belonging and purpose.

   - Spend time with community members, especially leaders in the community, to demonstrate that you value them.

Nurturing shared values

Diversity is great, but people tend to gravitate toward others who share their values and away from people who don't. Even people who value diversity tend to shun those who don't, which is kind of weird. How can you convince people that you're right when you don't interact with them? Be that as it may, when you're building community, acknowledge the fact that people generally hang out with others who share their values. So to build a community, you must recognize the values of the people who will ultimately form the community and nurture those values, whatever they may be.

Have you ever seen commercials or visited the websites of real estate investment gurus who sell books and host seminars on getting rich by investing in real estate? They're usually trying to cater to people who are driven by the promise of money and possessions. They wear a lot of bling and show off their cars, boats, and private airplanes — all presumably made possible by the profits they earned investing in real estate. When they build communities of real estate investors, one of the shared values they nurture is materialism.

To build your community, you must answer these questions:

>> What are the shared values of community members that I want to nurture?

>> How am I going to nurture those values?

To answer those questions, follow these steps:

1. **Deepen your relationship with your customers so that they'll be more willing to open up to you about what they value most.**

   Engage them in conversations about their lives, their personal and professional goals, and how they define success. Most important, listen to them.

2. **Review your brand's values (see Chapter 3), and identify areas where your brand's values align with those of your customers.**

   Throughout this process, be prepared to adjust your brand's values to bring them more in line with the shared values of the community.

3. **Start a list of ways you can demonstrate your brand's commitment to those values.**

   Here are a few ideas:

   - Think, act, and express yourself in ways that are consistent with those values. Don't just talk the talk; also walk the walk. People will pick up on any hint of hypocrisy.

   - Share stories of community members demonstrating their commitment to the community's values.

- Publish blog posts and social media content that highlight and promote the community's values.

- If you have employees, allocate some time for them to engage in activities that support what the community values.

- Support a common cause (see the next section).

Support a common cause

One of the best ways to reinforce your brand's mission — its purpose — while strengthening and growing the community around it is to support a common cause and possibly even rally community members around it. Choose a cause that aligns with what your brand and the community value. Here are a few examples:

» Clothing brand Ivory Ella donates 10 percent of its annual profits to saving elephants.

» Home Depot helps military veterans secure housing, provides natural-disaster relief to communities in need, and helps people become skilled tradespeople.

» During the COVID-19 pandemic, online pet-supplies retailer Chewy partnered with The Humane Society of the United States, donating and distributing $1 million in pet food and supplies to help families keep their pets.

» American fashion designer Tory Burch launched the Tory Burch Foundation to help women entrepreneurs by providing access to capital, entrepreneurial education, and mentoring and networking opportunities.

» Norwegian Cruise Line partnered with the Ocean Conservancy to work toward cleaning up and protecting the oceans.

» My brand, Girl Gang, has a community on social media dedicated to supporting female-owned businesses and female artisans.

Increasingly, people are choosing brands that are committed to a cause. Several sports organizations are committed to ending racism. Numerous organizations are working to reduce the effects of pollution and global warming. Many groups help military veterans and the homeless. Some brands are even built on a cause. The eco-conscious clothing company Everlane (https://www.everlane.com), for example, is in the forefront of the movement to reduce the use of plastics in the fashion industry by creating products made mostly from recycled plastic.

Creating Safe Spaces

To build a community, you must make members feel welcome, safe, and heard. Take the following steps to create and manage safe spaces (online or offline) for members:

1. **Post clear policies, such as the following:**

   - No abusive language is allowed.
   - No explicit or offensive content is permitted.
   - Respect others.
   - Bullying is not allowed.
   - Stay on topic.
   - Don't post anything as fact that you haven't thoroughly researched.

   A podcast support group I belong to requires anyone who shares an image of a traumatic event to flag it with a trigger warning, notifying others that the image may be upsetting. This policy allows members to connect and share their stories freely, yet avoid seeing something that may make them uncomfortable.

2. **Greet new people, and welcome them to the community.**

   See "Welcoming newbies" later in this chapter for details.

3. **Monitor the safe spaces you established for any policy violations.**

4. **Enforce your policies.**

   For minor offenses, you may want to start with a gentle but firm reminder of the policy, but if the bad behavior persists, you may need to block or banish the offender from the community.

REMEMBER

If you have an in-person meetup or are hosting an event (see Chapter 11), have ground rules in place, along with a plan for enforcing those rules and securing the safety of attendees.

Stimulating Engagement

Whenever you're at the center building a community, you're like the host at a dinner party. You're responsible for ensuring that everyone's comfortable and having a good time. You meet and greet guests, show them around, introduce anyone who's new to the group, and keep the conversation rolling. If the sizzle starts to fizzle, you change up the music or engage guests in a game of charades or Pictionary. Your goal is to facilitate and stimulate positive interactions so that everyone has a good time and feels enriched and connected by the time the party winds down.

When you're building a community, your objective is similar, but the group is larger. You may not have the time and energy to meet, greet, and interact with everyone; besides, that's not healthy for the community. You want to build a community that's pretty much self-sufficient where all members feel welcome, contribute to the discussion, ask and answer questions, work together to meet common goals, and welcome new members warmly. All you need to do is give them a little nudge now and then and apply the spark to ignite discussion. In this section, I show you how.

REMEMBER

Moderate discussions, especially on topics that are controversial or sensitive. You don't want to act like the thought police, squelching lively interaction, but you don't want to let things get out of hand either.

Welcoming newbies

When people join a community, they're at their most vulnerable stage of participation. Any uncomfortable encounter or experience could send them running in the opposite direction, so try to make them feel welcome.

Some social media platforms make it easy for administrators to welcome new members. If you have a Facebook group, at the top of the Add Members box is a list of new members. You click the Write Post button next to that list, and a dialog box pops up with a welcome message followed by the entire list of new members. You can edit the welcome message and add photos, videos, or other content. When you're done editing, click the Post button.

I strongly encourage you to go above and beyond a generic welcome message. Ask new members to introduce themselves to the group; then comment on each introduction. Encourage everyone in the group to welcome the newbies. Offer to answer their questions and address their concerns. Ask them to chime in on an ongoing discussion or share their story of how they first encountered the brand.

TIP

Consider welcoming new members with a gift — such as a free sample, a discount, or a branded sticker or pen — or include them in a drawing when your group meets a specified membership goal.

Asking thought-provoking questions

I'm always surprised when I hear from bloggers about the low engagement numbers on their blogs and find out that they never ask what their readers think. They post great content, but they pass up the opportunity to add a simple statement at the end of each post to open the floor to discussion — something along the lines of "Post a comment to let us know what you think" or "We'd like to know what you think. Please share your thoughts by posting a comment."

On your brand's blog or social media accounts, you can spark a lively discussion simply by sharing a brief post followed by a thought-provoking question.

REMEMBER

What you're after here is *user-generated content* — text, images, audio, or video posted to your blog or social media accounts by people other than you. Your brand benefits from having fresh, relevant content that you don't have to invest time and effort in creating. As fresh content is added, it boosts your brand's profile in the eyes of search engines, which can increase that content's search engine ranking, drawing more eyes to your brand.

Sharing user-generated content

Speaking of user-generated content, whenever someone inside or outside your community posts content that's relevant and interesting, share it with your community. Sharing content demonstrates that you're listening to what others have to say and are generous in sharing your platform, even with outsiders. When you share content posted by community members, you shine the spotlight on them and provide an opportunity for their content to spread across your platform.

TIP

When sharing user-generated content, be sure to include a comment about it (and a link to it, if appropriate), explaining why you think it's of interest and value to the community and thanking the person who posted it. Suppose that you're building a community around ocean conservation, and someone named Sheryl Green posts a piece on her blog about a beach cleanup she organized in Galveston, Texas. You could share that post with a comment like this: "Here's a shout-out to Sheryl Green from Galveston, Texas, who recently organized a beach cleanup and collected more than two tons of plastic! Thanks to Sheryl and her volunteers for doing their part to preserve our beautiful beaches." If Sheryl finds out that you're sharing your platform with her, what are the chances that she'll join your community and share her platform with you?

Responding to questions and comments

One of the easiest and most obvious ways to stimulate engagement is to respond to community members who post questions and comments. Your responses demonstrate that you're listening and you care.

WARNING

Before posting a response, be sure that you clearly understand the question or comment. Ask questions to clarify. Then compose a thoughtful response. If you have an emotional reaction to a comment, wait until you're ready to respond rationally. Far too often, people post knee-jerk responses before they fully understand a person's intended meaning, which can trigger pointless arguments. See "Remaining Positive At All Times" later in this chapter.

TIP

Make your responses personal by signing off with your name, even when the response is coming from the brand. Clarifying who's talking gives your responses a more personal touch.

Tagging people in posts

One way to engage with community members and possibly extend your brand's reach into other communities in your industry and related industries is to tag people in your social media posts. Tagging someone links the person to the post and notifies them that they've been tagged.

The person you tag in a post, photo, or video must be a member of the social media platform you're using. Assuming that the person is a member on the platform you're posting to, simply link their username to the post or photo. On Instagram, for example, post the photo with the person you want to tag, click the three dots above the photo, select Edit and then Tag People, start typing the person's name or username, and select the name from the list that pops up.

TIP

Friend or follow influencers in your community and industry in general, and occasionally tag them in posts that present them in a positive light. Tagging can initiate a conversation between you and the person you tagged, generating interesting content for your community while potentially giving you some exposure to the other person's community.

WARNING

Don't overdo tagging, and don't tag people in photos or posts unless you're absolutely sure that they'll be happy you tagged them. If you have any doubt, contact the person first and ask whether it's okay.

Taking a poll

Taking a poll is a great way to find out more about the people in your community and engage them in a group activity that brings them together and sparks discussion.

You can create polls on your website or blog by using a polling plug-in, such as Responsive Poll or WPForms for WordPress. Also, most social media platforms (including Facebook, Instagram, and Twitter) have a feature that makes it easy to conduct polls. Check the platform's help system for specific guidance.

Recognizing and rewarding community leaders

A community is only as good as its most active and influential members are motivated, so be sure to recognize and reward your community's leaders. Here are a few options to consider:

>> **Public appreciation** may be the most powerful way to reward leaders, singling them out for going above and beyond to deliver value to the community. You can show public appreciation by posting to your blog or social media accounts or acknowledging leaders at in-person events.

>> **Free items and discounts** are great to reward community members for serving the community and strengthening your brand. They're also great for motivating other members to play a greater role.

>> **Exclusive access to products, services, and events** is another powerful reward and motivator. Consider reserving this access for community leaders in your inner circle. The more exclusive you make it, the bigger the perceived reward.

Empowering Your Community

Community is all about working together to improve the lives of all community members in some way and enabling community members to achieve their personal and professional goals.

To empower your community, post and share content and stimulate discussion that enriches and inspires community members, helping them solve problems and overcome challenges relevant to the community. By "relevant to the community," I mean relevant to the context of your community's overarching theme, such as fashion, innovation, camping, fitness, sports, video gaming, women in business, environmentalism, or whatever it may be.

Here are a couple of specific ways to empower your community:

>> **Provide information, tools, and tips for community members to better their lives.** At Girl Gang, we interview ambitious career women and feature their favorite books and podcasts. These interviews inform and inspire community members, and suggest additional resources (books and podcasts) that offer more guidance and inspiration to help them achieve their goals.

>> **Co-create with your community.** Tap your community for ideas. Are you struggling to decide which design to use for your new packaging? Take a poll. Need ideas for improving your product? Ask. Engaging your community in the creative process and your business decisions empowers members and gives them an important role in your brand's success. It makes your brand *their* brand.

Remaining Positive At All Times

Building, maintaining, and growing a vibrant community takes time and effort. It can be rewarding, but it can also be frustrating. People don't always behave and interact the way you want them to. They don't always live up to your expectations.

They may even go negative, attacking others in the community or lashing out at you and your brand.

Through it all, you must remain positive. Act with *grace* — elegance or beauty of form, manner, motion, and action. You may need to be firm at times, but be firm gracefully, without anger or bitterness. Don't let others drag you down to their level. Remain above the fray even when you're in the middle of it.

REMEMBER

You set the tone for your community, so set a positive tone, and model the behaviors you expect from other community members. Here are a few specific suggestions for creating and maintaining a positive tone across your community:

>> Compliment, praise, and thank community members for their contributions.

>> Acknowledge achievements.

>> Encourage members to collaborate with one another and play a greater role in community activities.

>> Don't complain yourself, and encourage others not to vent in your public forum.

>> Be sensitive as you work to address members' needs and challenges.

4
Feeding and Caring for Your Brand

Extend your brand's reach beyond the niche market in which it started. Conduct a brand audit, create a plan to scale your brand, and (if desired), outsource some responsibilities to lighten your load.

Build customer loyalty and earn customers for life by rewarding loyalty, surveying customers to find out what you can do better and different, targeting offers to different customer tiers, and transforming customers into brand advocates.

Protect your brand against external threats from competitors and any upstarts seeking to capitalize on your creativity and innovation. Trademark your brand, patent your ideas, and seek legal advice at the first signs of trouble.

IN THIS CHAPTER

» **Scoping out your scaling options**

» **Auditing your brand to see how it's performing**

» **Developing a plan to increase brand reach and awareness**

» **Scaling up production while maintaining quality standards**

» **Beefing up your staff so you can focus on higher-level tasks**

Chapter **17**

Scaling Your Brand Identity

You built a successful brand. Congratulations! Now what?

You can rest on your laurels and let your brand continue to generate revenue, or you can scale it up to make it even more successful. If you just let it be, sales and revenue could increase on their own, but it's just as likely — if not more likely — that sales and revenue will plateau, taper off, and eventually decline to a point at which the brand could be declared dead. Like most things in life, a brand that isn't growing is dying.

Consider Amazon. Jeff Bezos started it as an online bookstore and built it into the number-one online retailer in the world. (Walmart is bigger, but it's a hybrid online/ bricks-and-mortar retailer.) Did Bezos rest on his laurels? Did he settle for being a hugely successful online retailer? Heck, no! He continued to expand — into groceries, streaming audio and video, movies and television series, book publishing, cloud computing services, and more. He's even dabbling in outer-space tourism.

When he was starting out, Bezos was no different from any other entrepreneur; he had a vision, some management skills, and access to capital. What he did, you can do too — maybe not on such a grand scale, but you can scale your brand up and out to increase its reach and its impact. In this chapter, I offer some guidance on how to do just that.

Surveying Different Approaches to Scaling a Brand

Scaling a brand simply means growing it, and you can scale your brand in a variety of ways:

>> **Ramp up your marketing efforts.** Do more of what you're already doing: building community on social media, advertising, blogging, podcasting, pursuing promising partnerships . . . everything I discuss in earlier chapters.

>> **Set up an affiliate program.** Recruit people to sell your products or services, and pay them a small commission. An affiliate program is a great way to build a sales force without having to go through the formalities of hiring and managing a dedicated sales team.

>> **Pursue new market segments.** Throughout this book, I encourage you to focus on specific markets for maximum impact. Well, now may be the time to add some new market segments to the mix.

>> **Add new products or services.** Expand your product/service line to offer customers more. Just make sure that the products and services you add are consistent with your brand.

>> **Expand into other businesses or industries.** Follow the lead of Amazon and Virgin by adding new business units. You may not have the bandwidth to start your own airline or music streaming business, but you can branch out into different product or service categories.

WARNING

Don't lose focus. I recommend ramping up your marketing efforts to promote what you already have in place before branching out into new product lines, businesses, or industries.

Conducting a Brand Audit

REMEMBER

Before you invest one iota of effort in scaling your brand, conduct an audit to evaluate your brand's current condition and determine whether it's performing up to your expectations. Scaling a brand makes no sense if it's not already headed in the right direction; you'll just end up going farther in the wrong direction.

A brand audit provides insight into whether your brand's image (in the minds of customers) aligns with the brand identity you envisioned and how well your brand is performing in the market compared with its competitors and your expectations.

Recognizing the benefits of a brand audit

Conducting a brand audit offers the following benefits:

TIP

>> Enables you to gauge your brand's performance

>> Reveals any disparity between what customers think and feel about your brand and what you want them to think and feel

Disparity isn't necessarily bad. It could reveal something about your target market that you overlooked. When you encounter a disparity between what customers think and feel and what you want them to think and feel, ask yourself, "Is that a bad thing or a good thing?" These thoughts and feelings may be things you want to nurture to your brand's advantage.

>> Uncovers any inconsistencies in how your brand guidelines are being practiced across your organization (See Chapter 6 for more about brand guidelines.)

>> Highlights your brand's strengths and weaknesses, along with possible improvements you can make to strengthen your brand

>> Identifies any emerging threats and opportunities

Auditing your brand

Take the following steps to conduct your brand audit:

1. **Identify the areas of focus for your brand audit, such as the following:**

   - Your branding goals (see Chapter 4) and whether you're on track to meet those goals

   - The alignment of what your customers think and feel about your brand with what you want them to think and feel

- Threats to your brand posed by competitors, changes in legislation or regulations, or other marketplace challenges

- Threats to your brand internally from people who aren't following your brand guidelines or from a toxic work environment that's reflecting poorly on your brand

- The people you're serving and their needs, desires, and values, which can change over time, creating a disconnect between your brand and the people you're trying to reach

2. **Survey your customers and prospective customers to find out what they think and how they feel about your brand.**

   Ask questions such as the following:

   - What words would you use to describe our brand?

   - How does our brand compare with competing brands?

   - If you were searching online for a brand like ours, what keywords would you use in your search?

   - What could we do to improve our brand?

3. **Survey suppliers, vendors, and any employees to find out what they think and how they feel about your brand.**

   Ask questions such as the following:

   - How would you describe our business culture?

   - What could we do to improve the way we do business?

   - Do we practice what we preach? or Do our business practices align with our stated mission and values? If not, please describe the misalignment.

4. **Review your branding guidelines (see Chapter 6).**

   Identify anything that needs to be changed to achieve better alignment between what people think and feel about your brand and what you want them to think and feel about it.

5. **Review your website, blog, webstore, and other online properties.**

   Determine whether what you're doing online is strengthening or weakening your brand, and highlight any areas that need improvement.

6. **Review your marketing campaigns, paid advertising, and email marketing.**

   Determine whether they're strengthening or weakening your brand and highlight any areas that need improvement.

7. **Examine your market closely.**

   Your aim is to spot potential threats from competitors, regulations, emerging technologies, and anything else that might disrupt your supply chain or other business operations.

8. **Examine your market closely for potential opportunities that would be a good fit for your brand.**

REMEMBER

Although branding is about consistency, your brand audit is about alignment. You're looking for inconsistencies that cause misalignment between what you're doing and what you're trying to accomplish in terms of strengthening your brand.

Before you start to invest time and effort in scaling your brand, address any issues that your audit reveals.

Creating a Scaling Plan

Scaling a brand is like starting one, in that planning helps ensure success. Every scaling plan is a little different, depending on the nature of the industry, business, and brand and on how you're planning to scale — such as by increasing your marketing efforts or adding a new business to your brand. In most cases, a scaling plan should cover the following areas:

>> **Strategy:** Your strategy is how you've decided to scale the brand. Refer to "Surveying Different Approaches to Scaling a Brand" earlier in this chapter.

>> **Goal:** your branding goal (what you hope to accomplish by scaling your brand) and how it aligns with your overall branding goals. (See Chapter 4.)

>> **Management:** Decide who's going to lead the scaling initiative. The person who starts a business often isn't the best candidate to grow the business. If you're currently in charge, be honest: Are you the best person for the job? If you're great at innovation and starting things but not so good at following through, you may want to hire or partner with someone who's better at managing a growing business.

>> **Documented procedures and policies:** Small-business owners often run their businesses without formal, documented procedures and policies in place. Everyone involved just knows what to do or learns through on-the-job training. That approach doesn't work for larger operations. Any scaling plan should include the development of documented procedures and policies so that the business can essentially run itself, without the direct involvement of executive leadership.

>> **Capital:** Small-business owners often finance their own operations, but a growing business often needs capital in the form of grants, debt, or equity:

- *Grants* are free money from government agencies, corporations, people, or not-for-profit organizations that believe in or stand to benefit in some way from what another organization is doing. What's great about grants is that you don't have to pay them back or give up any control of your business.

- *Debt financing* involves borrowing money, usually from a bank, but also potentially from private lenders.

- *Equity financing* involves selling a stake in the business, such as selling shares of stock to investors.

See Chapter 2 for more about finding capital to build or grow a brand.

>> **New technologies:** A new technology can be the driving force behind a business expansion. It may enable you to create better products or lower their cost, improve or automate customer service, or deliver new products or services to the market.

WARNING

As many successful entrepreneurs advise, "Failing to plan is planning to fail." Growth doesn't always lead to success. If scaling isn't planned and managed properly, it can destroy a previously successful company, usually due to cash-flow problems (more cash flowing out than in).

Setting milestones

With plan in hand, establish milestones for all your objectives — everything you need to accomplish to scale your brand, including hiring, documenting procedures and policies, securing financing, and integrating new technologies or methodologies. Milestones enable you to break down large, complex projects into manageable tasks, and they keep you and your team on track and accountable for progress.

REMEMBER

Set a milestone for each step of every objective you must meet, along with a brief description of what must be accomplished (the deliverable) by the specified date. If you're going to hire an assistant to reduce your workload, for example, specify the dates on which you'll start and end the recruiting process, the date by which you'll select candidates to interview, the date by which you'll choose a candidate, and the date by which the person you choose will be in place.

Sourcing products at larger quantities without sacrificing quality

If you're scaling a product brand, one of the biggest hurdles involves increasing production without sacrificing quality or taking a big hit on your profit margin.

If you outsource production to a manufacturer or obtain products from suppliers (who buy them from manufacturers and sell them to you), the first order of business is contacting your manufacturer or supplier to discuss your plans to scale and find out whether they can deliver the quantities you need. In other words, find out whether they can scale along with you.

REMEMBER

You and your manufacturer/supplier have, or should have, a mutually beneficial relationship; their sales and revenue growth is directly dependent on yours. They should be happy and eager to scale along with you. If they're not, you may need to find a new partner or another one to pick up the slack.

You can find manufacturers and suppliers by searching the web for the name or a description of the product followed by "manufacturer" or "supplier." Alibaba (https://www.alibaba.com) can connect you with suppliers in China, and other online directories are available to aid you in your search (both in the United States and internationally), including the following:

>> Maker's Row (https://makersrow.com)

>> Kompass (https://www.kompass.com)

>> IndiaMART (https://www.indiamart.com)

>> Sourcify (https://www.sourcify.com)

As you contact suppliers, gather the following information:

>> Whether they can manufacture/supply the product you need in the quantities you need to your specifications

>> Lead times (when you can expect to receive products after placing an order)

>> Cost per unit

>> Any discounts for bulk orders (and what constitutes a bulk order)

>> Shipping costs

>> Minimum order quantities

>> Intellectual-property protections (if the supplier will be manufacturing a product that you invented)

>> Setup fees

>> Defect/return policy

>> Reputation and reliability (check references and sample products)

If you manufacture your products yourself, figure out what you need to ramp up production, such as

>> Additional materials and supplies

>> Technology or machinery that saves time and effort

>> A bigger space

>> Hiring personnel or outsourcing work to freelancers (see the later section "Outsourcing Responsibilities to Lighten Your Load")

Scaling a service brand

If yours is a service brand, you basically have two ways to scale: get more clients or provide more service to existing clients. If you're a one-person business (you are the business), scaling up is especially challenging, because you need to increase efficiency to have the time and other resources to fuel your growth. Here are a few suggestions for scaling a service brand:

>> **Focus on increasing efficiencies first.** Analyze all your business processes with an eye toward maximizing efficiency.

>> **Examine your existing client pool with an eye toward serving them better.** Can you improve existing services to do a better job of meeting your clients' needs? Can you offer any additional services to expand your business by meeting more of their needs?

>> **Examine your best clients to find out who they are, which channels they came from, and what they value most about you.** This information gives you insight into where to find more best clients and how to pitch to them most effectively.

>> **Delegate and deputize.** Ask yourself whether you're working *in* your business or *on* it. If you're working in it (doing everything), you're not a business owner; you're an employee. You want to create a business that can run on its own, without you, so that you can use your time and resources to improve and grow the business. Your ultimate goal should be to create a business you can sell, whether you decide to sell it or not.

REMEMBER

For a service-based business, keep a close eye on *variable costs* — materials and wages or time you need to deliver the service. Because a service-based business focuses on someone performing the service, your variable costs will rise as you scale up. Just be sure that your profits will increase enough to more than make up for the rise in costs.

Outsourcing Responsibilities to Lighten Your Load

As your brand evolves, especially if it's growing faster than expected, delegating and deputizing to free your time and energy for higher level tasks can be a challenge. You built the brand from the ground up, so you may struggle to trust others to take it to the next level. Keep in mind, however, that you're not doing your brand any favors by trying to do everything yourself. You'll do more good at the top — and there is no top without people below you to handle the daily operations (or at least some of them). You just need to hire the right people and train them well.

REMEMBER

Think in terms of the three Ps: people, positions, and processes. Hire the right people for the right positions, and give them effective processes to follow, and your success is almost guaranteed.

Hiring the right people

Hiring the right people and putting them in the right positions is first and foremost. The most valuable part of any business is its people. Whether you hire contractors or employees, screen them carefully. Pay special attention to the following criteria:

>> **Competence:** Does the person have the knowledge, skills, and experience to do the job?

>> **Confidence:** Confident people with positive attitudes tend to succeed even in the face of adversity. They're willing to take risks and don't feel threatened or insulted when a superior offers help or guidance.

>> **Reliability:** You want people you can count on to show up and do their jobs.

>> **Strong values that align with your brand:** Do the person's core values fit with your brand and with the work that needs to be done? Some values are important across your organization, such as honesty, integrity, and a strong work ethic. Other values may be job-specific, such as innovation, creativity, independence, and collaboration.

>> **Familiarity with your industry:** This quality may not be essential, but it's good to have people who "get it" — who understand how the industry operates and how your brand fits in that ecosystem.

>> **Personality:** Does the person have a personality that's right for the job and that fits with your brand's identity? If your brand is built on creativity and innovation, for example, someone who's more practical and systematic may not be the right fit.

>> **Communication and interpersonal skills:** Does the person have the communication and interpersonal skills necessary to play well with others on your team?

Choosing a contractor or employee

You can outsource work and responsibilities to employees or contractors. Which of the two is right for you depends on the situation:

>> If you have steady work and need someone who's available onsite and during business hours, hire an employee — someone who's dedicated to serving your business.

>> If you have specific jobs or responsibilities that a contractor can handle offsite and outside normal business hours, you're probably better off hiring a contractor.

Hiring a contractor is often a good way to test-drive someone before adding them to your team as an employee. It's also a good approach if your business is seasonal and needs to scale up and down over the course of the year.

REMEMBER

The gig economy is exploding. More and more people are freelancing, so they can pick and choose the work they want to do, the businesses they work for, and the hours they work, all while maximizing their income. Be prepared to make accommodations for gig workers; you may be able to attract better workers for less money by being flexible.

Using your brand style guide for training

Whether you hire employees or contractors, you should have procedures, policies, and standards in place to ensure that the work is performed to your expectations. To ensure consistency for your brand, be sure to include your brand style guide in your training. All members of your team — especially those in marketing, sales, and customer service — need to review the brand style guide so that they have intimate knowledge of the desired look and feel of the brand and how you want customers to perceive the brand.

As you bring employees and contractors up to speed on your brand's look and feel, highlight the following elements in your brand's style guide:

>> Mission/vision statement

>> Core values

>> Brand identity

>> Key differentiators (what makes your brand different from and better than the other options on the market)

>> Customer avatars

>> Your brand's voice and tone

REMEMBER

Having clear branding guidelines in place simplifies the process of outsourcing work to contractors and educating new employees on your brand's essentials.

See Chapter 6 for more about creating and using a brand style guide.

Chapter **18**

Building on Customer Loyalty and Longevity

When you have some customers under your belt, they can help you get more customers. After all, word of mouth is the most effective and affordable way to build brand recognition and grow sales. Everyone knows that, right? The million-dollar question is this: How do you spark the wild-fire of word of mouth? In this chapter, I answer that question by presenting several techniques to energize your base.

In this chapter, you discover how to identify your best customers; keep track of them; and reward them in ways that encourage them to promote your brand to their friends, family members, and (via social media) complete strangers. I explain how to gain insight from existing customers into what you do well and where you can use some improvement. And I explain how to create a hierarchy of customers to optimize your success with less effort and expense. Finally, I offer guidance on how to put your customers to work for you, building brand recognition and recruiting more customers.

Identifying Your Top Customers

Before you can transform your top customers into brand advocates, you need to find out who they are and get to know a little about them.

In this section, you establish criteria you can use to assess relative customer value and start to gather and analyze data about your customers to find out which ones have the greatest potential for promoting your brand.

Defining criteria for evaluating customer value

Every business has great customers, average customers, and high-maintenance customers — those who aren't worth the trouble. To identify your best customers, start by creating a list of the qualities you value in a customer. Use the following as inspiration to create your own list:

My best customers . . .

» Buy frequently

» Spend more than others

» Subscribe to my newsletter

» Promote my brand to others (act as a source for referrals)

» Rarely, if ever, complain

» Rarely, if ever, return products or demand a refund

» Serve as a source of innovation and continuous improvement

TIP

Do your best to establish quantifiable criteria — criteria you can measure based on data collected from transactions and interactions with customers. Linking your criteria to customer data you already collect routinely is the ideal approach.

Collecting and organizing customer data

Chances are good that customer data is already being collected, regardless of whether you're intentionally doing so. If you sell products on Shopify, for example, the platform collects point-of-sale (POS) data for every transaction and provides you access to that data. You simply need a means for consolidating and organizing customer data from all available sources. You have two options:

>> **A customer relationship management (CRM) system:** A CRM system such as Salesforce (www.salesforce.com), Monday CRM (https://monday.com), or ZOHO CRM (www.zoho.com) is your best option, especially for high-volume brands. A CRM system is useful not only for managing sales funnels and customer relationships, but also for building your brand. You can use it to organize and follow up with leads and to build relationships with first-time buyers.

>> **Spreadsheet software:** You can create a spreadsheet in a program such as Microsoft Excel (Microsoft.com) or Google Sheets (docs.google.com) and manually input information about your customers or export information from your POSes. If you use Shopify, you can export your sales data in CSV format and paste it into your spreadsheet.

TIP

I recommend that you subscribe to a cloud-based CRM system and learn how to use it instead of wasting time with clunky spreadsheet software that you'll quickly outgrow. CRM systems are built to facilitate the collection, management, and analysis of customer data; to scale as your brand grows; and to use customer data to manage targeted email marketing and online advertising campaigns.

All CRM systems are different, so I can't provide specific instructions on how to set up and use such a system to collect and organize customer data, but here's some guidance on the types of customer data to collect:

>> **Customer details:**

- Customer's name

- Date of first contact

- Contact info (email address, mailing address, phone number)

- Preferred mode of contact

- How/where customer was acquired (such as online search, social media site, retail store, or trade show)

- Customer's birthday

- Hobbies and interests

- Income level

- Info about the customer's family (spouse's name, anniversary date, number of children)

>> **Transaction data:**

- Items purchased

- Categories of items purchased

- Total dollar amount of each purchase
- Payment method(s)
- Returns and exchanges

>> **Engagement info:**

- Response to emails you sent
- Response to different message types (such as informational messages and promotions)
- Social media membership and communication
- Record of phone-call interactions

>> **Customer feedback:**

- Complaints the customer has made
- Customer survey results
- Ratings and product reviews the customer has posted
- Customer sentiment toward the brand

Your CRM system should be able to pull this data automatically from a variety of sources, including the following:

>> POS systems

>> Email communications

>> Sales and customer service calls

>> Social media channels

>> Customer surveys

>> Web analytics

Rewarding Customer Loyalty

Rewarding customer loyalty and targeting incentives to your best customers are great ways to build a strong base and transform your most loyal customers into brand advocates. Here are a few ways to reward customer loyalty:

>> Offer exclusive items or discounts to customers for their next purchase.

>> Create tiers for subscriptions, such as $9.99 monthly, $99.99 annually, and $249 for three years. Or, for a six-month subscription, the customer receives one month free.

>> Give your best customers early or exclusive access to events.

>> Issue loyalty cards that you stamp or punch for every purchase a customer makes. You can design and order custom loyalty cards online at websites such as UPrinting.com (www.uprinting.com) and Vistaprint (https://www.vistaprint.com).

TIP

Consider using a digital loyalty card that customers can access easily via your website or by using an app on their smartphone. Companies such as LoopyLoyalty (https://loopyloyalty.com) provide the tools and guidance to create, promote, and manage digital loyalty cards. They also collect data on card use that you can use for business analytics.

Creating a customer loyalty program

A *customer loyalty program* rewards customers for placing larger or more frequent orders. These programs are great for increasing sales and improving customer retention.

As part of your customer loyalty program, consider including one or more of the following:

>> **Stamp cards or punch cards** provide an effective and affordable means of rewarding customers, usually for in-store purchases. Digital cards can be used to track both in-store and online purchases, with the advantage of enabling you to collect additional data about the customer.

>> **Membership cards** are usually tied to a customer account. Airlines, for example, offer their passengers memberships and then award them frequent-flyer miles and other incentives.

>> **Personal identification numbers (PINs)** can be used alone or in tandem with membership cards. You can even use a customer's phone number as a PIN. PINs function like membership cards to identify customers.

>> **Smartphone apps** are perhaps the best (though most expensive) means of creating and managing a customer loyalty program. They can deliver instant notifications, coupons, and discount codes, and even monitor a customer's location and offer special discounts when a customer is near one of your retail locations. Smartphone apps can also collect valuable data about customers that help you serve them better.

To lay the groundwork for your customer loyalty program, take the following steps:

1. **Decide what you're going to offer as an incentive, and tie your offers to specific milestones.**

   You may have different offers for reaching different milestones, such as example, free shipping for orders over $50 and a 10 percent discount on top of that for orders over $100.

2. **Build the incentive offering into your marketing budget.**

   If you're offering a $5 discount, account for that discount in your marketing budget.

3. **Decide on a redemption method.**

   A customer might present a physical punch card at checkout to receive a free product, or you might email the customer a discount code after a specific online purchase.

4. **Set goals for your loyalty program.**

   Goals might be increasing your average order value, the number of repeat customers, or the number of orders from repeat customers.

TIP

The easiest way to create and manage a customer loyalty program is to outsource the work to a specialized service provider, such as Repeat Rewards (https://loyalty.repeatrewards.com), Spendgo (https://www.spendgo.com), or Perkville (https://www.perkville.com). Most of these providers offer flexible solutions that cover direct email, branded websites, social media, and mobile apps so that you can offer rewards wherever your customers spend their time.

Creating and issuing discount codes

One of the best and easiest ways to implement a loyalty program for an ecommerce business is to use a discount code. A *discount code* is like a digital coupon; the shopper can input the code online, usually during checkout, to redeem the discount.

Most e-commerce platforms include a feature for creating, managing, and issuing discount codes. The platform may charge extra to unlock the feature, or you may need to install a widget or plug-in to add this functionality to your ecommerce website. Check your platform's help system for details.

The process for using the feature varies depending on the platform or promotional software you use. On Shopify, the process goes like this:

1. **Log in to your account, and go to your Admin page.**

2. **Click Discounts (in the menu bar on the left side of the screen).**

3. **Click Create Discount (top right).**

   The Create Discount dialog box appears.

4. **Click Discount Code.**

   The Create Discount Code dialog box appears.

5. **Type your discount code in the Discount Code text box.**

   The discount code is what customers will enter at checkout to claim their discount.

TIP

Use a short name that welcomes the customer to your brand community; such as JAVAJOESVIP, or something simple for a customer's second purchase, such as WELCOMEBACK.

6. **Choose a discount code type: Percentage, Fixed Amount, Free Shipping, or Buy X Get Y.**

   The options below the list of discount types change depending on the type you choose.

7. **Enter additional details about the discount as prompted.**

8. **Specify any use limits for the discount.**

   You may be able to limit it to one item or one use per customer.

9. **Specify the minimum requirements to qualify for the discount (such as none, a minimum purchase amount, or a minimum quantity of items purchased), or enter details about customer eligibility.**

10. **Enter the range of dates during which the discount will be available.**

    If you have no expiration date in mind, don't specify an end date.

TIP

Specify a deadline for your discount to create a sense of urgency for customers that compels them to act on the discount sooner rather than later.

11. **Click Save.**

    Your discount is available.

Now that you have a discount, use it to reward your loyal customers, drive sales, and promote your brand. Here are a few ways to get your discount code into the hands of your customers:

>> If you have a physical location, you can create a physical discount code card to hand customers when they make a purchase. I use UPrinting.com and Vistaprint to create my promotional materials.

>> Add your discount code to your email marketing campaigns.

>> Include your discount code on any website, blog, or other online property you own.

>> Send a personalized email message to your best customers that includes the discount code. Here's an example:

Hi Angela,

Thanks for supporting our small business. As a token of our appreciation, I'd like to offer you 10% off your next online order. Just shop as you normally do at GirlGangtheLabel. com, and when you're ready to check out, enter the discount code HEYGIRL to claim your discount by the end of the month.

Happy shopping!

Amy

Expanding your offers

TIP

Keep the ball rolling by surprising customers with additional discounts after they make a purchase. You can continue offering discounts when customers reach certain milestones. If a customer has placed two orders, for example, you can email a new discount code with a new offering to show your appreciation for their business. At Starbucks, members earn points with every order and can redeem them for freebies. The more stars a member accumulates, the better the freebie:

Number of Stars	Freebie
25	Drink customization (extra shot of espresso, dairy substitute, or dash of flavored syrup)
50	Brewed hot coffee, bakery item, or hot tea
150	Handcrafted drink, hot breakfast, or parfait
200	Lunch sandwich, protein box, or salad
400	Select merchandise or at-home coffee

The Starbucks app enables members to log in at any time to check their points, and points expire after a certain number of days. These are great ways to encourage members to return to Starbucks.

To create offers for customers on different tiers, take the following steps:

1. **Review your customer loyalty program to ensure consistency.**

   See the earlier section "Creating a customer loyalty program."

2. **Set tiered milestones.**

   You may want to set different milestones based on the total dollar value of orders placed or frequency of purchases, such as different tiers for customers who placed 5, 10, 20, or 50 orders.

3. **Budget for the additional rewards.**

   You don't want to go broke offering discounts and other perks.

4. **Implement your reward tiers.**

   Use your e-commerce platform, app software, or loyalty program administrator to set up discounts and rewards for customers at the tiers you established.

5. **Advertise your tiered rewards.**

   Hang a sign in any retail locations, send an email blast to your customers, post details about your rewards programs on your website, blog about it, and do anything else you can think of to spread the word.

Getting Customer Feedback

One of the best ways to nurture customer loyalty is to treat your relationships with customers as a partnership. After all, your success depends on their satisfaction.

The hard part is figuring out whether your customers are satisfied and what you can do to make their lives even better. Small-business owners often feel as though they're operating behind a curtain, having to guess what their customers think about the business. You can't always figure out what customers are thinking by looking at a bunch of numbers. Sometimes, the only way to find out what's on your customers' minds is to ask them.

Getting customer feedback via email or an online survey is often as valuable as conducting a focus group. It can provide you with insight into both the products you're selling and the service you're providing while sending a subtle message to customers that you value their opinions and are committed to continuous improvement.

Requesting feedback via email

One of the easiest ways to solicit feedback from customers is to send your request via email. You can create an automated email that's sent to all first-time buyers, asking them about their experience with your products or services, or blast an email to all your customers or a select group.

TIP

To improve your response rate, offer a perk to any customers who provide feedback — positive or negative.

Here's a sample request for feedback you can use as is or modify to suit your purposes:

> As a new business, we'd greatly appreciate your feedback on our products and your shopping experience. If you could let us know how we're doing and what we can do to improve by emailing support@joescoffee.com, we'd really appreciate it. As a token of our appreciation, we'll give you a 20% discount on your next order as soon as we receive your feedback.

Your email message may contain a request for general or specific feedback or a link to a form that prompts the customer to answer a series of questions. Your email may even include surveylike selections that the customer can click, as shown in Figure 18-1.

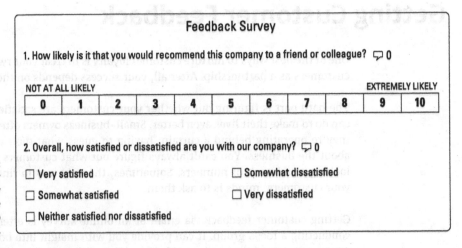

FIGURE 18-1:
Your request for feedback may contain a range of options to select.

You can use an email program such as Mailchimp (`https://mailchimp.com`) or a CRM platform to blast your feedback request to multiple customers. See Chapter 14 for details on email marketing.

TIP

When composing automated emails for feedback, use your email client's mail-merge feature to personalize the request by inserting the customer's name into the greeting. Mail merge can pull names from your customer database and insert them into outgoing messages. This personalized touch will reinforce your brand identity.

Conducting an online survey

Conducting customer surveys has never been easier now that you can conduct them online. Many social media sites, including Facebook and Instagram; e-commerce platforms, such as WooCommerce (`https://woocommerce.com`); and dedicated survey platforms such as SurveyMonkey (`https://www.surveymonkey.com`), Google Forms (`https://www.google.com/forms/about`), and Qualaroo (`https://qualaroo.com`) feature tools for composing and distributing surveys and then collecting and analyzing the results.

All you do is design your survey form, add your questions, specify the recipients (or upload your customer contacts), and click a button to distribute your survey via email or text to your customers. Another option is to add a survey form to your website by using a special widget or plug-in. Some shopping platforms include a survey feature, and many dedicated survey platforms integrate with popular shopping platforms, including BigCommerce, Twilio, and eBay.

REMEMBER

Social media can be a great place to get feedback. Nearly every platform has a survey feature for soliciting member or follower feedback. On Instagram, for example, you can conduct a survey via an Instagram Story poll by using your smartphone:

1. Open Instagram, and swipe left.
2. Choose to post to Story (below the record button).
3. Take the video or picture you want to post.
4. Click the sticker icon (top right).
5. Scroll down, and choose the desired poll type.
6. Type your question and responses.

7. **Click Send To.**

8. **Choose the option to share your poll to your story.**

REMEMBER

If you have employees, they can be valuable brand advocates too. Be sure to survey your employees regularly to find out what you can do to create a more enjoyable, comfortable, and productive work environment and to improve your business overall. Your customer service reps may also have insight into your customers and possible ways to improve products and service.

Soliciting testimonials

If you have a service-based business, testimonials serve as great proof of value, giving instant assurance to new customers that you're legit and trustworthy. Here are a few ways to encourage customers to post testimonials:

» Create a separate Testimonials page on your website or blog, complete with a form for posting a testimonial, to make it as easy as possible for customers to post. Most platforms for creating and managing websites or blogs have third-party widgets or plug-ins you can install that enable you to create and post survey forms.

» Use a dedicated testimonials platform, such as TestimonialTree (https://get.testimonialtree.com) or Spectoos (http://spectoos.com). A testimonial platform typically provides a plug-in or widget you can use to add a testimonial form to your website or blog, a way to aggregate testimonials from across the web, and a way to request and receive testimonials from customers.

» Email your best customers and strongest brand advocates, requesting that they post a testimonial for your business. In your message, give your customers the option to click a link to access your Testimonials page or the option to include their testimonial in their response.

» On social media platforms, you can subtly request testimonials by asking your followers how you're doing.

WARNING

Don't offer any sort of compensation or discount in exchange for positive testimonials. You don't want to get a reputation for buying praise, and there's a remote chance that doing so could land you in legal trouble.

Gathering feedback via your blog

If you have a blog, it can serve as the perfect vehicle for soliciting and collecting customer feedback. All you need to do is post relevant and valuable content to encourage and facilitate discussion among your readers. Whichever blogging platform you use, you can find plenty of plug-ins that let you add surverys to your blog posts quickly and easily.

Beauty brand Glossier used its blog to develop its initial product run. The company posted a blog entry asking customers to comment what they wanted to see from the company. (See Chapter 12 for more about blogging.)

Requesting feedback at checkout

An effective way to get immediate feedback about a customer's online shopping experience is to request feedback at checkout. Then you can use the feedback to optimize your site for a better shopping experience.

All you need to do is add a feedback call to action to your checkout page, which is easy to do on most of the leading e-commerce platforms (see Figure 18-2). Just go to your online store settings, choose the option to edit or customize your checkout page, and add your feedback call to action. You won't need to add any code to change the checkout message, but you'll need to add a link that customers can click to submit a feedback form or email message.

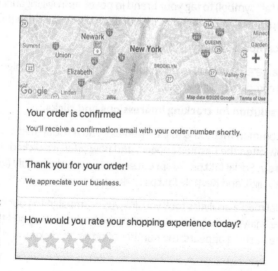

FIGURE 18-2:
A sample checkout page with a feedback call to action.

Encouraging Customers to Share Why They're Loyal to Your Brand

The best proof of concept for your brand is real customers sharing their actual experiences. At this point, you transform loyal customers into brand advocates and put your customers to work for you promoting your brand. When loyal customers sing the praises of your brand, prospective customers listen and begin to envision your product or service fitting into their lives.

TIP

Make it easy for customers to share why they love your brand by providing clear feedback calls to action and making your social handles easily accessible.

You recruit loyal customers to promote your brand via *user-generated content* (UGC) — text, images, audio, or video posted by users (as opposed to your business or brand) to promote your brand. To start a UGC campaign, follow these steps:

1. **Choose the social media channels you want to use.**

   When choosing social media channels to focus on, consider where your targeted customers are already posting.

2. **Create recognizable, branded social media handles.**

   A social media handle is your brand's public-facing name, which can be used with @ (the "at" symbol) to tag your brand in posts, as in @girlganglabel. You'll be using your social media handles in your campaign's calls to action.

3. **Give your campaign a unique name.**

   A unique name enables you to distinguish this marketing campaign from others and compare their success.

4. **Arrange a solution for tracking impressions and clicks.**

   The most common method is to use hashtags and a social media analytics tool to track how often the hashtag appears and how often it's clicked. These tools include Sprout Social (https://sproutsocial.com), Hashtagify (https://hashtagify.me), and Keyhole (https://keyhole.co).

   With a social media analytics tool, you link your campaign to your hashtag. As soon as the analytics tool starts to monitor the hashtag, it reports the number of times the hashtag appears, the number of times it's clicked, and how users are responding to and sharing your content. Users can also click the hashtag to access relevant content posted by other users.

Come up with a hashtag that's short, catchy, and unique, such as #oatmilklattes.

5. **Compose a call to action that includes your handle and the hashtag for this campaign.**

   Here's an example: "Show us how much you're loving our new Oat Milk Lattes by tagging us on Instagram @JoesCoffeeCo #oatmilklattes."

6. **Post your call to action on your social media properties, blog, and anywhere else that makes sense.**

7. **Respond to users who participate in your campaign.**

   People like to see that their actions are having some impact. When customers post their response, respond in kind, and let them know what others have written (when appropriate). Demonstrate that you're hearing what they have to say.

Chapter 19

Dealing with Competition and Other Threats to Your Brand

P art of your responsibility as a brand owner is to protect it from threats, both external and internal — from competitors, intellectual-property thieves, and negative publicity (typically the result of carelessness or dissent within an organization). Your approach needs to be both proactive and reactive; you must take steps to prevent bad things from happening and be prepared to respond when they do happen.

In this chapter, I provide guidance on how to protect your brand against the most common and serious threats from within and without.

Remaining Sensitive to the Changing Needs of Your Target Market

The biggest threat to your brand is complacency. Many brands achieve some degree of success and decide to rest on their laurels, forgetting that the world and their customers' needs and preferences are changing continuously. As their customers change, they remain fixed in what they do, allowing competitors to swoop in and gain market share at their expense. Imagine a clothing line that never changes. It's still pushing skinny jeans when all its competitors have followed the trend toward wide-legged pants.

Here are a few ways to remain sensitive to changes in your target market:

>> **Stay laser-focused on your customers' needs and preferences.** A brand's success ultimately boils down to customer enthusiasm.

>> **Listen closely to your customers.** Sources for gaining insight into what customers want include the following:

- Your sales team
- Your customer service reps
- Discussions on social media that mention your brand, a competitor's brand, or the types of products or services you sell
- Returns and exchanges
- Surveys

>> **Look for trouble.** Every problem, pain point, and challenge your customers face is an opportunity for your brand to serve their needs.

>> **Keep an eye on the competition while remaining proactive.** You don't want to merely react to what your competition is doing. By knowing what they're up to, you have a better chance of outcompeting them in innovative ways.

>> **Monitor market conditions.** Buying habits shifted considerably starting in 2020 in response to the COVID-19 pandemic, for example. Keep an eye out for big changes in the world, and think about how any given change might affect your customers' needs and preferences.

REMEMBER

Monitor any changes within your organization as well, and think about their impact on your brand. As your business grows, for example, it may gradually become less innovative and responsive, and focus more on the quality and reliability of existing products. If your brand identity is closely associated with innovation, you'll need to find ways to reinvigorate that aspect of your business or rebrand it if you think that your customers' evolving values make the change necessary.

Keeping the Competition at Bay

With branding, one thing's for certain: When you achieve success, someone or something will come along and try to take it from you. They'll mimic you, steal your idea, or do you one better. Chances are good that you're doing the same with your brand — trying to unseat an established brand by offering something superior — and that's okay (assuming that what you're doing is legal and ethical). Competition drives development, makes stuff more affordable, and improves the lives of consumers. Unfortunately, it can also drive you and your brand out of business. What happened to Blockbuster, for example, can happen to you (see "Staying abreast of changes in your industry" later in this chapter).

To maintain your competitive edge and ensure that your brand continues to thrive, you must remain vigilant for anything that's competing against it or threatening to replace it and respond quickly to any threats. In this section, I show you how.

Identifying your competition

Most brand owners can identify their competition, both direct and indirect:

>> **Direct competition** is another brand that competes in the same market with a nearly identical product. Starbucks, McDonald's, and Dunkin', for example, are all vying to become the go-to place for great coffee.

>> **Indirect competition** is another brand that competes in the same market with a substantially different product. Starbucks, for example, competes against several companies that sell premium teas, including Tazo and Twinings.

I have a broader interpretation of competition: Competition is anything else that someone in your target market can spend their money on. I have a fashion brand, so I'm obviously competing against other fashion brands, but my customers can choose to spend their money on all sorts of things — entertainment, travel, pets, gym membership, beauty supplies, home décor, you name it. I'm competing for every discretionary dollar my customers spend. To win their business, I need to give them a compelling reason to spend that dollar on my products instead of anything else they have a choice to spend it on. I recommend that you take the same approach.

Striving to go beyond quality and value

In today's world, most products and services have become indistinguishable from their competition. If you're focused solely on delivering the highest-quality product or service or the greatest value, you'll likely end up working too hard while watching every penny be squeezed out of your profit margin. You need to deliver something else, such as a unique experience, a special feeling, or a sense of belonging. Branding is all about making people feel an emotional connection to what you're offering — an emotional connection that your competitors can't possibly offer.

Here are a few ways you can start to nurture an emotional connection to your brand:

» Tell and share stories that evoke an emotional response.

» Share your vulnerabilities. Reveal the human/emotional side of your brand.

» Express a genuine interest in the lives of your customers. Be empathetic. Show that you care.

» Engage and interact with customers authentically. Don't be afraid to be you.

» Connect with customers on *their* emotional level. Are they afraid, lonely, or insecure? If your brand can fill a void in their lives, it will create a deep and lasting bond.

» Build a thriving community around your brand. Most people want to be part of something greater than themselves. By building a thriving community and offering membership to that community through your brand, you build and strengthen brand loyalty.

» Rally your customers around a common cause. Nothing creates a stronger sense of community than a worthy cause.

Staying abreast of changes in your industry

Earlier in this chapter, in the section "Remaining Sensitive to the Changing Needs of Your Target Market," I encourage you to keep an eye on the changing needs and preferences of your customers, as well as changes in your industry. Otherwise, you're likely to get blindsided by new technologies, techniques, products, services, and other innovations.

Blockbuster is the poster child for brands that got blindsided by disruptive technologies. It was the leading video rental company in the world. Then, thanks to high-speed Internet and cable TV, streaming video became possible, making VHS and DVD rentals obsolete. Soon thereafter, Blockbuster locations across the country began to disappear.

Here are a few ways to stay abreast of changes in your industry:

REMEMBER

>> Read your industry's leading trade journals and newsletters regularly.

>> Network with other people in your industry, including any vendors you may use or businesses you sell to.

>> Visit your competitor's websites and blogs to see what they're up to.

>> Engage in discussion forums related to your industry.

Check LinkedIn for industry-specific discussion forums.

>> Join and participate in professional organizations related to your industry.

>> Set up Google news alerts to notify you of any news that's relevant to your industry.

Focusing on innovation

One of the best ways to keep your competitors at bay is to outinnovate them — develop products, services, and practices they haven't thought of. Some of the most innovative companies develop products and services before market demand for them exists. They deliver what consumers want before consumers even know they want it. Case in point is the smartphone. When IBM introduced the first smartphone — the Simon Personal Communicator — in 1994, it didn't exactly fly off the shelves. Now most people can't imagine living without one.

Innovation isn't restricted to technology, however. It's important in every sector — including transportation, agriculture, education, hospitality, fashion, and entertainment — and it encompasses everything from what's made to how it's made, marketed, distributed, sold, and supported. When most people think of the fast-food industry, for example, they don't think innovation, but just consider how much has changed over the years, from drive-ins to drive-throughs, from paying with cash to paying with credit cards, and from ordering at the counter to ordering via apps and kiosks.

As you think about innovation, consider all aspects of your business, and always ask yourself this question: "What improvements can I make to enhance the customer experience?"

Protecting Your Brand

Before you introduce a new brand, product, or process to the market, take steps to protect it. If you haven't done so already, now may not be too late. As long as someone else hasn't trademarked the same brand or patented a very similar product or process, you still have time to protect your intellectual property — ideas that may have commercial value.

In this section, I bring you up to speed on the legal protections available and offer guidance on getting legal advice during the process and in the event that anyone infringes on your rights.

Registering your business with government agencies

The first step to protecting your business and brand is registering your business. If you conduct business under your own name and don't have employees, you're not necessarily required to register your business, but doing so is a good idea. Registration can help you qualify for personal liability protection, as well as legal and tax benefits, and it can facilitate the process of applying for a trademark or patent. On the other hand, if you're operating under an assumed name or a fictitious name, you *are* required to register your business.

Registration requirements vary at the federal, state, and local levels and according to your business structure: sole proprietorship, limited liability company (LLC), S corporation (S corp), or C corporation (C corp). See Chapter 2 for details about different business structures and guidance for registering your business name.

Trademarking your brand

A *trademark* is any word, phrase, symbol, design, or combination of those four things that identifies your goods and services and distinguishes your brand from competing brands. It identifies the source of your goods or services, provides legal protection for your brand, and helps guard against counterfeiting and fraud.

Trademarks come in two flavors:

>> **Trademark,** which is used for goods

>> **Service mark,** which is used for services

For the purposes of this book, I use the term *trademark* to refer to both trademarks and service marks.

REMEMBER

The primary purpose of a trademark is to prevent unfair competition. A business might create a similar brand to cause confusion in the marketplace to the detriment of the trademark's creator, for example. Or another business in an entirely different sector may use the same name as a name you trademarked, and you'd have little, if any, legal cause to file a trademark-infringement lawsuit against that business.

TIP

I recommend hiring a law firm that specializes in registering trademarks to conduct the search for you. (For details on hiring a qualified attorney and getting help paying for one if you don't have the money to cover the cost, visit `https://www.uspto.gov/trademarks/basics/why-hire-private-trademark-attorney#Find%20attorney`.)

CORRECTING COMMON TRADEMARK MISCONCEPTIONS

Over the years, several misconceptions have arisen about what trademarks are and the protections they provide. Here are some common misconceptions clarified:

Myth: You can trademark a word, phrase, or logo to prevent others from using it for commercial purposes.

Fact: A trademark protects only how the word, phrase, or logo is used with specific goods and services. If you trademark a name and logo for your carpet-cleaning business, that trademark doesn't prevent a different type of business, such as a fashion retailer, from using the same name and logo.

Myth: A trademark that describes your goods or services is sufficient for protecting your name, logo, and other brand assets.

Fact: A highly creative and unique name, logo, and design makes for a much stronger trademark. In addition, using the name, logo, and design continuously and extensively, and challenging any infringement of the trademark in court, strengthens your rights.

Myth: A trademark must be registered to secure legal protections.

Fact: Your trademark is legally protected as soon as it's used in the marketplace. Registering a trademark enables the use of the registered trademark symbol (®), establishes the presumption that the registrant owns the mark, precludes others from registering a similar mark, and strengthens the basis for filing trademark infringement claims in the United States.

Conducting a trademark search

The first step in trademarking your brand is conducting a trademark search to ensure that you're not infringing on someone else's trademark. Conducting a thorough trademark search is a complicated process requiring the following three types of searches:

WARNING

>> **Federal:** A federal trademark search involves searching the U.S. Patent and Trademark Office (USPTO) database of registered trademarks, which you can access at https://www.uspto.gov/trademarks/search. You enter the name you want to trademark, and the search indicates whether the name is already registered.

Don't limit your search to an exact match. Also search for similar names, names with the same meaning, foreign-language equivalents, and any anything else that may be similar. When a trademark registration application is denied, it's usually because at least one variation of the trademark already exists, not because the name is identical to that of a registered trademark.

>> **State:** Every state has its own database of trademarks registered in that state. If you're going to do business in only one state, you don't need to search the databases of all 50 states, but if you ever expand nationally, you could become the target of a trademark-infringement lawsuit if someone registered an identical or similar trademark in any state. You can find links to state trademark databases at https://www.uspto.gov/trademarks/basics/state-trademark-information-links.

>> **Common-law:** Because a name, logo, or design is trademarked as soon as it's used, and because people don't always go to the trouble of registering their trademarks at the state or federal level, you also need to conduct a common-law trademark search. This process involves searching the web, newspaper and TV sources, trademark lawsuit databases, business directories such as The Real Yellow Pages (https://www.yellowpages.com), and public and private company records.

Now you know why I recommend hiring a law firm.

Establishing a common-law trademark

The easiest way to obtain trademark protection is to start using your brand name, logo, design, and anything else that's unique to your brand. Assuming that nobody else is already using the same elements or very similar ones, you gain legal rights by being the first to use them. Use *TM* (trademark) or *SM* (service mark) in superscript next to your mark as a further indication that you're claiming rights to it.

Assuming that you establish a common-law trademark, you should still proceed with registering the trademark, as discussed in the next section. Here's why:

>> A common-law trademark is protected only where the trademark has been used.

>> A common-law trademark doesn't provide legal protection as strong as that afforded by a registered trademark.

>> Without the rigorous vetting of the registered trademark registration process, you're at greater risk of being legally liable for infringing on someone else's trademark.

Obtaining a registered trademark

If you make it to this point, most of the hard work is behind you. Now you simply need to complete and submit the official forms. Which forms you use depend on whether you want protection just in the United States or in other countries as well:

>> To obtain the forms for registering your trademark in the United States, visit https://www.uspto.gov/trademarks/apply/index-all-teas-forms.

>> To obtain the forms for registering your trademark in more than 100 countries through a single registration, visit https://www.wipo.int/madrid/en.

As soon as you receive your registered trademark, but no sooner, you can and should begin using the registered trademark symbol (®) immediately and continuously in at least one prominent location on every product you're your packaging and in every document and brand communication. Position the symbol in superscript to the right of your brand name, logo, or other unique mark. If you don't use the mark, you'll have a tough time claiming any damages for trademark violation.

REMEMBER

Use your trademark often, and defend it against any suspected trademark infringement. The more you use it, and the more vehemently you defend it in the court of law, the stronger it becomes. Also, be sure to file the required maintenance forms and pay the maintenance fees by the specified deadlines to prevent your registration from expiring or being canceled; visit `https://www.uspto.gov/trademarks/basics/maintaining-registration` for details.

Defending your trademarks

The USPTO doesn't defend your trademarks for you. You need to remain vigilant of any infringement of or threats to your intellectual-property rights. Here are several actions to take to protect and defend your trademarks:

» Use your registered trademark on your logo, press releases, business cards, packaging, website, and anything else in the public eye. Use it within six months of obtaining it, and use it continuously and extensively.

» Maintain your registered trademarks by filing the renewal forms and paying the associated fees by the USPTO deadlines.

» Remain vigilant, both online and off, for marks or products that are identical or similar to your marks. Be on the lookout for *counterfeiting* (a mark that's identical to or nearly indistinguishable from yours), *infringement* (anything that's similar enough to your mark to cause substantial confusion in the marketplace), *dilution* (anything that's similar enough to your mark to reduce its distinctiveness), and *mislabeling/false advertising* (anything that misleads the consumer or end users in a way that causes confusion or damage to the trademark).

TIP

Check *Trademark Official Gazette* (`https://www.uspto.gov/learning-and-resources/official-gazette/trademark-official-gazette-tmog`), published every Tuesday, for new registered trademarks. The *Gazette* also includes a record of trademark renewals and cancellations.

» Record your trademark with U.S. Customs and Border Protection (`https://iprr.cbp.gov`), which will enforce your mark at the borders, primarily for counterfeit goods. You'll need to pay a fee, but it's well worth the cost if you're concerned about bad actors from foreign countries infringing on your rights.

» Take legal action as soon as you suspect any infringement of your intellectual-property rights. The longer you wait to act, the weaker your position in court will be. If you suspect infringement of your rights, I encourage you to consult an attorney who specializes in that type of litigation.

Preventing and Recovering from Publicity Disasters

No business is immune from public relations (PR) disasters. Given the popularity and pervasiveness of social media, good or bad news can go viral in an instant.

As with any potential difficulty, prevention is best. Certainly, you can't prevent everything bad from happening. A product defect, an angry customer or disgruntled employee, an environmental accident, or even an ad that offends a sensitive audience can damage your brand. But you can take a few proactive steps to prevent negative PR, such as the following:

>> Establish clear, firm policies and guidelines that govern anything anyone in your organization might say or do, during or outside work hours, that could reflect negatively on your brand. Include social media policies. (Many companies publish their policies or code of conduct online if you need examples to follow.)

>> Establish policies and procedures for securing and sharing customer data. A great deal of negative publicity these days arises from customer data falling into the wrong hands or being shared without express permission.

>> Monitor online news and discussions that mention your brand, and respond immediately to any negative comments or criticism.

>> Be vigilant for and address any workplace issues that could result in disgruntled employees going negative on your brand. Put a no-tolerance policy in place for sexual harassment, bigotry, and unethical business practices, and enforce it.

>> Put a system in place to handle grievances internally before they have a chance to spill over into public view.

If you experience a PR crisis, take the following steps to minimize the damage and begin to restore your brand's positive reputation:

1. **Accept it.**

    Acknowledge the problem. Don't deny the problem, ignore it, or pretend that it doesn't matter. If others perceive a situation to be a big problem, it is.

2. Own it.

Take responsibility, and show empathy to anyone who was harmed by what was done, said, or written. You're the person in charge; the buck stops with you.

3. Correct it.

Take the necessary action to fix the problem and prevent it from happening again.

4. Stay in front of it.

Monitor discussions to remain on top of all the publicity, and respond quickly and appropriately, correcting any misinformation or misinterpretation.

5. Be contrite.

Even if you weren't directly responsible for the problem, express remorse on behalf of your brand about what occurred.

5

The Part of Tens

Find ten ways to make a marketing campaign go viral. Craft a catchy marketing campaign slogan, leak to the press, promote posts on social media, leverage the power of email marketing, and more.

Check out ten ways to differentiate your business/ brand from what's already on the market. Deliver quality products and service, set fair prices and guarantees, engage with customers and prospects, and look for ways to deliver value.

Explore ten ways to drive or draw traffic to your website, blog, or online store. Create your own mini-web with all your online brand assets promoting one another, place your site address on all your marketing materials, harness the power of influencers, and much more.

Chapter 20

Ten Ways to Make Your Marketing Campaigns Go Viral

The ultimate goal for any marketing campaign is for it to go viral. You want to build a campaign that gets people buying your products and promoting your brand long after you launch your campaign.

My husband and I launched a viral marketing campaign for the second brand we created. The product was a custom coloring book; customers provided the photos, and we turned them into a coloring book. We originally pitched the product to BuzzFeed, and it went viral. Unfortunately, we were ill-prepared for the blessings of success. We couldn't keep pace with demand.

After witnessing firsthand what happens when a business isn't prepared to scale, I decided to share our story with other entrepreneurs to help them avoid making the same mistakes. In this chapter, I share what we did right and steer you clear of what we did wrong so that you can create a viral marketing campaign without the setbacks and aggravation we experienced.

Plan for Phenomenal Success

When they're starting a business, many entrepreneurs wonder what they'll do if they fail. Few give much thought to what they'll do if they succeed beyond their wildest dreams. When success happens, they're unprepared to capitalize fully on a golden opportunity.

That's what happened when my husband and I launched our personalized coloring book on BuzzFeed. We'd hoped to generate a few dozen orders, but we had no plan in place for what would happen next. Our article quickly became the number-one trending topic on BuzzFeed and was picked up by 500 media outlets, including *The Today Show*. We had a problem that comes with phenomenal success: thousands of orders for just the two of us to fill, with no plans in place to scale production.

When you come up with a great idea for a marketing campaign, you'd better have an equally great plan for meeting the increased demand it'll generate. Follow these steps to plan for success:

1. **Consider what'll happen if your marketing campaign goes viral.**

   Will call volume increase? Will you have more email messages to answer? Will sales go through the roof? Will you lose customers due to an inability to serve them or deliver product?

2. **Figure out what you'll need to do to meet increased demand.**

   Will you need to hire more people, ramp up production, or outsource some work? Identify potential pain points and bottlenecks. If you manufacture a product, will you need to have extra material and supplies on hand?

   TIP

   If you're testing a product or campaign, you're not sure what to expect in terms of demand, and you don't want to invest heavily in something that might not be successful, consider one of the following options:

   - Offer a limited quantity, and give customers the option of adding their name to a waitlist if you run out of stock.

   - Have customers preorder the product so you can gauge demand without going all in.

3. **Estimate the time required to upscale.**

   Can you scale immediately, or will it take days or weeks?

4. **Prepackage as much as possible.**

   If you're selling day planners, and you use the same mailer, product, and inserts for every order, you can prepackage those items. This approach allows you to print shipping labels and stick them to the packages as orders come in. Any time-saving measures can be useful in handling unexpectedly high demand.

5. **Manage customer expectations.**

   Suppose that you're a handmade-candle merchant who typically produces 400 candles a month to fill 100 orders a week. You're about to launch a marketing campaign that could generate sales of 200 or more candles a week. You can manage customer expectations with a message such as "Thank you for your interest in Pretty Cool Candles. Please note that our candles are handmade by a small team of dedicated makers. You can order items shown as 'Out of Stock,' but they may take up to two weeks to ship. You won't be charged for anything you order until the day it ships."

TIP

Selling out isn't necessarily a bad thing. In fact, you can use a sellout to your advantage by stating "Limited quantities are available" or something along those lines. You don't need to worry too much about selling out so long as you have a plan for that possibility.

REMEMBER

Being transparent with customers is crucial, especially when you experience an influx of interest. Knowing what you can promise realistically and sharing that information with customers helps you establish a positive relationship with them.

Build Your Email List

One of the most valuable tools for driving a viral marketing campaign is a well-populated email list of people who have shown some interest in your brand or signed up specifically for the launch. To start capturing email addresses, install an email capture or lead generator plug-in or widget on your website that encourages and rewards visitors for providing their email addresses. Email capture tools include OptinMonster (https://optinmonster.com), SleekNote (https://sleeknote.com), Bloom (https://www.elegantthemes.com/plug-ins/bloom), and Constant Contact (https://www.constantcontact.com).

TIP

Most people are reluctant to share their email addresses, so provide a compelling reason or an incentive for them to do so — an exclusive offer or content that they can access only by providing the information.

Some e-commerce sites give their merchants an option to add a subscription preference at checkout so that customers can opt in or opt out of receiving email messages from the merchant. In Shopify, you can activate this feature by following these steps:

1. **Log in to Shopify, and go to your Admin screen.**

2. **Choose Settings > Checkout.**

3. **Scroll down to the Email Marketing section and select Show a Sign-up Option at Checkout.**

   During the checkout process, visitors will be able to enter their email addresses to sign up for your list.

4. **(Optional) Check Preselect the Sign-up Option.**

   This option automatically signs up the customer for a subscription unless they opt out. If a customer has already opted out, the Sign-up option won't be preselected.

   See Chapter 14 for more about email marketing.

Get Emotional

To have any hope of going viral, your campaign needs to appeal to your target customers' feelings. If you can tap into a consumer's emotions, you can inspire them into action, such as sharing a post about your brand, subscribing to your newsletter, ordering your product or service, or recommending you to a friend or family member.

Many of the most successful marketing campaigns get emotional through humor. In 2018, Burger King ran a Whopper Neutrality commercial to demonstrate how ridiculous net neutrality would be if it were applied to operations at its popular fast-food restaurants. When customers ordered a Whopper, they were given the option to pay more for faster service. They could choose to pay $4.99 for a Slow MBPS Whopper, $12.99 for a Fast MBPS Whopper, and $25.99 for a Hyperfast MBPS Whopper. Customer reactions were hilarious, and the video went viral.

Compose a Catchy Campaign Slogan

Every marketing campaign has a message designed to stick to the consumer's brain like Velcro. When composing your campaign message, make sure that it meets the following criteria:

>> Concise (suitable for use in social media captions, press releases, and email subject lines)

>> Buzzworthy (interesting, funny, or emotive)

>> Related to the targeted consumer's interests, needs, or desires

>> Descriptive of the uniqueness and benefit of the product or service

For our personalized coloring book, we wanted to emphasize the idea of turning photos into coloring-book images. When we launched our company in 2016, Instagram was a popular way to share photos with friends and family members, and we saw it as the perfect venue for marketing our product. To appeal to Instagram users, we came up with the tagline "You can turn your Instagram photos into a coloring book!"

Other tag lines we experimented with included the following:

>> "The first ever custom coloring book!" This one didn't make the cut because it wasn't related to the targeted customer.

>> "Want to wow them with this personalized gift?" This one was too broad; it didn't describe the uniqueness and benefit of the product.

REMEMBER

Your marketing message is all about generating hype and creating demand. You want consumers to feel as though they have an opportunity to get in on something new, unique, or exclusive. In some cases, you may want to add something to your marketing message to communicate a sense of urgency. Your message might point out that limited quantities are available or that an offer will be available for a limited time, for example.

Never Underestimate the Power of Visuals

Every marketing campaign needs a catchy text-based message, but visuals (graphics and videos) are more likely to go viral, especially if they're interesting, informative, or funny. Consider creative ways to express your marketing message in an impactful and memorable graphic or video that reveals how special what you're offering really is.

Several years ago, Squatty Potty produced a hilarious commercial featuring a unicorn that poops tutti-frutti soft-serve ice cream. The company posted it on YouTube, where it has racked up more than 39 million views. You may not have the resources to produce a slick commercial, but you don't need high-quality video to make your campaign go viral. Every day, homemade videos are going viral on YouTube and TikTok. Memes (images combined with text) provide additional opportunities to spread the word with visuals.

Choose Media Outlets Strategically

Pull together a list of media outlets that your target demographic turns to for news and information, such as newspapers, magazines, TV, radio, and online media. If you're marketing an educational product for children, having an article or a positive review of your product in *Parents* magazine would certainly get your brand noticed. If you're launching an app for organizing travel documents, you may want to focus on travel magazines and technology news and information websites. If you're a local business, consider reaching out to local TV and radio stations.

TIP

Search the web for relevant media outlets. If your product or service is travel-related, search for "travel magazines," "travel advice," "travel websites," and "travel blogs." As you conduct your search, keep a record of each outlet's name, website address, and any contact information you find.

Pitch Your Brand to the Media

When you have a few prospective press contacts, send them information about your brand, explaining how it might be a good fit for their audience. Keep in mind that people in the media constantly receive pitches, so be succinct while presenting the following information:

>> A few sentences about your brand crafted in a way that suggests how it's relevant to the media outlet's audience

TIP

Having an angle and a story in place before pitching to the media is the most important and most overlooked step. As you compose your pitch, think about how your brand fits with the media outlet's mission and audience. Be authentic while making your brand's story relatable to the target audience.

>> Where/how to obtain the product or service

>> Price info

>> A link to your website, blog, or social media

>> A statement that you can provide additional info and images (such as "If you're interested in doing a piece on my brand, I'm happy to answer any questions and can provide product and lifestyle images")

These details provide journalists everything they need to write a story.

WARNING

Hold off on sending any images or attachments until after you receive a response, because emails with attachments often get flagged as spam or junk.

TIP

You'll have more success if you build relationships *before* pitching your brand. Find common ground, and get involved in the communities that form around relevant media outlets. Like and share their articles. Contribute to discussions on their websites and social media channels *without* blatantly advertising your brand. When journalists see that you're supporting their interests, you may find it easier to pitch being featured on their platforms because you can share a portfolio of work that aligns with their audiences' values.

Extend Your Reach with Promoted Posts on Social Media

Nearly every social media channel provides some way to advertise, because advertising is how they make their money. On most social media channels, you can use paid advertising to build an ad. Some channels provide an additional option to create ads from posts. Facebook calls the option *boosting* a post, and Instagram calls it *promoting* a post. Whatever it's called, it's just another form of advertising, one that you may find easier and more convenient than traditional forms of advertising.

REMEMBER

Advertising and promotions may be available only to business user accounts, not personal accounts. If you're not seeing these features in your social media account, check your profile settings to make sure that you have a business account.

If the social media channel features a way to boost or promote posts, you'll find the option near the content you posted. On Instagram, you click the post you want to promote, click Promote (below the post's image), and enter your preferences.

Preferences include where you want users to be sent when they click the call to action, destination/location, audience demographics, budget, and duration.

Use Hashtags to Generate Buzz

To extend the reach of marketing campaign, use one or more hashtags promoting your brand in any content you post or share. A *hashtag* is a keyword or phrase with a pound sign before it, such as #Branding4Dummies. Make sure that your hashtag meets as many of the following requirements as possible:

>> Short and memorable

>> Easy to read

>> Clear (difficult to misread or misunderstand)

>> Unique (unless you're intentionally piggybacking on a popular hashtag)

>> Actionable (suggesting a call to action)

TIP

Consider using a hashtag that has fewer than 100,000 posts already associated with it. This approach gives your posts a better chance of appearing near the top of the list when users search for that hashtag. Make it specific enough to narrow the scope but not so specific that it fails to catch anyone's interest.

Make Your Message Easy to Share

People will share your marketing message only if it's worth sharing and easy to share. They're not going to copy and paste your message into an email and blast it out to all their contacts, but if they can click a link and share it instantly with all their Facebook friends or Twitter followers, they're more than happy to do it.

Social media channels make it easy to share content with other members, but if you're posting content to your own website, e-commerce site, or blog, be sure to include buttons that users can click to share your posts quickly and easily with their friends and followers on Facebook, Instagram, Twitter, and other popular social media channels.

Most website and blog platforms have a selection of plug-ins or widgets that enable you to add this functionality to a website or blog and allow you to choose which social media channels to link to.

Chapter **21**

Ten Ways to Distinguish Your Brand from the Competition

Making your brand stand out from the competition can feel like a daunting task when you're getting started, especially if you're launching your brand in a crowded industry or one that a few brands already dominate.

In this chapter, I share ways to differentiate your brand from all the others so that prospective customers will know how your brand is different and why it's better. By implementing at least a few of these tactics, you can take your brand to the next level and build a loyal, growing customer base.

Offer Quality Products/Services

Nothing you do to create a strong brand can make up for a lousy product or service, so bake quality into everything you do, starting with what you're selling. Quality attracts customers, keeps them coming back, and inspires them to recommend specific products and service providers to their friends, family members, and colleagues. Think about it — when's the last time you recommended a poor-quality product or service to someone?

REMEMBER

The importance of quality isn't exclusive to physical products. It applies to service providers and digital products too.

Before launching a new brand, product, or service, check its quality. Here are a few quality-assurance checks you can perform even if you're a tiny startup:

» **Send product prototypes to a few people in your personal network.** Suppose that you invented a new toy that your dog loves. You can post something on Facebook along the lines of "I just invented a new toy that my dog loves. Will other dogs love it too? I need to figure that out before I take out a second mortgage to produce 10,000 of these things. If you have a dog, please help! Message me with your mailing address and cell number or email address, and I'll send you a prototype to test."

When you send your samples, include a note indicating how to use the product and what kind of feedback you're looking for, and ask for any suggestions they may have for improving it. Also include a deadline for obtaining feedback. Ask for honest feedback, not a pat on the back. You can even ask directly about the quality with a simple call to action: "Please rate the quality of this product on a scale of 1 to 10."

» **Create an informal focus group to test your service.** Ask close associates who match your target demographic to try your service for a limited time. If you're a personal trainer with plans to launch an online training program for $50 a month, you can record a video of a few sample sessions and send it to focus-group members for feedback. Request specific feedback, such as how likely the person would be to sign up for such a course and the reason for their answer, how much they'd be willing to pay for it, anything in the video that turned them off, and anything you could do to improve the classes.

The feedback you receive can help ensure that you're providing a valuable service at an appropriate price point for the customers you're targeting. You might receive feedback along the lines of "I really enjoyed the training sessions, but I wouldn't pay $50 a month. $20 a month would be more in line with what I'd pay. Maybe you could charge more for higher-level sessions."

>> **Monitor quality carefully.** I can't count the number of negative product reviews I've read on Amazon due to a brand's outsourcing its manufacturing or choosing a cheaper supplier that let quality slip. If you're selling products, at least spot-check each batch. If you're selling services, keep in touch with customers to make sure that their satisfaction rating isn't declining.

Consumers read labels, research products, and talk with one another. If you change suppliers, and customers are no longer getting the high-quality product they've come to expect, they'll know why, and they'll tell everyone they know. Don't try to pinch pennies unless you're sure that a new manufacturer or supplier will meet or exceed your quality standards. Develop close relationships with your manufacturers and suppliers so that you're working as a team toward a shared goal: pleasing your customers.

Deliver Exceptional Customer Service

Exceptional customer service can go a long way, especially during the early stages of a company's development. The late Tony Hsieh, an early investor in and former chief executive officer of Zappos, wrote the book *Delivering Happiness* (Grand Central Publishing), which credits exceptional customer service for the growth and success of the company.

At Zappos, customer service is more than just a department that serves customers; it's also a culture that applies to the treatment of employees. By focusing on the happiness of its employees and investing in their personal and professional growth, Zappos created a company culture that places people first.

Here are two key points to keep in mind about customer service:

>> If you drop the ball on customer service, your customers are likely to take their business elsewhere, assuming that they have a choice, and they almost always do. Getting them back can be costly or even impossible.

>> Providing quality customer service requires little more than being responsive, friendly, reasonable, and helpful. Yes, this process takes time and effort and may require some financial investment, but it's cheaper and far less trouble than acquiring new customers and earning their trust.

Target a Price Point

Pricing can be a great way to differentiate your brand from the competition. If all your competitors are selling high-end, high-priced items, you have an opportunity to supply the market comparable lower-end products at a lower price point. You can see how this approach works for nearly every product on the market, from clothing to tools to kitchen appliances. Some consumers must have the best; others just want something that's inexpensive and gets the job done. Conversely, if the market is already crowded with inexpensive, low-end products, there's a potential opportunity for a higher-end product you can charge more for.

My first job was as marketing director at Tower Paddle Boards. Our differentiating factor was our price point: Our paddleboards were less expensive than those currently on the market. We could sell the same-quality paddle boards for less by creating a direct-to-consumer model instead of a wholesale model that required a markup. Whereas the other companies were focused on getting retail accounts selling their product through surf shops, we leaned into the idea of bringing customers in directly online and offering a price point that our competitors couldn't afford to offer.

REMEMBER

This discussion of price point is only in the context of doing something to differentiate your brand from the competition. When choosing a price point, you need to consider other factors, such as ensuring that you're not pricing yourself out of a profit.

Offer a Guarantee or Warranty (or Both)

Offering a guarantee (and honoring it) builds instant trust, especially with first-time buyers. Here are a few types of guarantees and warrantees to consider:

» **Time-limited guarantee:** You can provide a 90-day money-back guarantee, for example. If customers aren't satisfied, they can return the product within the specified time frame and receive a full refund.

» **Warranty:** A warranty promises a refund, repair, or replacement for a product that proves to be defective or unsatisfactory within a certain period — typically, one year or less.

>> **No-hassle returns and exchanges:** Retail giant Nordstrom is known for its liberal return policy. You can exchange or return an item at any time at any location.

>> **Exchange only:** Offering exchanges or in-store credit isn't quite as satisfactory as a money-back guarantee. If you can't risk the potential burden of giving refunds, but you want to offer customers some form of reimbursement, exchange only is an option.

Cash in on Your Good Looks: Design

In branding, appearance counts . . . a lot. Everything from the appearance of your product and packaging to your website and social media, your online and bricks-and-mortar stores, and your signage and business cards create a strong and respected brand identity. Every touchpoint is an opportunity to reinforce your brand identity.

Conduct a design audit. Identify any areas of your business where you can take your design up a notch. Maybe your website or web store could use a facelift. Maybe your logo could benefit from a redesign. If you have public-facing employees, having them wear branded polo shirts may help promote your brand. Think of all the ways customers encounter your brand and then consider ways to increase your brand's impact in those areas.

Revisit your product and branding with a similar focus on design. Look for ways to be impressively unique.

CREATING AN "UNBOXING EXPERIENCE"

Golden Rice Co., owned by Sophia Parsa (the tech editor of this book), is a Los Angeles-based pop-up style restaurant focused on bringing to life her Persian home cooking. Her product is often described as an "unboxing experience." When you receive an order from Golden Rice, the box has a standout design that pops open and lays flat under your takeout food. It's unique and impressive. On top of that (literally), you get a nutritious, delicious meal. The experience is sort of like coming for the box and staying for the meal. Parsa's unboxing experience has been featured in various media outlets, including *The Los Angeles Times*.

Become a Disrupter

Lately, the term *disrupter* has become a buzzword to describe companies and innovations that threaten the existence of traditional products, services, business models, or even entire industries. Uber and Lyft, for example, became disrupters by introducing a business model that threatens the taxi industry. Netflix crushed the DVD rental market, sending Blockbuster into bankruptcy. When manufacturers began installing cameras in cellphones, they destroyed demand for traditional film cameras.

If you succeed at becoming a disrupter, your brand will stand head and shoulders above even the most deeply entrenched existing brands, at least for a short time as your competitors struggle to change course or another brand comes along to disrupt yours!

To become a disrupter, start thinking like one:

>> **Mine problems for solutions.** Necessity is the mother of invention for a reason: Many (most?) inventions are inspired by problems. If you discover a unique way to solve a problem, you can create a new product or industry. Case in point is the digital no-touch thermometer. If you've ever tried to take a baby's temperature, you know that the problem it solved. Or how about the Keurig coffeemaker? Or are you still brewing coffee and then microwaving cold coffee by the cup? Figure 21-1 demonstrates one process to consider to mine problems for solutions.

<figure>
Identify a Problem to Solve

Define your industry:
Stand-up paddleboards.

Ask your customers a need they have in the industry:
A less-expensive option.

Research the problem in depth:
Prices are high due to the wholesale model and a 2.5X standard markup.

Create a solution:
Sell paddleboards direct to customers and take away the wholesale markup.
</figure>

FIGURE 21-1:
Examine problems to discover opportunities.

>> **Look for ways to improve old processes.** Many innovations come from ideas about how to do things better, often by applying new technologies to traditional services. Machine learning applied to personal finances, for example, helped give rise to robo-advisers, which automate the process of managing investment portfolios.

>> **Keep tabs on changes in government regulations.** Government regulations often drive innovation as businesses and individuals struggle to comply with those regulations. The auto industry is a prime example. Government regulations pertaining to gas mileage and exhaust continuously challenge automakers to design more fuel-efficient and cleaner engines.

>> **Keep an eye on your competition.** Competition is a powerful driver of innovation, so monitor what your competitors are doing, and seek ways to deliver something different and better to the market. Also be careful to avoid taking a "me too" approach and simply following your competitors' lead. If you're following your competitors, you'll always be at least one step behind.

Create a Unique Brand Experience

Creating a unique branding experience is all about engaging customers and making them part of something unique, exclusive, and exciting. Customers will go out of their way to participate in the brand, making it stronger. Here are a few ways to create a unique brand experience:

>> **Post and share awesome content.** When content goes viral, it builds and strengthens the community that forms around your brand. See Chapter 8 for more about developing quality content.

>> **Host exciting events.** Bringing people together to share in and celebrate your brand makes them feel personally connected to your brand and committed to its success. Do things right, and you'll convert followers to fans and perhaps even your most enthusiastic brand advocates.

>> **Build a branded website.** Use colors, a unique font, and graphics to visually communicate what your brand is all about. (See Chapter 7 for more about building a branded website.)

>> **Create Instagram-able moments.** If you have a physical store or if you host events, create moments and spaces that inspire your customers to take photos and share them on their social media accounts. I first encountered this tactic when I was shopping at a Glossier pop-up shop on Melrose Avenue in Los Angeles. The space was filled with flowers retail assistants wore matching

white jumpsuits; soft pink engulfed visitors as soon as they stepped through the door, and the signage made them feel that they were part of something special. The experience in the store made me want to take photos and share without the company's having to explicitly ask me to do this.

Carve Out a Niche for Yourself

If you're hoping to get into a large or crowded industry but feel intimidated by competition, a great way to stand out is to focus on a niche within that industry. If you want to create a skin-care line that's really different from what the competition offers, think about starting with one product, such as an eye cream, and excelling at that.

Another way to create a niche product is to use different materials. If you're in consumables, consider exploring vegan or gluten-free options. If you're looking to make your mark in fashion, explore sustainable clothing; ecofriendly fabrics comprise a small but growing market that appeals to consumers who are strongly committed to ecology.

You can also identify a niche by looking for opportunities with an underserved demographic. In the United States, for example, the Hispanic market is underserved by most brands.

REMEMBER

In any broad market or industry, take the time to research underserved customers or clientele to find a niche that's a good fit for your expertise and passion.

Build Community Around Your Brand

Community is the soul of a brand and can play a key role in differentiating your brand from the competition. As you build a strong community, your brand's followers and fans will feel invested in your mission, have an emotional connection to it, and form relationships with people instead of just to your products. Numerous techniques are available to build community; see Chapter 16 for details.

REMEMBER

Customers who identify with your brand not only spend more, but also have the potential to become your biggest and best referral-marketing microphones. Some of them may also become *whales*: customers who spend far more than your average customers and typically become powerful influencers.

Be a Force for Good

All other things being equal, consumers generally prefer to buy goods and services from businesses that are committed to making the world a better place. Being one of those businesses can help you stand out from the competition. Amazon's Smile program, for example, donates a percentage of each purchase to a customer's chosen charitable organization. Here are a few ways you can position your brand as a force for good:

>> **Donate a product or service to the cause.** If you sell water purifiers, you can donate 1 for every 100 you sell to a community that has limited access to clean water. If you're a motivational speaker, you can do a certain number of free presentations at local not-for-profit organizations.

>> **Join a cause.** If you sell tools or building materials, you can donate a portion of your team's time to working on Habitat for Humanity homes. If your brand is built around ecofriendly products, you can support an organization dedicated to restoring ocean health or preserving rainforests.

>> **Rally the troops.** If you have lots of successful business associates, organize them to support a worthy cause. As an organizer, you can often do more good with less of an investment of your own money, although the time and effort you invest could be substantial.

TIP

Whenever possible, align your charitable program with your brand's core mission. If you sell school supplies, focus your efforts on supporting and improving education. You may commit to something like this goal: "For every 10 backpacks we sell, we'll donate a backpack full of school supplies to the Good Samaritan Community Center for distribution to at-risk children attending local schools."

Chapter **22**

Ten Ways to Drive Customers to Your Website

After you go through all the trouble (and cost) of designing and building a branded website, it'd be a shame if nobody visited it. Yet that's often what happens. Small-business owners build great websites and are surprised when they get little to no traffic. Usually, nothing's wrong with the site; it's just that people don't know (or care) about it.

Ironically, the tool you invested so much in to market your business and brand needs marketing. Visitors don't show up magically; you need to lead them there. This chapter delivers ten proven methods to make that happen.

Treat Your Website as Brand Central

Imagine a bicycle tire with a hub in the center and spokes radiating out from it toward the rim. In a similar manner, you can use your website as your marketing hub and link it to all your other online properties: your blog, social media accounts, press releases, articles, white papers, e-commerce stores, and so on. You use all those properties to drive traffic toward your hub with the added benefit of increasing its relevance in the eyes of search engines, such as Google, Bing, and DuckDuckGo. (Search engines consider external links to a site to be signs that the site is relevant and of some value.)

REMEMBER

Make sure that all your branding assets point back to your website hub, including the following:

>> Social media profiles

>> Any brand or business profiles or pages you create on social media platforms

>> Your blog

>> Any business directory listings, such as on Yelp

>> Your business cards

>> Your email signature (check your email client's help system for details)

>> Any marketing materials you send out, such as press releases

>> Any content you compose or contribute to that's posted on other websites or blogs

With multiple paths leading to your hub, your site becomes a bigger target for search engines, and you increase your website's chances of being discovered.

Use SEO to Your Advantage

Search engine optimization (SEO) is a technique for improving a site's search engine ranking by populating the content of the site with relevant words and phrases. SEO is used to generate organic traffic as opposed to traffic from paid advertisements.

When you build your website and as you add content to it, be sure to use relevant keywords and phrases in the following areas:

- » **Your website's name, address, and title tag**: The title tag is a descriptive element that's hidden from users but can be read by search engines.

- » **Your website's meta description**: Like the title tag, the meta description is hidden from visitors but describes the website's contents and mission to search engines so that they can index your site properly.

- » **All content you post on your site**: Presenting content that's relevant to visitors' interests and that includes keywords and phrases enables search engines to determine the relevance of a website or specific pages when someone conducts a search.

- » **Headings (H1 through H6)**: Search engines check page titles and headings for valuable information that describes the contents of a page. When composing web pages or posts, use headings to label blocks of content.

- » **Image alt text**: *Alt text* is a description of an image in words. If a visitor can't view the image or chooses not to have the browser display it, they can still figure out what the image is by reading the alt text. Likewise, search engines use alt text to determine the nature of the content on web pages and in blog posts.

See Chapter 8 for more about SEO.

WARNING

Don't commit *keyword stuffing* — intentionally packing content and meta tags with keywords and phrases to manipulate a site's search engine ranking. This technique is considered to be a form of spam and is likely to do more harm than good. Search engines penalize sites for this practice by ranking them lower or not including them in search results.

Deliver Content That's Fresh, Relevant, and Valuable to Your Target Market

People and search engines love to see fresh content that's relevant and valuable, so don't create a static website that attracts more dust than visitors. Continuously populate it with valuable content — text, images, audio, and video. Make your site as interactive and multimedia as possible. Remove or revise old content. Add something new at least weekly.

TIP

One of the easiest and best ways to keep your site populated with fresh content is to add a blogging component. In most content management systems, such as WordPress, you can build a combination website/blog by adding a separate tabbed page for your blog. Posting a couple times a week is easy, it keeps your site fresh, and it encourages visitors to post comments that add an ever-flowing stream of fresh content to your site.

Promote Your Content on Social Media

When you develop a following on any social media platform, you can use it to drive traffic to your website. Whenever you post any new content on your website or blog, post a teaser on all your social media accounts where it makes sense to do so — Facebook, Twitter, Instagram, Reddit, and so on — with a link back to the fresh content. Instead of having to generate traffic (which is hard), you simply redirect it from a site that has loads of traffic to your website. (See Chapter 13 for more about promoting your brand on social media.)

REMEMBER

Keep in mind that social media is social. It's not business media, marketing media, or advertising media. When posting any content or commenting on personal accounts, take a low-key approach. If you're constantly pitching products or services, you're going to lose a lot of friends and followers. People are drawn to social media to connect and share in a friendly, social environment. Your goal should be to enhance their lives, not your bank account.

Spread the Word via Email

Email is a great tool for driving traffic to your website, assuming that you have a respectable list of email addresses for receptive contacts. It's likely to be far more effective than social media just based on the numbers. If you have a list of 10,000 email addresses, your message will go to 10,000 recipients. By contrast, if you have 10,000 followers on Instagram, your teaser post will reach only about 1,000 of them (about 10 percent, according to 2021 Instagram stats).

Here are three ways to use your outgoing email messages to drive traffic to your site:

>> Include your website address in the signature of all outgoing email messages. (Check your email client's help system to find out how to use its signature feature.)

>> Whenever you post something new and of interest on your site, blast an email teaser with a clear call to action to everyone on your email list. If you post a blog entry, compose a brief description of it followed by a "Click here to read more" link that takes the recipient to the page with the blog entry.

>> Offer an incentive. You might offer a discount on merchandise or a free cool sticker to the first 1,000 people who visit your site and confirm their visit by entering their email and mailing addresses.

Take Advantage of Guest Blogging

Guest-blogging is a two-way street that often benefits both the guest blogger and the host. Think of guest blogging as a late-night talk show; interesting guests draw viewers and boost the show's relevance, and the show provides the guest increased exposure or a way to plug their latest book or movie. It's a win–win situation, right? Well, the viewers also benefit, so it's a win–win–win situation.

In the same way, you can benefit from guest blogging in two ways:

>> **Host a popular guest blogger on your blog.** Having a popular blogger post something that's relevant to your customers on your site increases your site's credibility while potentially increasing your exposure to the guest blogger's followers, especially if the guest blogger makes a point of posting about the experience on their own blog.

>> **Be a guest blogger on a popular blog.** When you contribute to a blog, you definitely increase your exposure to the host's audience, and you have the opportunity to leave them with a favorable impression of you and your brand. In most cases, the host will allow you to link back to your site, which drives traffic to your site while increasing its relevance in the eyes of the search engines.

Another perk of hosting a guest blogger is that the blogger contributes fresh content that you don't have to create yourself. It can also increase the variety of content available to the community that follows your blog.

Engage with Your Visitors

Small-business owners often create great blogs and post exceptional content but fall short by not following up with people who take the time to comment on their posts. As a result, they lose a golden opportunity to connect with customers and prospects. Even worse, visitors who aren't acknowledged aren't likely to return and certainly won't recommend the site.

REMEMBER

If you're investing in creating a blog and developing quality content, spend some time engaging with your visitors. Think of the blog as a party, and you're the host. Your job is to go around and make sure that everyone knows where the food and drinks are and is having a good time. If you see someone who appears to be lost, greet the person, talk with them, offer them a drink, show them around, maybe introduce them to some people they might like. Don't ignore them.

Post Useful Content on Reddit

Reddit, self-proclaimed as "the front-page of the Internet," is a social news aggregator where members post, rate, and comment on content in communities organized around their interests. Community members are treated to closely curated selections of the top posts in each category, and they vote thumbs-up or thumbs-down on posts based on their relevance and value.

A great way to use Reddit to drive traffic to your site is to submit quality content to a *subreddit* (a specific category) and link it back to your website. If you created an ecofriendly cup, and you plant a tree for every cup you sell, you can share the product and information on a subreddit that focuses on sustainable products. Used appropriately, Reddit can be a valuable tool for driving website traffic and extending the reach of your brand.

WARNING

Go easy on the self-promotion. If you're blatantly promoting your brand or using Reddit merely to drive traffic to your website without offering anything of value to Reddit communities, you're likely to have your content flagged and your account suspended. An example of content that probably would get flagged by a moderator is a post that promotes a fashion business but offers nothing of value to community members.

Recruit Influencers

An *influencer* is a person who has the power to affect other people's purchasing decisions as a result of their knowledge, authority, or position. You're probably more likely to buy a kitchen appliance recommended by Martha Stewart than one recommended by Eva Mendes, who has stated that she has too much respect for food to spend time destroying it in a kitchen.

Influencers typically recommend products or brands, but you can also use them to steer traffic to your website or web store simply by changing the call to action.

TIP

An easy and inexpensive way to find an influencer is to monitor your blog and social media accounts for charismatic leaders and then approach them privately about the possibility of working with them to promote your product or service. You can also find professional influencers on platforms such as HYPR (https://www.hyprbrands.com) and Heepsy (https://www.heepsy.com). (See Chapter 13 for more about teaming up with influencers.)

Answer Questions on Quora

To establish yourself as an authority on a product or service, consider answering questions on Quora, a platform where anyone can ask and answer questions. You can link your answers back to your website or blog to increase traffic and grow your own following.

When you create a professional Quora profile page, you have the opportunity to include your website's URL (address), specify the market your business serves, list your qualifications, and link to projects or social media properties you want to promote.

REMEMBER

Be highly selective about the questions you answer. Start by searching Quora for topics in your area of expertise. Then look for questions that have lots of followers, lifetime views, and answers or questions that have a low quality rating. I'm talking thousands of followers and in excess of hundreds of thousands of lifetime views. You want to answer questions that have the potential to drive hordes of people to your website or blog.

Index

A

A/B testing, 247–248, 266

accent colors, 89

Adidas, partnership with Kanye West, 147

Adobe Audition, 196

Adobe Creative Cloud, 91

Adobe Spark, 211, 212

advertising
- as activity of brand promotion, 22
- boosting brand awareness with paid advertising, 251–266
- as branding activity, 62, 65
- choosing the right advertising agency for your brand, 265
- creating and running a Facebook ad, 258–259
- getting started with paid advertising, 253–263
- knowing when to outsource, 264–265
- paying influencers and other talent to promote your brand, 260–262
- in print media, 263
- promoting your Instagram posts, 257–258
- running TV and radio ads, 262–263
- search engine marketing (SEM), 254
- selling of to monetize your content, 215
- on social media platforms, 256–257
- tapping power of search engine marketing and pay-per-click advertising, 254–256
- through popular podcasts, 259–260
- tracking results of, 265–266
- weighing pros and cons of paid advertising, 252–253
- working with advertising agencies, 264–265

advertising copy, 126–127

Alfred Coffee, partnership with Recess, 146

Alibaba, 287

alignment, for typographical guidelines, 89

Alliance for a Healthier Generation, McDonald's partnership with, 75

Amazon, 54, 281

Amazon Web Services, 107

analogous colors, 88

analytics, 67, 68, 118–121, 164

Anchor, all-in-one podcasting platform, 196

answering questions, on Quora, 347

app, branded one, 21, 100–101, 122–123

Appery.io, 123

Apple, 54

application or use, brand positioning focus on, 45

Appy Pie, 123

artist, hiring of to design logo, 92

Asana, 68

Attention, Interest, Desire, Action (AIDA), as formula for writing marketing copy, 135

Audacity, 196

audio/video scripts, writing copy for, 127

AutoZone vehicle parts and supplies, as inspirational example of brand naming, 57

Ayla, Sivan, Lux Unfiltered, 275

B

backdating, defined, 162

benchmarks, establishing of for launch campaign, 163–164

benefits (of products or services), brand positioning focus on, 45

Bezos, Jeff (Amazon founder), as not resting on his laurels, 281–282

BigCommerce, 303

Bing, 115, 255

blacklisted, 236, 237

brand promotion, activities involved in, 22

brand purpose, 9

brand recognition
  as brand metric, 67
  defined, 44, 60
  increasing of, 60–61

brand style guide
  benefits of, 84–85
  creating color palette, 86–89
  creation of, 21, 84–94
  defined, 84
  designing logo, 90–92
  establishing typographical guidelines, 89–90
  primary purpose of, 84
  setting corporate guidelines, 86
  setting guidelines for voice and tone, 93–94
  specifying guidelines for photos, illustrations, and other artwork, 92–93
  use of for training, 290–291

branded app, launching of, 122–123

branded email account, 121–122

branded house (monolithic), 13, 14

branded template, creating your own, 96–98

branding efforts, monitoring and evaluating success of, 66–68

branding goals, 59–65, 69

branding objectives, identification of, 60–65

branding plan, creating your one-year branding plan, 66

branding process, steps of, 19–23

Buffer, 233

Burger King, Whopper Neutrality commercial, 326

business brand
  with debt and equity, 40–41
  defined, 26
  described, 10
  information that helps to define, 27
  as type of brand, 11

business credit cards, as alternative financing option, 42

business financing
  alternative financing options, 41–42
  budgeting for your business/brand, 37–38

creating business plan, 38–39
  getting grants, 39–40

business name, registration of, 35–36

business plan, creation of, 38

buzz, using hashtags to generate, 330

BuzzFeed, author and husband pitching custom coloring book to, 323, 324

Buzzsprout, 197

C

C corporation (C corp), 34–35

call-to-action options, in email marketing, 239

campaign slogan, composing a catchy one to make your marketing campaigns go viral, 327

Canva
  Color Palette Generator, 87, 88
  creating custom template in, 97–98
  logo maker, 91
  online photo editor, 229

capital
  considerations of in scaling plan, 286
  raising of, creating brand for, 18

cardioid microphone, 195

career, furthering yours, creating brand for, 16–17

Cascading Style Sheets (CSS), 111

catalog copy, 129

celebrity, becoming one, creating brand for, 17

changes
  remaining sensitive to changing needs of your target market, 310–311
  staying abreast of changes in your industry, 312–313

charisma, benefits of in personal brand, 17

Cheat Sheet, 4

checkout page, requesting feedback at, 305

Chewy, supporting a cause, 271

clicks, as advertising metric, 266

click-through rate, 250, 266

cloud server, 107

Coca-Cola, 8, 54, 90, 268

color, for typographical guidelines, 89

color associations, 86–87

crowdfunding, as alternative financing option, 42

customer avatar
  defined, 69
  defining and refining yours, 69–77
  defining your brand's, 20
  describing yours in your own words, 77–78
  putting yours to work, 79
  redefining yours as it evolves, 78

customer feedback
  conducting an online survey, 303
  gathering of via your blog, 305
  getting, 301–302
  requesting feedback via email, 302–303
  requesting of at checkout, 305
  soliciting testimonials, 304

customer loyalty
  building on, 293–307
  creating and issuing discount codes, 298–300
  creating customer loyalty program, 297–298
  encouraging customers to share why they're loyal to your brand, 306
  expanding your offers, 300–301
  rewarding of, 296–297

customer loyalty program, defined, 297

customer relationship management (CRM) system, 295–296

customer service
  brand positioning focus on, 46
  delivering exceptional customer service, 333–334

customer value, defining criteria for evaluation of, 294

customers
  collecting and organizing customer data, 294–296
  defining criteria for evaluating customer value, 294
  identifying top customers, 294
  knowing you can't please everyone, 75–76
  ways to drive them to your website, 341–347

D

Dafont, 90

Dairy Queen ice cream, as inspirational example of brand naming, 57

data, collection and analysis of, 68

DBA (doing business as), 33

debt financing, 40–41, 286

dedicated server, 107

Delivering Happiness (Hsieh), 333

design, cashing in on your good looks, 335

design audit, conducting of, 335

developer, hiring of, for building website, 100, 102–104

DevTeam.Space, 123

differentiation, 11, 29

digital loyalty card, 297

Digital Photography For Dummies, 7th Edition (King), 228, 235

direct competitor, 47, 311

discount codes, for customer loyalty program, 298–299

discovery, as compared to search, 136–137

Disney, sense of purpose, 268

disrupter, 336–337

doing business as (DBA), 33

Dollar Shave Club, Our Blades are F**ing Great YouTube video, 171

domain name, 104–105

dominant colors, 89

Dr. Pepper, partnership with Bonne Belle, 147, 148

Drano drain opener, as inspirational example of brand naming, 57

Dry Bar, as using color to enhance brand identity, 85

DuckDuckGo, 115, 255

dynamic microphone, 194

E

eBay, shopping platform, 303

editorial calendar, 133–134

EIN (employer identification number), 33–34, 181

Elegant Themes, 111

headphones, adding of to podcast setup, 195

Heepsy, 346

hiring
  of artist to design logo, 92
  choosing contractor or employee, 290
  content creators, 229
  qualified attorney for protection of brand, 315
  the right people, 289–290
  using your brand style guide for training, 290–291

Hispanic market (in US), as underserved by most brands, 338

holidays and observances, that provide great brand launch opportunities, 161–162

Home Depot, 271

Hootsuite, 232

HostGator, 104

hosting service, 104, 105–106, 107

house of brands (freestanding brands), 13, 14

Hsieh, Tony (Zappos CEO), 333

HubSpot, 236, 249

hues (of color), defined, 87

Hypertext Markup Language (HTML), 114

HYPR, for finding professional influencers, 346

I

IBM, logo, 90

icons, explained, 3

IG Live, 177, 222

IGTV, 222

images
  adding of to website, 113
  including of in email marketing, 246–247

iMovie, 211

impressions, as advertising metric, 266

incentives, for initial customers, 162–163

incorporation, 32, 33–35

Indeed, 133

IndiaMART, 287

indirect competitor, 47, 311

influencer campaign, 61

influencer marketing, defined, 230

influencers
  creating brand for becoming one, 17
  defined, 260–261, 346
  macro influencer, 231
  micro influencer, 231
  paid influencer versus organic influencer, 231
  paying influencers and other talent to promote your brand, 260–262
  recruitment of, 346
  teaming up with, 230–231

innovation, focusing on, 313

in-person experiences
  as activity of brand promotion, 22
  creation of, 175–189
  getting products into stores, 181–185
  pop-up shop, 176–181
  taking advantage of marketing event opportunities, 186–189

Instagram
  conducting survey on, 303–304
  creating Instagram-able moments, 337–338
  for creating virtual pop-up shop, 177
  described, 222–223
  girlgangthelabel profile on, 218
  girlgangthelabel story highlights on, 219
  as huge photo library, 228
  promoting posts on, 257–258, 329–330
  as social media platform, 217

Instagram For Dummies, 2nd Edition (Herman, Butow, and Walker), 223

Instagram Reels, 223

iTunes, 197

Ivory Ella, 271

J

jockey for position, use of phrase, 44

K

kerning, for typographical guidelines, 90

key performance indicators (KPIs), 67

keyword stuffing, 116, 139, 343

Khoros, 172

Kompass, 287

L

launch campaign

budgeting for your launch, 164–165

choosing metrics for success and establishing benchmarks, 163–164

confirming your key target audiences, 159

creating launch calendar, 162

creating to-do list for, 159–160

deciding where to launch, 158

improving your campaign's chances of going viral, 170–172

launching your brand internally, 165–166

planning yours, 157–166

preparing incentives for initial customers, 162–163

tapping power of the press in, 166–170

timing launch for maximum impact, 160–162

Levi Strauss & Co., partnership with Pinterest, 147

Libsyn, 197

license, getting of or not, 36

limited liability company (LLC), 34

line sheet, defined, 182

LinkedIn, 52, 133, 224

Linktree, 226

livestream events, charging for as way to monetize your content, 215

Logic Pro, 197

logo, 90–92

LoopyLoyalty, 297

Louis Vuitton, 57

loyalty program, use of to drive sales, 65

Lux Unfiltered, 275

Lyft, as disrupter, 336

M

macro influencer, 61, 231

Mailchimp, 97, 236, 246, 249, 303

Maker's Row, 287

marketing campaigns, ways to make yours go viral, 323–330

marketing copy

defined, 126

formulas for writing, 135–136

marketing event, defined, 186

Mayfair Group, launch of clothing line, 170

McDonald's, 75, 90

media, pitching your brand to make marketing campaign go viral, 328–329

media kit, 94–96

media outlets, choosing them strategically to make marketing campaign go viral, 328

meet-and-greet, hosting of as in-person experience, 189

Mendes, Eva (influencer), 346

merchandise, as way to monetize your content, 215

merchant cash advance, as alternative financing option, 41–42

messages, making them easy to share to make marketing campaign go viral, 330

meta text, 116, 138

metrics

advertising metrics, 265–266

choice of, 67

choosing of for launch campaign, 163–164

defined, 66–67

email metrics, 249–250

purpose of, 67

micro influencer, 61, 231, 262

microblog, Twitter as, 221

microloans, as alternative financing option, 42

microphones, choice of for podcasting, 194–195

Microsoft Advertising, 255

Microsoft Azure, 107

Microsoft Excel, 296

Microsoft Publisher, 102

Microsoft Video Editor, 211

Milled.com, 246

mission statement, use of, 52

Mobile Roadie, 123

Monday CRM, 295

monetization of content, 215

monochromatic color palette, 88

monolithic (branded house), 13, 14

Mr. Clean household cleaner, as inspirational example of brand naming, 57

music, adding of to podcast intro and outro, 199

MXToolbox, 237

N

net promoter score (NPS), as brand metric, 67

networking, benefits of, 141

new business, opening of, creating brand for, 15

new markets, expansion into, creating brand for, 18

new product or service, introduction of, creating brand for, 16

niche market

 carving out a niche for yourself, 338

 identification or creation of, 29–32

Nike, 90, 268

99 designs, 103

nonfungible token, defined, 150

nongovernmental organization brand, as type of brand, 13

Nordstrom, 22, 46, 185

Norwegian Cruise Line, partnership with Ocean Conservancy, 271

not-for-profit, fundraising for, creating brand for, 18

NPS (net promoter score), as brand metric, 67

O

Ocean Conservancy, partnership with Norwegian Cruise Line, 271

one-year branding plan, creation of, 66

online branding activities, use of web analytics to improve, 118–121

online business line of credit (LOC), as alternative financing option, 42

online survey, conducting of, 303

online videos

 building brand recognition with, 209–215

 creating branded thumbnail, 212–213

 creating branded YouTube channel, 213–215

 editing of, 211

 recognizing different genres you can use to promote your brand, 209–210

 recording of, 210–211

 uploading to YouTube, 211–212

open house, hosting of as in-person experience, 189

open rate, 243, 250

opportunities, brand style guide as guiding selection of, 85–86

OptinMonster, 325

Oreo, Dunk in the Dark tweet, 171

organic influencer campaigns, 231

organic marketing, 252, 254, 256

organic traffic, 136

outsourcing, 289, 290–291

P

Parsa, Sophia (owner of Golden Rice Co.), 335

partners, brand style guide as guiding selection of, 85–86

partnership

 limited liability partnership (LLP), 34

 limited partnership (LP), 34

PAS (Problem, Agitate, Solution), as formula for writing marketing copy, 135

patent, getting, 36

pay-per-click (PPC) advertising, 254, 255–256, 266

Pedialyte, 45

perceived quality, as brand metric, 67

perceptual map, 49

personal brand, 12–13, 28–29

photos, harnessing the power of, 228–230

Q

Qualaroo, 303
quality
  brand positioning focus on, 46
  striving to go beyond, 312
quality control, brand style guide as facilitating, 85
Quora, answering questions on, 347

R

radio, running ads on, 262–263
reach (of advertising), 254
Recess, partnership with Alfred Coffee, 146
recording space, choosing and prepping of for podcasting, 195–196
Red Bull, partnership with GoPro, 147
Reddit, 346
registered trademark symbol (®), 317
registering (your business), 35
Resonate, 202
Responsive Poll, 276
return on investment (ROI), as email metric, 250
Riverside.fm, 197

S

S corporation (S corp), 35
sales
  as brand metric, 67
  driving of, 65
sales funnel, 129
Salesforce, 68, 295
SBA (U.S. Small Business Association). See U.S. Small Business Association (SBA)
scaling, defined, 282
scaling plan, 285, 286–288
scaling your brand identity, 281–288
search, as compared to discovery, 136–137
search engine marketing (SEM), 254

search engines, making your site attractive to, 115–116
self-funded brand, 38
seminars, hosting seminars in your area of expertise, 187–188
SEO (search engine optimization)
  cautions with, 116
  defined, 342
  maximizing your reach with, 136–137
  strategy for, 138–139
  using it to your advantage, 342–343
service, defined, 11
service brand, 11–12, 28, 288
service mark, for your brand, 314–316
shades (of color), defined, 87
shared server, 107
Shell, logo, 90
Sherwin-Williams, partnership with Pottery Barn, 149
shock mount, 195
Shopify
  as all-in-one-solution, 101, 104
  as blogging platform, 204
  for choosing and registering domain name, 104
  for collecting and organizing customer data, 296
  for creating, managing, and issuing discount codes, 299
  for e-commerce, 138
  indicating subscription preference on, 326
Shopify Experts Marketplace, 103
Similarweb, 47
Simplecast, 197
Sintillia, as focused on discovery, 137
sitemap, defined, 103
size, for typographical guidelines, 89
SleekNote, 325
slogan, composing a catch campaign slogan to make your marketing campaign go viral, 327
SM (service mark), 316–317
small get-together, hosting of as in-person experience, 189

About the Author

Amy Will is an entrepreneur and marketing maven who earned her B.A. in Communications and Marketing from California Lutheran University. During her college years, she spent several sessions abroad studying Media Globalization in Tokyo, Japan, Fashion at the Université Paris Sorbonne (Paris IV), and Trend Spotting at Central Saint Martins in London. During those same years, she also had internships in marketing and public relations at National Lampoon, Universal Music Group, and MTV Network. During her final semester, Amy interned at Monrow Attire in its warehouse, where she learned about the process of scaling a fashion brand.

Fresh out of college, Amy served as director of marketing for Tower Paddle Boards, after which she started her first business (at 24 years old) — 6D Hair Ties. Since then, she has founded and co-founded additional successful brands: Color Me Book (a custom coloring book company she formed with her husband, Cory), Pretty Cool Stuff, Inc. (a B2B company specializing in developing one-of-a-kind promotional products), Girl Gang (a line of fashion and other merchandise), and Evolving Vegan, with her business partners Cory Will and Mena Massoud (a cookbook highlighting vegan eateries across North America).

Girl Gang was born from Amy's passion to connect with and inspire women. It began as a merchandise line with its flagship product — a "Support Your Local Girl Gang" t-shirt — and grew into a full line of products and partnerships.

Along with the label, Amy hosts *Girl Gang the Podcast*. She travels the world as she interviews strong, ambitious women who hold leadership positions at the leading brands, including Burberry, Nike, British Vogue, Beboe, and Uber. Her goal is to facilitate and nurture authentic connections among women so that every woman can achieve her full potential.

To further her goal, Amy is developing a directory of female-owned businesses to encourage female entrepreneurs and others who are dedicated to women empowerment to support one another in their commercial endeavors.

This next chapter of Amy's career is focused on investing in female-owned small businesses, mentoring female founders, and raising money for girls to acquire education in computer science programs, business, and financial literacy.

Dedication

To my partner in business and life, Cory. Thank you for inspiring me and working with me to bring our ideas to life.

Author's Acknowledgments

It takes a village to publish a book, and this book is no exception. Thanks to Wiley senior acquisitions editor Tracy Boggier for kick-starting this project and choosing me to write the book. Thanks also to project manager Charlotte Kughen and copy editor Keir Simpson for polishing my prose and carefully shepherding my text and illustrations through the production process. Completing this project during a pandemic with multiple ongoing projects would have been a monumental challenge without the skilled assistance of these professionals.

Special thanks to technical editor Sophia Parsa for contributing her time, effort, and marketing expertise. Sophia went above and beyond the call of duty to not only check the manuscript for technical errors and errors of omission but also to add her own expertise and insight to significantly improve and enhance the book.

Thank you to Morgan Evans for making this possible by running and growing our brands during the writing process.

Publisher's Acknowledgments

Sr. Acquisitions Editor: Tracy Boggier

Project Editor: Charlotte Kughen

Copy Editor: Keir Simpson

Technical Editor: Sophia Parsa

Sr. Editorial Assistant: Cherie Case

Production Editor: Tamilmani Varadharaj

Cover Image: © tiero/iStock/Getty Images

Leverage the power

Dummies is the global leader in the reference category and one of the most trusted and highly regarded brands in the world. No longer just focused on books, customers now have access to the dummies content they need in the format they want. Together we'll craft a solution that engages your customers, stands out from the competition, and helps you meet your goals.

Advertising & Sponsorships

Connect with an engaged audience on a powerful multimedia site, and position your message alongside expert how-to content. Dummies.com is a one-stop shop for free, online information and know-how curated by a team of experts.

- Targeted ads
- Video
- Email Marketing
- Microsites
- Sweepstakes sponsorship

20 MILLION PAGE VIEWS EVERY SINGLE MONTH

15 MILLION UNIQUE VISITORS PER MONTH

43% OF ALL VISITORS ACCESS THE SITE VIA THEIR MOBILE DEVICES

700,000 NEWSLETTER SUBSCRIPTION TO THE INBOXES OF *300,000* UNIQUE INDIVIDUALS EVERY WEEK

# of dummies

Custom Publishing

Reach a global audience in any language by creating a solution that will differentiate you from competitors, amplify your message, and encourage customers to make a buying decision.

- Apps
- Books
- eBooks
- Video
- Audio
- Webinars

Brand Licensing & Content

Leverage the strength of the world's most popular reference brand to reach new audiences and channels of distribution.

For more information, visit dummies.com/biz

PERSONAL ENRICHMENT

Staying Sharp

9781119187790
USA $26.00
CAN $31.99
UK £19.99

Facebook

9781119179030
USA $21.99
CAN $25.99
UK £16.99

Guitar

9781119293354
USA $24.99
CAN $29.99
UK £17.99

Investing

9781119293347
USA $22.99
CAN $27.99
UK £16.99

Beekeeping

9781119310068
USA $22.99
CAN $27.99
UK £16.99

Digital Photography

9781119235606
USA $24.99
CAN $29.99
UK £17.99

Meditation

9781119251163
USA $24.99
CAN $29.99
UK £17.99

Pregnancy

9781119235491
USA $26.99
CAN $31.99
UK £19.99

Samsung Galaxy S7

9781119279952
USA $24.99
CAN $29.99
UK £17.99

iPhone

9781119283133
USA $24.99
CAN $29.99
UK £17.99

Crocheting

9781119287117
USA $24.99
CAN $29.99
UK £16.99

Nutrition

9781119130246
USA $22.99
CAN $27.99
UK £16.99

PROFESSIONAL DEVELOPMENT

Windows 10

9781119311041
USA $24.99
CAN $29.99
UK £17.99

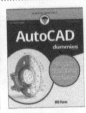

AutoCAD

9781119255796
USA $39.99
CAN $47.99
UK £27.99

Excel 2016

9781119293439
USA $26.99
CAN $31.99
UK £19.99

QuickBooks 2017

9781119281467
USA $26.99
CAN $31.99
UK £19.99

macOS Sierra

9781119280651
USA $29.99
CAN $35.99
UK £21.99

LinkedIn

9781119251132
USA $24.99
CAN $29.99
UK £17.99

Windows 10

9781119310563
USA $34.00
CAN $41.99
UK £24.99

SharePoint 2016

9781119181705
USA $29.99
CAN $35.99
UK £21.99

Fundamental Analysis

9781119263593
USA $26.99
CAN $31.99
UK £19.99

Networking

9781119257769
USA $29.99
CAN $35.99
UK £21.99

Office 2016

9781119293477
USA $26.99
CAN $31.99
UK £19.99

Office 365

9781119265313
USA $24.99
CAN $29.99
UK £17.99

Salesforce.com

9781119239314
USA $29.99
CAN $35.99
UK £21.99

Coding

9781119293323
USA $29.99
CAN $35.99
UK £21.99

dummies
A Wiley Brand